CONTROL FREAKS

CONTROL
FREAKS

7 Ways Liberals Plan to Ruin Your Life

TERENCE P. JEFFREY

Editor-in-chief of CNSNews.com

Since 1947
REGNERY PUBLISHING, INC.
An Eagle Publishing Company • Washington, DC

Library of Congress Cataloging-in-Publication Data

    Jeffrey, Terence P.
     Control freaks : 7 ways liberals plan to ruin your life / by
Terence P. Jeffrey.
       p. cm.
     ISBN 978-1-59698-597-1
     1. Liberalism–United States. 2. Social control–United
States. 3. United States–Social policy–1993- I. Title.
     JC574.2.U6J44 2010
     320.51'30973–dc22

2010024256

Published in the United States by
Regnery Publishing, Inc.
One Massachusetts Avenue, NW
Washington, DC 20001
www.regnery.com

Manufactured in the United States of America

10 9 8 7 6 5 4 3 2 1

Books are available in quantity for promotional or premium use. Write to Director of Special Sales, Regnery Publishing, Inc., One Massachusetts Avenue NW, Washington, DC 20001, for information on discounts and terms or call (202) 216-0600.

Distributed to the trade by:
Perseus Distribution
387 Park Avenue South
New York, NY 10016

For Julie

Contents

Introduction

Who's In Control?

I n the quest for freedom in our everyday lives, we are ultimately confronted with a practical, not a philosophical, question: Who is in control?

When we make the major decisions in our lives, we are free. When someone else makes them, we are not free. When government makes them, we live in tyranny.

The liberals discussed in this book advocate imposing unnecessary, or even unjust, government controls on the lives of individuals. Modern American liberals, as demonstrated in these pages, would like to see the government exercise more control over our movement, our retirement income, our health care, our private property, our speech, whether we live or die, and even whether we are allowed to live according to our consciences or raise our children to love and embrace the God-given moral law that forms the only foundation of a free society.

This work seeks to illuminate how these liberals are pushing America away from liberty toward forms of government control that will ruin our nation.

Many Americans, who know they owe their children the same great nation our parents gave to us, are already calling our leaders back to the matchless governing principles of the Constitution and the eternal values of the Declaration of Independence, that, together, are the guides that will lead us home to the land of the free.

Chapter 1

Coercing People Out of Their Cars

Liberals Want to Control Your Movement

"He would be a rash prophet who should assert that the expansive character of American life has now entirely ceased. Movement has been its dominant fact, and, unless this training has no effect upon a people, the American energy will continually demand a wider field for its exercise."[1]

—**Frederick Jackson Turner**
"The Significance of the Frontier in American History," 1893

"The days where we're just building sprawl forever, those days are over."[2]

—**President Barack Obama**
Fort Myers, Florida, February 10, 2009

"It is a way to coerce people out of their cars, yeah."[3]

—**Transportation Secretary Ray LaHood**
National Press Club, May 21, 2009

L iberals love Ray LaHood because he is the type of Republican who wants government to control more of American life. When President Obama named him secretary of transportation, it was not so much an act of bipartisanship as an expression of ideological solidarity.

About a month into his tenure, LaHood told the Associated Press that the administration should consider taxing people for every mile they drive their car, a system that would require tracking people's movements. "We should look at the vehicular miles program where people are actually clocked on the number of miles that they traveled," he said. "What I see this administration doing is this—thinking outside the box on how we fund our infrastructure in America."[4]

The Associated Press reported that the system LaHood had in mind "would require all cars and trucks be equipped with global satellite positioning technology, a transponder, a clock and other equipment to record how many miles a vehicle was driven, whether it was driven on highways or secondary roads, and even whether it was driven during peak traffic periods or off-peak hours." A similar system proposed in Massachusetts, the wire service noted, had "drawn complaints from drivers who say it's an Orwellian intrusion by government into the lives of citizens."[5]

LaHood's big-brother-like suggestion proved too much even for Obama, who had just pushed a $787 billion stimulus law through Congress and was preparing to launch an ambitious campaign to enact a national health program. Within twenty-four hours, White House Spokesman Robert Gibbs told reporters the president would not back the driver-tracking plan.[6] As we shall see, however, the president would back other ideas LaHood had for controlling how people move.

While a member of the U.S. House of Representatives, LaHood had served on the Appropriations Committee, the panel that decides each year how the federal government will spend trillions of dollars of other people's money. He once spoke with arresting candor about why he wanted to serve on this committee. "The reason I went on the Appropriations Committee, the reason other people go on the Appropriations Committee," he said, "is they know that it puts them in a position to know where the money is at, to know the people who are doling out the money and to be in the room when the money is being doled out."[7]

Before Obama drafted him for his Cabinet, LaHood had become one of the biggest-spending Republicans on Capitol Hill. The *New York Times* described him as a "backer of earmarks,"[8] the Associated Press called him a leader "in distributing largesse,"[9] Citizens Against Government Waste awarded him its January 2009 "Porker of the Month" award,[10] and fellow Illinoisan Rahm Emanuel—who would become Obama's chief of staff— praised him for his "leadership, his thoughtfulness and his character."[11]

In LaHood's view, the transportation secretary's highest duty was not to build highways and facilitate freedom of movement, but to use government to change the way people live. Early on, he announced what he called a "livability initiative"[12] and formed a partnership with the Department of Housing and Urban Development and the Environmental Protection Agency aimed at creating "sustainable communities."[13] As Ronald Utt of the Heritage Foundation observed, the partnership LaHood's department formed with HUD, together with a rhetorical attack launched by President Obama on suburban "sprawl," seemed to indicate the administration's "intent to re-energize and lead the Left's longstanding war against America's suburbs."[14]

Utt noted that "the Smart Growth and New Urbanist movements want Americans to move into higher density developments—such as townhouses and high-rise apartment buildings—which, the antisuburbanists contend, can be better served by public transportation (hence the commitment to 'transportation choice,' a process whereby commuters are bribed or coerced into an inconvenient mode of transportation that most would not choose on their own)—thereby freeing the hapless American people from relying on their automobiles."[15]

LaHood first described what he had in mind using benign-sounding words in testimony given to the House subcommittee that allocates gas-tax money. "If a large share of the traveling public could walk or bike for short trips, it is estimated that the nation could save over one million gallons of gas and millions of dollars in motor fuel costs per day," he said. "Transit-oriented development also has the potential to contribute significantly to the revitalization of downtown districts, foster walkable neighborhoods, and offer an alternative to urban and suburban sprawl and automobile-focused commuting."[16]

The administration, he conceded, wanted to "influence how people choose to travel." But their goal was to increase the "independence" of those who do not drive rather than limit the independence of those who do.

"Mixed-use neighborhoods with highly-connected streets arranged in small blocks promote mobility for all users, whether they are walking, bicycling, riding transit or driving motor vehicles," he said. "Benefits include improved traffic flow, shorter trip lengths, reduced vehicle-miles traveled, safer streets for pedestrians and cyclists, lower per-capita greenhouse gas emissions, reduced dependence on fossil fuels, increased trip-chaining, and independence for those who prefer not to or are unable to drive."[17]

A couple of months after this testimony, LaHood lunched with columnist George Will. Will discovered that the former Republican congressman had come all the way out of the closet as an advocate of using government to alter the way Americans live. "I think we can change people's behavior," LaHood told Will.

Government "promoted driving" by building the Interstate Highway System, LaHood said. He intended to reverse that. "People are getting out of their cars, they are biking to work," he said, pointing to Portland, Oregon, as an example of the type of place where government has promoted this trend. Appalled, Will wrote a column dubbing Lahood "the Secretary of Behavioral Modification."[18]

In a question-and-answer session at the National Press Club a few days later, LaHood defiantly restated his intention to use government to stop people from driving. "Some in the highway supporters and motorists groups have been concerned by your livability initiative," said the moderator, reading a reporter's question. "Is this an effort to make driving more torturous and to coerce people out of their cars?"

"It is a way to coerce people out of their cars, yeah…" said LaHood. "Now, look it, every community is not going to be a 'livable community,' but we have to create opportunities for people that do want to use a bicycle or want to walk or want to get on a street car or want to ride a light rail."

"And the only person that I've heard of that objects to this," he said, "is George Will."

This elicited laughter from the room full of Washington journalists. But the moderator followed up. "OK," she said. "Speaking of, some conservative groups are wary of the livable communities program, saying it's an example of government intrusion into people's lives. How do you respond?"

"About everything we do around here is government intrusion in people's lives," said LaHood. "So have at it."

The reporters laughed again.[19]

Freedom Seekers

The people who created America were freedom seekers. They left their homelands and traveled vast distances seeking individual liberty and economic opportunity. On an undeveloped continent, they went where they wanted, when they wanted, and they built a nation of, by, and for freedom of movement.

When the French and Indian War ended in 1763, France retreated from the North American mainland, leaving England uncontested ownership of the Ohio Valley.[20] America's colonial frontier leapt westward from the crest of the Appalachians to banks of the Mississippi. Across the river sat the vast Louisiana territory that, for the moment, France had ceded to Spain—and that eventually would become yet another open space on the American frontier.

From almost the instant they set foot on this continent, our forbearers saw the lands beyond the mountains as a place for new settlements—a vast territory where an independent people could own the soil they lived on and thrive in self-sufficient freedom. Historian Samuel Eliot Morrison observed that Americans in the pre-revolutionary era "were not security minded but liberty minded."[21] They were ready to risk life in the wilderness in return for liberty. They did so not just for themselves, but for their children and grandchildren.

In 1759, foreseeing England's victory in the war and the end to French claims in the West, a Boston clergyman delivered a sermon on America's prospects. He spoke of his countrymen's dreams. "What fair hopes have we of being completely delivered from that enemy, that has so often interrupted our tranquility, and checked our growth," asked the Reverend Samuel Cooper. "What scenes of happiness are we ready to figure for ourselves, from the hope of enjoying, in this good land, all the blessings of an undisturbed and lasting peace? From the hope of seeing our towns enlarged; our commerce increased; and our settlements extending themselves with security of every side, and changing the wilderness into a fruitful field."[22]

Six years later, John Adams—a proud New England farmer as well as a Boston lawyer—exhorted his countrymen to remember that America's spirit was a pioneering spirit. Our ancestors, he told them, turned their backs on old-world oppression to bravely face an untamed wilderness.

> Let us read and recollect and impress upon our souls the views and ends of our own more immediate forefathers, in exchanging their native country for a dreary, inhospitable wilderness. Let us examine into the nature of that power, and the cruelty of that oppression, which drove them from their homes. Recollect their amazing fortitude, their bitter sufferings—the hunger, the nakedness, the cold, which they patiently endured—the severe labors of clearing their grounds, building their houses, raising their provisions, amidst dangers from wild beasts and savage men, before they had time or money or materials for commerce. Recollect the civil and religious principles and hopes and expectations which

constantly supported and carried them through all hardships with patience and resignation. Let us recollect it was liberty, the hope of liberty for themselves and us and ours, which conquered all discouragements, dangers, and trials.[23]

King George III and his allies in Parliament looked at the American frontier differently than the likes of Reverend Cooper and John Adams. They did not see the opening of the West as an opportunity for the colonies to expand and prosper. They did not see the territory across the mountains as a sanctuary for individual liberty. They saw the potential settlement of those distant landlocked regions as a threat to English control of North America. They feared that if colonists settled beyond the Appalachians, it would spark conflict with the Indians, put Americans beyond the reach of England's political grasp, and unravel a trading system in which America served as a captive market for England's manufactured goods and as England's exclusive domain for securing raw materials.[24]

Eight months after England signed the peace treaty with France and Spain that obligated France to withdraw from North America, George III issued a proclamation. It set the boundary lines for four new English colonies in the North American lands secured by the war. These included Quebec, East Florida, West Florida, and Grenada. All could be reached by the English Navy and governed under her guns.

The proclamation also instructed the governors of England's North American colonies to give generous land grants to the officers, soldiers, and sailors who had served in North America during the war. Field officers were to receive massive estates of 5,000 acres; captains, 3,000 acres; lesser officers, 2,000 acres; and non-commissioned officers, 200 acres. Even the lowliest private was to receive a grant of 50 acres for risking life and limb for his king.

The same proclamation, however, included a provision that significantly diminished the value of these grants. It prohibited any settlement at all in the "Lands and Territories lying to the Westward of the Sources of the

Rivers which fall into" the Atlantic. Americans were barred from moving over the mountains. "And We do hereby strictly forbid, on Pain of our Displeasure," said the king, "all our loving Subjects from making any Purchases or Settlements whatever, or taking Possession of any of the Lands above reserved, without our especial leave and Licence for that Purpose first obtained."[25]

At least one former officer—a Virginian named George Washington— did not intend to see his real-estate development plans thwarted by this royal proclamation. He refused to take it seriously. In 1767, he wrote William Crawford, a fellow veteran who had moved from Virginia to the western edge of Pennsylvania, and asked for his help in locating a tract of first-rate land beyond the legal line of settlement that the king had emphatically drawn. Washington was convinced the king would rescind his proclamation, and he wanted to preempt the best land for himself. He asked Crawford to travel into the forbidden territory—as if on a hunting trip— and find a good 2,000 acres Washington could formally claim when the time was right.[26]

"I offered in my last to join you in attempting to secure some of the most valuable lands in the King's part, which I think may be accomplished after a while, notwithstanding the proclamation that restrains it at present; and prohibits the settling them at all; for I can never look upon that proclamation in any other light (but this I say between ourselves) but as a temporary expedient to quiet the minds of the Indians," Washington wrote Crawford.

"It must fall, of course, in a few years, especially when those Indians consent to our occupying the lands," wrote Washington. "Any person, therefore, who neglects the present opportunity of hunting out good lands, and in some measure marking and distinguishing them for his own, in order to keep others from settling them, will never regain it."

Washington was adamant that Crawford keep his plans private so as not to alert potential competitors or those who might be shocked at his disregard for the king's edict.

I recommend that you keep this whole matter a secret, or trust it only to those in whom you can confide, and who can assist you in bringing it to bear by their discoveries of land. This advice proceeds from several very good reasons, and, in the first place, because I might be censured for the opinion I have given in respect to the King's proclamation, and then, if the scheme I am now proposing to you were known, it might give the alarm to others, and, by putting them upon a plan of the same nature, before we could lay a proper foundation for success ourselves, set the different interests clashing, and, probably, in the end, overturn the whole. All of this may be avoided by a silent management, and the operation carried on by you under the guise of hunting game, which you may, I presume, effectually do, at the same time you are in pursuit of land.[27]

Washington was wrong to believe George III would soon allow Americans to settle beyond the mountains. He never did. In March 1775, less than a month before British regulars exchanged fire with American minutemen on Lexington Green, Edmund Burke delivered a speech in Parliament urging conciliation with the colonies. Burke caustically pointed to the unenforceable folly of stopping Americans from moving west and attacked a more recent proposal that would go beyond the Proclamation of 1763 by completely stopping all new colonial land grants as a means of checking colonial population growth.[28]

Burke, alas, did not express the prevailing English position. General Thomas Gage, the king's commander in America, did. On the eve of the revolution, the short-sighted Gage was still insisting it would "be for our interest to keep the Settlers within reach of the Sea-Coast as long as we can and cramp their Trade as far as it can be done prudentially."[29] George III's refusal to allow Americans to move west was one of the forces that drove Americans to declare their independence.

The people who founded the United States refused to allow government to control their movement.

Significance of the Frontier

One hundred thirty years after King George III drew his line at the Appalachians, a University of Wisconsin professor named Frederick Jackson Turner began arguing in a series of essays that it was the process of populating the wilderness beyond the line that made America an exceptionally free and democratic country.

"The frontier individualism has from the beginning promoted democracy," he wrote. "The forest clearings have been the seed plots of American character."[30]

Turner believed that Americans who were willing to pass over the mountains into an undeveloped wilderness—where they would be wholly responsible for their own families and their own destiny—were making a fundamental break with the Old World way of life. They were becoming a new people, a distinctly American breed of men and women, who would bow neither to the arbitrary power of kings nor to European-style class distinctions determined by law, ancestry, or ideology. These pioneers were individualists, who would not tolerate a government that told them what to do.

"Complex society is precipitated by the wilderness into a kind of primitive organization based on the family," wrote Turner. "The tendency is antisocial. It produces antipathy to control, and particularly to any direct control. The tax-gatherer is viewed as a representative of oppression."[31]

Americans who ventured into the forests bringing only their wits and whatever they could load on a wagon or a mule understood that their future prosperity and security depended on their own industry and ingenuity, as well as on the liberty they knew awaited them in the wilds.

"Almost every family was a self-sufficing unit, and liberty and equality flourished in the frontier periods of the Middle West as perhaps never before in history," wrote Turner. "American democracy came from the forest and its destiny drove it to material conquests, but the materialism of the pioneer was not the dull contented materialism of an old and fixed society. Both native settler and European immigrant saw in this free and competitive movement of the frontier the chance to break the bondage of social rank, and to rise to a higher plane of existence."[32]

Freedom of movement, self-reliance, self-government, and material prosperity were inextricably linked in the mind of the American pioneer. Central planning was unheard of.

"This democratic society was not a disciplined army, where all must keep step and where the collective interests destroyed individual will and work," wrote Turner.

> Rather it was a mobile mass of freely circulating atoms, each seeking its own place and finding play for its own powers and for its own original initiative. We cannot lay too much stress upon this point, for it was at the very heart of the whole American movement. The world was to be made a better world by the example of democracy in which there was freedom of the individual, in which there was the vitality and mobility productive of originality and variety.[33]

Turner rebutted those who argued that when the American people ran up against the far boundaries of the western frontier, their nature must change, that they must surrender their pioneering spirit and with it their individualism and mobility.

> Since the days when the fleet of Columbus sailed into the waters of the New World, America has been another name for opportunity, and the people of the United States have taken their tone from the incessant expansion which has not only been open but has even been forced upon them. He would be a rash prophet who should assert that the expansive character of American life

has now entirely ceased. Movement has been its dominant fact, and, unless this training has no effect upon a people, the American energy will continually demand a wider field for its exercise.[34]

Turner believed it was America's destiny to reject European socialism and aristocracy and to carry the pioneering individualism of our forefathers into the centuries ahead.

"It would be a grave misfortune if these people so rich in experience, in self-confidence and aspiration, in creative genius, should turn to some Old World discipline of socialism or plutocracy, or despotic rule, whether by class or by dictator," he wrote. "Nor shall we be driven to these alternatives. Our ancient hopes, our courageous faith, our underlying good humor and love of fair play will triumph in the end."

"As we turn from the task of the first rough conquest of the continent," he concluded, "there lies before us a whole wealth of unexploited resources in the realm of the spirit."[35]

The Walled City

Just like King George in 1763, liberals today want to draw lines on the map and stop people from moving to the other side. In their vision of America's future, our cities are ringed by regulatory walls designed to force people to live near downtown and use mass transit.

When Ray LaHood talked about his department's "livability initiative" and the administration's "sustainable communities" program, the word "Portland" was never far from his lips. He invoked Portland to George Will, mentioned it at the National Press Club, cited it in congressional testimony and spoke of it on national television. He even visited the city to publicly hold it up as an example of what the Obama administration hoped to do to the rest of America.[36]

Portland, LaHood said on C-SPAN, has been a "model over the years of getting people out of their cars and creating a livable community idea."[37]

"Portland's way ahead of the curve," he told PBS. "They are the example of a livable community. They're the example, and we want to replicate that in other communities around the country."[38]

"I came here today because Portland is the transportation capital of our country," LaHood said on his visit. "Portland is the green capital of our country. Portland is the streetcar capital of our country. And Portland is the livable community capital of America."[39]

Speaking to the editorial board of the local newspaper, LaHood explained the Obama administration's transportation strategy: "Take what you've done here in Portland and try to replicate it around America. It's not that complicated."[40]

So what did they do in Portland that the administration would like to replicate nationwide? In 1973, Oregon enacted a law requiring all cities and counties to develop comprehensive development plans. The law established a state commission to set development goals that local jurisdictions would follow when formulating their plans. In the late 1970s, the people in the Portland area set up a new regional government, the Metro Council, to oversee development in an area that included territory in three counties.[41]

Oregon's state commission established development goals—and regulations for enforcing them—that would convert the state's metropolitan areas into modern liberal versions of the walled city. Unlike medieval walled cities, where physical bulwarks protected the community from external threats, the modern walled cities envisioned in Oregon would be surrounded by regulatory walls erected to keep people in and prevent them from threatening the environment.[42] These regulatory walls were called "urban growth boundaries," which were supposed to accommodate a metropolitan area's growth over a period of twenty years.[43]

"Urban growth boundaries shall be established and maintained by cities, counties and regional governments to provide land for urban development needs and to identify and separate urban and urbanizable land from rural land," said Oregon's Statewide Planning Goals & Guidelines. "Land within urban growth boundaries shall be considered available for urban development consistent with plans for the provision of urban facilities and services."[44]

The regulations implementing this goal called on local governments to use transportation, zoning, and tax policies to keep development inside the line.

"The type, design, phasing and location of major public transportation facilities (i.e., all modes: air, marine, rail, mass transit, highways, bicycle, and pedestrian) and improvements thereto are factors which should be utilized to support urban expansion into urbanizable areas and restrict it from rural areas," they said.[45]

For Oregon's regulators, traffic jams were a good thing. They wanted to make it more difficult for people to drive in the hope that people would give up the freedom of movement cars provide. In their perverse view, clogged highways increased an area's "livability."

"Within metropolitan areas, coordinated land use and transportation plans are intended to improve livability and accessibility by promoting changes in the transportation system and land use patterns," said one of the regulations promulgated by the Oregon government in support of its planning goals. "A key outcome of this effort is a reduction in reliance on single occupant automobile use, particularly during peak periods. To accomplish this outcome, this division promotes increased planning for alternative modes and street connectivity and encourages land use patterns throughout urban areas that make it more convenient for people to walk, bicycle, use transit, use automobile travel more efficiently, and drive less to meet their daily needs."[46]

The regulations required metropolitan areas to set a standard for transportation development that would "result in a reduction in reliance on automobiles" and would be "likely to result in a significant increase in the share of trips made by alternative modes, including walking, bicycling, ridesharing and transit."[47]

For Oregon's regulators, parking spaces were a bad thing. In a well-planned community, people who persisted in driving would get stuck in traffic whenever they wanted to go some place and would not be able to find parking, when or if they got there. Metropolitan areas, the Oregon regulations say, must implement a "parking plan" that results in a 10 percent reduction in parking spaces available over the life of their development plan. "This may be accomplished through a combination of restrictions on development of new parking spaces and requirements that existing parking spaces be redeveloped to other uses."[48]

If all goes as planned in the development of one of Oregon's walled cities, once the people largely give up driving and parking, they will all settle in to densely populated "transit-oriented developments" inside the urban growth boundary and within walking or biking distance of a government-sponsored-and-scheduled mass transportation system. "Transit-Oriented Development means a mix of residential, retail and office uses and a supporting network of roads, bicycle and pedestrian ways focused on a major transit stop designed to support a high level of transit use."[49]

Rather than use the people's tax dollars to develop a transportation infrastructure that accommodates the mobile lifestyle that car-loving Americans have freely chosen, Oregon wants to use taxes and regulations to make the people adopt a new lifestyle that will conform to the transportation infrastructure chosen by the government. Simply put, Oregon wants to control where, when, and how people move.

Nor is Transportation Secretary Ray LaHood the only fan of what Oregon is doing. The Sierra Club of California, for example, has published a statement presenting "policies designed to achieve the Sierra Club's vision for the future of California."[50] It, too, calls for cities walled by regulations that keep people in and inhibit freedom of movement.

> All cities and unincorporated urban centers must establish permanent urban growth boundaries (UGBs) that will define the area of ultimate urbanization and protect the county's or region's open

space lands. Development shall be directed toward areas within UGBs, in order to avoid adverse impacts upon productive agriculture, wildlife habitat, critical watershed lands, historical and archeological resources, open space lands, and scenic values.... Lands within the urban boundary will be devoted to compact residential, commercial, and industrial development that makes efficient use of land and infrastructure. Natural systems and environmentally sensitive habitat areas within the urban boundary must be protected. Lands outside of the urban growth boundaries—lands that form the area's greenbelt—will encompass recreational open space, watershed, agricultural, wetlands, wildlife habitat/corridors, shoreline, forest/woodland, and other lands which are essential. To protect biodiversity, these lands must be zoned for uses and in parcel sizes consistent with economically viable units for the agricultural, recreational or resource conservation uses proposed.[51]

Like Oregon's regulators, the futurists of the Sierra Club see human beings densely packed into urban cages, moving, when they must, on government and "nonmotorized" transit. "Residential densities and commercial floor area ratios must be sufficient to facilitate public transit and nonmotorized transportation and to achieve increased energy efficiency and affordability of housing," says the Club's plan for California.[52]

In California, according to the Sierra Club's vision, planners should seek to limit parking not just where people work and shop, but also where they live. "Parking in business, commercial and industrial centers shall be limited or made more expensive in order to encourage transit use," says the club's plan. "Residential parking should be limited to half the number of driving age population."[53] If the Sierra Club actually succeeded in remaking America along these lines, a husband and wife who both wanted to own a car would either have to rent an unused parking space from a non-driving neighbor if one were available, or give up the mobility a second car allows.

"Those Days Are Over"

In his 1991 book *Edge City—Life on the New Frontier*, journalist Joel Garreau examined the new commercial centers Americans were building in the age of the interstate freeway. Dubbed "Edge City," these places— such as Tysons Corner in northern Virginia, the Galleria area in Houston, Texas, and the Livermore Valley east of San Francisco—designed for car owners. Garreau argued that the typical real estate developer (who built such places) and the typical urban planner (who loathed them) looked at the world through dramatically different eyes. The developers wanted to make money by satisfying the freely made choices of consumers. The planners disapproved of those freely made choices and wanted to change people's behavior in pursuit of some abstract ideal of what they believed a community should be like. The planners, for example—as Ray LaHood might put it—wanted to coerce people out of their cars.

"The crazy quilt of Edge City made perfect sense if you understood the place as the manifest pattern of millions of individual American desires over seventy-five years," wrote Garreau.

> The developers viewed Edge City the same way they viewed America itself: as problem driven, not ideology-driven. In this way, their perspective was quite the opposite of the designers'. The planners seemed to think that human behavior was malleable, and that nobody was better equipped by dint of intelligence and education than they to do the malleting. They believed that the physical environment they wanted to shape could and would shape society. The places they would like to plan would lead, they believed, to fundamental, welcome, and long-overdue changes in human mores and human attitudes.[54]

Garreau asked a British-born urban planner working in Houston what he would do if he were "handed a magic wand" that gave him the power to remake that city into the place he thought it ought to be. After saying he would increase the population density and move people into "smaller, less individual residences," the planner took aim at what he considered the excessive freedom of movement in America.

> I'd raise the gasoline tax by 300 percent. I'd raise the price of auto-
> mobiles enormously. I mean I would just limit movement. I'd
> limit movement completely and there would be a massive rush to
> live near your work, your social or commercial activity. And then
> I would put enormous costs on parking. I think just take trans-
> portation alone, you could change these places dramatically.[55]

While leading liberals in American government today might not share this planner's precise policy prescriptions, they do share his desire to limit free-dom of movement as a means of remolding American society. That is one of the reasons they routinely divert gas-tax revenues from building roads that people want to mass transit systems they do not want. That is why they respond to rising gas prices by choking off supply, resisting new oil drilling in northern Alaska, off the coast of California, or in the Gulf of Mexico. And that is why President Obama said what he did at a town hall meeting in Fort Myers, Florida, only a few weeks after his inauguration.

At that meeting, a city councilman from a nearby community asked Obama about his transportation policies. In framing his question, the coun-cilman made it clear that he supported government-funded mass transit programs and opposed oil drilling in the nearby Gulf of Mexico. He sig-naled, in other words, that he had the world view of Garreau's typical urban planner, not his typical real estate developer. In responding to this man, Obama would have known he was speaking to a kindred spirit—a fellow control freak. "I would like for us to invest in mass transit because poten-tially that's energy efficient. And I think people are a lot more open now to thinking regionally, in terms of how we plan our transportation infrastruc-ture," Obama said. "The days where we're just building sprawl forever, those days are over."[56]

The days of building sprawl are over?

Who is President Obama to say this, or believe he has any say in the matter? He is not a monarch like George III; he has no arbitrary power over us. The people elected him to a four-year term in which he must at all times abide by the restrictions on federal authority written into the Constitution he swore to preserve, protect, and defend.

If our children and grandchildren decide their pursuit of happiness involves living in four-bedroom homes on half-acre lots a hundred miles from the nearest downtown, that is their right. If they want to go over the mountain to find a better life, that is not only their right, it is their particular inheritance as Americans. All of us, no matter where our ancestors came from or when they arrived here, are the moral descendants of pioneers. They gave us a free country and it is our duty to keep it free. That means rejecting government policies aimed at restricting freedom of movement.

The First Amendment guarantees the freedom to assemble, which is essential to representative government. But that freedom is meaningless unless it is coupled with the freedom of movement. If government controls how, when, and where we can go, government can stop us from getting where we need to be when we need to be there. The freedom to assemble not only describes what takes place when Tea Party patriots gather together to protest excessive government, it also describes what takes place when a family flees Nancy Pelosi's San Francisco, or Rahm Emanuel's Chicago, or Mary Landrieu's New Orleans, or Charlie Rangel's New York to settle down in a suburb, exurb, or small town where the values and views of their neighbors and the local government are more in keeping with their own.

The Founding Fathers developed the federal system of our Constitution so that citizens could check the power of a government by leaving its jurisdiction. If someone did not like the way Pennsylvania was governed, he could move to Ohio. The Tenth Amendment says: "The powers not delegated to the United States by the Constitution, nor prohibited by it to the States, are reserved to the States respectively, or to the people." Leaving aside the defense and external affairs of the nation which were necessarily vested in the federal government, the Constitution largely left to the people the power to govern themselves town by town, county by county, state by state. This created a political free market. To thrive, a community needed to persuade a mobile people that it was a nice place to settle down. If a community could not make that sale, the people would move on. In a nation so blessed with the freedom of movement and the never-dying spirit of the frontier, the natural variety in people's tastes would and did ensure a great variety in American communities.

This variety is partly reflected in the color-coded maps produced after recent elections that show liberal-leaning communities in blue and conservative-leaning communities in red. An obvious trend these maps reveal is that urban communities tend to be blue and non-urban communities tend to be red.[57]

It may be no coincidence that Portland, the city that Transportation Secretary Ray LaHood says the Obama administration wants to "replicate"[58] around the country, is enduringly blue.

When President Obama says the days of sprawl are over forever, what he means is that he and other liberals want to herd as many red-state Americans as possible into places like Portland and then choke off the avenues of escape until the whole country turns deeply and irreversibly blue.

Chapter 2

So-Called Social Security
Liberals Want to
Control Your Retirement

"In business and in politics we are still individualists. We habitually put our individual before our common interests, and even when we are conscious of our common needs we hesitate to intrust them to our common government. To correct these national characteristics is, in my opinion, the most important next step in social advance."[1]

— **Henry Rogers Seager**
Social Insurance: A Program of Social Reform, 1910

"There is still today a frontier that remains unconquered—an America unclaimed. This is the great, the nationwide frontier of insecurity, of human want and fear. This is the frontier—the America—we have set ourselves to reclaim."[2]

— **President Franklin D. Roosevelt**
Radio Address on the Third Anniversary
of the Social Security Act, August 15, 1938

"Turn me loose, set me free, somewhere in the middle of Montana, and give me all I got coming to me. And keep your retirement and your so-called social security. Big City, turn me loose and set me free."[3]

— **Merle Haggard and Dean Holloway**
"Big City," 1981

E stablishing Social Security was the greatest mistake Congress made in the twentieth century. It started the transformation of America from a nation of self-reliant individualists into a nation of people dependent on government.

The founding fathers of Social Security rejected the pioneering spirit of can-do individualism celebrated by Frederick Jackson Turner, and saw the individual liberty enshrined in the Constitution by the Founding Fathers of the United States as an obstacle to the welfare state they dreamed of building.

In their view, the family values and self-reliance that served Americans so well on the frontier were unsuited to modern urban life. If American leaders of the Founding era viewed this nation as a model of republican liberty for the rest of the world to emulate, the leaders of the social security movement pointed to European nations as the model for the welfare state they believed America should become. Their America was not a shining city on a hill; it was a dim place in the shadow of enlightened Europe.

As Mark Levin explained in *Liberty and Tyranny*, one of the earliest advocates of "social insurance" in the United States was a Columbia University political economist named Henry Rogers Seager.[4] The Social Security Administration considers him one of its intellectual founders. This agency, which runs the Social Security system, has posted the entirety of Seager's 1910 book *Social Insurance: A Program of Social Reform* on its Web site.[5]

"The philosophy expressed by Seager would be the same general viewpoint favored by many of the founders of Social Security in America," the agency explains in presenting his work. "Seager's book expresses the thinking of Americans toward this new idea of social insurance which had its origins in Europe at the end of the 19th century."[6]

So what did Seager believe?

As Thomas C. Leonard, an economic historian at Princeton University, outlined in his essay "Retrospective: Eugenics and Economics in the Progressive Era," Seager, like a number of other progressive economists of his time, believed in eugenics.[7] He literally wanted to prohibit breeding among those members of the human race he viewed as inferior and incapable of becoming materially productive members of society.

Seager bluntly stated his views in a 1913 essay arguing for a minimum wage law.

> One important part of the program with reference to those who are defective from birth is to prevent that monstrous crime against future generations involved in permitting them to become the fathers and mothers who must suffer under the same handicap. If we are to maintain a race that is to be made up of capable, efficient and independent individuals and family groups we must courageously cut off lines of heredity that have been proved to be undesirable by isolation or sterilization.[8]

In the book posted online by the Social Security Administration, Seager advocated what can be fairly described as re-education-through-labor camps.

> The certainty of arrest and commitment to an industrial colony would deter many young men who are now attracted by the tramp's seemingly care-free existence from ever entering upon it. Those who were not deterred from the attempt to live without work, by such a policy, would in due course be sent to the farm colony, and there get the benefit of training in habits of industry...
>
> To legislate vagrants into suitable detention colonies appears to me to be a wise step, but it is equally important to correct, so far as we may, the conditions that create the vagrants. We must all agree that the chief of these conditions is the absence of suitable industrial training for boys and girls.[9]

Seager's desire to train American "boys and girls" to be good, compliant workers in an industrialized society proceeded from his vision of America as a place where individualism and self-reliance were not only outmoded but also—along with America's constitutional tradition of limited government—obstacles to building a better society.

Seager looked back at the same pioneering tradition historian Frederick Jackson Turner famously explored, but concluded it gave Americans an excessive focus on individual liberty:

> The variety and abundance of our resources have offered unrivaled opportunities for individual achievement. Dazzled by these, we have been absorbed in a mad struggle for individual success and blinded to our common interests. Nor is this all.
>
> As though it were not enough that heredity and environment combined to make us individualists, our forefathers wrote their individualistic creed into our federal and state constitutions. All these instruments give special sanctity to the right to liberty and property. As interpreted by the courts, a significance has been given to these constitutional rights that has seemed at times to make a fetish of the merely formal freedom of the individual. Thus it is not too much to say that Americans are born individualists in a country peculiarly favorable to the realization of individual ambitions and under a legal system which discourages and opposes resort to any but individualistic remedies for social evils.[10]

Seager wanted to end this American tradition. It might be all right for pioneers facing a wilderness, he argued, but not for city dwellers in a mature nation. Places "in which manufacturing and trade have become the dominant interests of the people, in which towns and cities have grown up, and in which the wage earner is the typical American citizen—the simple creed of individualism is no longer adequate," he said.

> For these sections we need not freedom from government interference, but clear appreciation of the conditions that make for the

common welfare, as contrasted with individual success, and an aggressive program of governmental control and regulation to maintain these conditions.[11]

To move America toward the "aggressive program of governmental control and regulation" he envisioned, Seager called for a comprehensive system of compulsory social insurance—and compulsory labor camps. America needed "collective remedies," he declared, for "protecting wage-earning families which have developed standards of living from losing them" and for "helping wage-earning families without standards to gain them."

These twin objectives required increasing the government's control over people's lives.

> The first end is to be accomplished by making obligatory for wage earners exposed to industrial accidents, illness, premature death, unemployment, and old age, adequate insurance against these evils. The second, by withdrawing from competitive industries the lowest grade of workers, the tramps and casuals, and giving them the benefit of industrial training in graded farm and industrial colonies, from which they shall be graduated only as they prove their ability to be independent and self-supporting. [12]

Seager argued that compulsory old-age insurance would be affordable because people would not receive benefits until they turned seventy, and most people would die before then. For the same reason, he believed it made little sense for Americans to save what they would need to provide for their own old age.

> Old age is a risk to which all are liable, but which many never live to experience. Thus, according to American life tables, nearly two thirds of those who survive the age of ten die before the age of seventy. Under these circumstances, for every wage earner to attempt

to save enough by himself to provide for his old age is needlessly costly.[13]

Seager further argued that social insurance would relieve children of the burden of caring for elderly parents, thus making families wealthier and the future brighter.

> Moreover, whatever the fact as regards saving for old age, there can be no doubt that the new policy will add to the incomes of families who feel the care of parents and grandparents a serious, even though not unwelcome, burden. The better provision for children that may result from this enlargement of family incomes should have a favorable effect on the rising generation.[14]

In 1934, when President Franklin D. Roosevelt announced his plan for a social security system, he echoed at least some of Seager's thinking. For Roosevelt, the frontier was closed. The era of American individualism and self-reliance was over. Americans could no longer depend on themselves and their families. They must now depend on government. In his elitist view, as in Seager's, it was naïve to think otherwise.

"In a simple and primitive civilization homes were to be had for the building. The bounties of nature in a new land provided crude but adequate food and shelter. When land failed, our ancestors moved on to better land. It was always possible to push back the frontier, but the frontier has now disappeared. Our task involves the making of a better living out of the lands that we have," Roosevelt said in his message to Congress, announcing the plan.

> So, also, security was attained in the earlier days through the interdependence of members of families upon each other and of the families within a small community upon each other. The complexities of great communities and of organized industry make less

real these simple means of security. Therefore, we are compelled to employ the active interest of the Nation as a whole through government in order to encourage a greater security for each individual who composes it.[15]

After the Social Security program was enacted in 1935, Roosevelt's administration started putting out propaganda telling Americans it was no longer possible for them to take care of themselves as Americans in previous eras had. They should now rely on the state.

"The colonists and frontiersman wanted independence. They wanted a chance for themselves and their children. They wanted a place of their own and an active share in the life of their times," a booklet published by Roosevelt's Social Security Board in 1937 said. "There is no reason to think that our wants have changed. These are the things most Americans ask today. What has changed is the way we take to get them. Families no longer can carve out security for themselves. Our security is the security of the people."[16]

In a 1938 radio address marking the third anniversary of the Social Security Act, Roosevelt turned the idea of the American frontier upside down. On the real frontier, Americans had traded a measure of security for matchless liberty. It was a place they went on their own and took care of their own. On Roosevelt's welfare-state frontier, Americans traded a measure of liberty for a modicum of security. It was a place where people in the government said they would take care of you.

"There is still today a frontier that remains unconquered—an America unclaimed," Roosevelt said. "This is the great, the nationwide frontier of insecurity, of human want and fear. This is the frontier—the America—we have set ourselves to reclaim."[17]

Packing the Court

Yet, the welfare state was not only contrary to America's pioneering cultural tradition, it was also contrary to America's constitutional tradition.

The Social Security Act that Roosevelt sent to Congress proposed more than just a federally run pension program for the elderly. It also included grants to the states to help state-based programs aid the elderly, grants to the states to help needy mothers and children, grants to the states to help the blind, and a federal payroll tax to fund state-administered unemployment insurance programs. The question that most worried the bill's authors, however, was whether legislation to force Americans to participate in a tax-funded, government-run retirement program would pass constitutional scrutiny—or whether it would be thrown out by a conservative majority on the Supreme Court.

Edwin E. Witte, whom Roosevelt appointed executive director of the Committee on Economic Security that drafted the Social Security Act, later reflected that the act moved through Congress and the Supreme Court in an historical window that was only open for a brief moment. This was when Roosevelt was at the height of his popularity and the Supreme Court made an unexpected lurch to the left. Twenty years after the bill became law, Witte recalled:

> A majority of the members of the Senate Committee on Finance believed old-age insurance to be unconstitutional, and it is my belief that several voted for it in the expectation that it would be invalidated by the Supreme Court. This also is to be said: while not then apparent, the timing of the Social Security Act was most fortunate. I doubt very much whether this or any similar measure could have passed, at least for many years, had it come before Congress later than 1935; also, whether it would have been held constitutional had this question come before the Supreme Court earlier than 1937.[18]

Thomas H. Eliot worked with Witte as counsel for the Committee on Economic Security. He later confessed that the bill's opponents made such a strong constitutional argument against compulsory tax-funded pensions that he was relieved he never had to testify on the point in Congress. "These arguments I found rather difficult to refute, and I'm glad I wasn't really called upon to do so as a witness before the committees of Congress because I had very grave doubts at that time about the likelihood of the Court's upholding the old-age insurance section of the bill."[19]

Advocates of compulsory old-age pensions had good reason for concern. The Supreme Court's decision in *Railroad Retirement Board v. Alton*, decided on May 6, 1935, three months before Congress took its final vote approving the Social Security Act, was a good indicator that the court might hold social security unconstitutional. The Railroad Retirement Act of 1934 had created what amounted to a social security program for workers in the railroad industry. It required all railroad employees to pay an initial 2 percent payroll tax to the federal government that would be credited to a trust fund overseen by a national board. The railroads themselves would pay a payroll tax at double the rate assessed against their workers. The funds raised by these payroll taxes would be used to pay a pension to all railroad workers who retired at age sixty-five or older. The law also ordered all railroad workers to retire at age seventy, even if they were still capable of doing their jobs and wanted to continue working.[20]

The court split six to three in declaring the Railroad Retirement Act unconstitutional. The six-member majority included the court's four-member conservative bloc — Pierce Butler, Willis Van Devanter, George Sutherland and James McReynolds — and the two swing votes, Chief Justice Charles Evans Hughes and Owen J. Roberts. The court's three liberals — Benjamin Cardozo, Louis Brandeis and Harlan Stone — dissented. Roberts wrote the majority's opinion, which was an unambiguous defense of the constitutional limits on federal power. The Constitution, he argued, simply did not give Congress the authority to force railroad companies to participate in a tax-funded, government-run pension program.

Roberts began the opinion by echoing the words of the Tenth Amendment, noting that the Constitution created a limited federal government that could only exercise the specific powers granted to it.

The federal government is one of enumerated powers; those not delegated to the United States by the Constitution, nor prohibited by it to the States, are reserved to the States or to the people. The Constitution is not a statute, but the supreme law of the land, to which all statutes must conform, and the powers conferred upon the federal government are to be reasonably and fairly construed with a view to effectuating their purposes. But recognition of this principle cannot justify attempted exercise of a power clearly beyond the true purpose of the grant.[21]

The Roosevelt administration had argued that forcing a pension program on the railroad industry was a legitimate act of federal power under Article 1, Section 8, Clause 3 of the Constitution, which authorizes Congress to "regulate commerce with foreign nations, and among the several states, and with the Indian tribes." As the court understood the government's argument, the idea was that if railroad workers knew that they would be financially secure in retirement, they would be happier at their work and the railroads would be safer—thus constituting an impact on interstate commerce. Roberts scoffed at this notion, and said it was beyond the constitutional power of Congress to create programs designed to achieve what Congress perceived to be desirable social ends—in this case, financial security for retired railroad employees. If the administration's interpretation of the Constitution were to prevail, he said, there would be no limit to the welfare state Congress could create. The next abuse of federal power, he speculated, might be mandatory free health care.

The theory is that one who has an assurance against future dependency will do his work more cheerfully, and therefore more efficiently. The question at once presents itself whether the fostering of a contented mind on the part of an employee by legislation of this type is, in any just sense, a regulation of interstate transportation. If that question be answered in the affirmative, obviously there is no limit to the field of so-called regulation. The catalogue of means and actions which might be imposed upon an employer in any business, tending to the satisfaction and comfort of his employees, seems endless. Provision for free medical attendance and nursing, for clothing, for food, for housing, for the education of children, and a hundred other matters, might with equal propriety be proposed as tending to relieve the employee of mental strain and worry.[22]

In 1935, this was an open-and-shut case for the majority of the Supreme Court. The Constitution did not empower Congress to create a welfare state, period. In his majority opinion, Roberts asked, "Can it fairly be said that the power of Congress to regulate interstate commerce extends to the prescription of any or all of these things? Is it not apparent that they are really and essentially related solely to the social welfare of the worker, and therefore remote from any regulation of commerce, as such? We think the answer is plain. These matters obviously lie outside the orbit of congressional power."[23]

Supporters of Roosevelt's Social Security proposal could not be blamed for drawing the logical conclusion from this decision: If the Supreme Court said Congress did not have the constitutional authority to create a compulsory tax-funded pension program for railroad workers, the court must also believe Congress did not have the constitutional authority to create a broader-based compulsory tax-funded pension program for employees across a wide range of industries and professions. Still, the administration pushed ahead with its legislation to create a compulsory, tax-funded pension program that would encompass most workers in the United States.

Few and Defined Powers

As it turned out, the Supreme Court did not follow through on the logical conclusion of its railroad-pension decision.

In December 1935, seven months after deciding the railroad case, the court heard arguments in *U.S.* v. *Butler*, a case testing the constitutionality of the Agricultural Adjustment Act of 1933. This act was designed to prop up the prices of farm commodities by placing an excise tax on food processing companies and using the proceeds to pay farmers not to farm. This time, the Roosevelt administration did not defend the law based on Congress's constitutional authority to regulate interstate commerce. Instead, it argued that the law was justified under Article 1, Section 8, Clause 1 of the Constitution, which says, "Congress shall have Power To Lay and collect Taxes, Duties, Imposts and Excises, to pay the Debts and provide for the common Defense and general Welfare of the United States; but all Duties, Imposts and Excises shall be uniform throughout the United States."

Taxing food processors and using the proceeds to pay farmers not to farm, the government argued, advanced the "general welfare of the United States."

This contention raised profound questions about the scope of federal power: could Congress spend money on a program it considered to be in the "general welfare" of the United States that was not clearly comprehended within the other powers specifically delegated to Congress in the rest of Article 1, Section 8 or elsewhere in the Constitution? If so, what were the limits on Congress's power to act in the "general Welfare"?

These were not new questions. The framers and ratifiers of the Constitution, and statesmen of the Founding era, had debated and discussed them, as well. As University of Montana Law Professor Robert G. Natelson, who studied the drafting, ratification, and history of the General Welfare Clause, concluded, the clause was not originally understood to grant the federal government any additional power. Instead it restricted Congress to using its taxing-and-spending power only to advance truly national interests as opposed to narrow special or local interests. Natelson wrote in the *University of Kansas Law Review*,

> On the contrary, the General Welfare Clause was an unqualified denial of spending authority. It did not add to federal powers; it subtracted from them. The General Welfare Clause was designed as a trust-style rule denying Congress authority to levy taxes for any

but general, national purposes. Because the Clause prevented Congress from using tax revenue for local or special interest purposes, the Clause indirectly qualified the appropriation power. Even if some enumerated power could be enlisted to support the appropriation, federal tax money was not to be used for the private benefit of a museum—however worthy—in Savannah, nor an artist—however struggling—in New York.[24]

In contrast to the Roosevelt government's position in 1935—that the General Welfare Clause justified their agricultural scheme—James Madison and Thomas Jefferson, key creators and framers of our nation's government, were leading voices in the Founding era who firmly asserted that the General Welfare Clause gave the federal government *no power* to take any action outside the scope of the other enumerated powers.[25]

In January 1788, Madison published Federalist 45, explaining that the yet-to-be-ratified Constitution divided power between the federal government and the states, leaving the federal government with "few and defined" powers that largely focused on the external, rather than internal, affairs of the nation.

> The powers delegated by the proposed Constitution to the federal government, are few and defined. Those which are to remain in the State governments are numerous and indefinite. The former will be exercised principally on external objects, as war, peace, negotiation, and foreign commerce; with which last the power of taxation will, for the most part, be connected. The powers reserved to the several States will extend to all the objects which, in the ordinary course of affairs, concern the lives, liberties, and properties of the people, and the internal order, improvement, and prosperity of the State.[26]

At the North Carolina ratifying convention later that year, Samuel Spencer, a state judge, expressed the views of many who, notwithstanding Madison's argument in the *Federalist,* advocated a bill of rights be created to more explicitly limit the power of the federal government.

> Our rights are not guarded. There is no declaration of rights, to secure to every member of the society those inalienable rights which ought not to be given up to any government. Such a bill of rights would be a check upon men in power. Instead of such a bill of rights, this Constitution has a clause which may warrant encroachments on the power of the respective state legislatures. I know it is said that what is not given up to the United States will be retained by the individual states. I know it ought to be so, and should be so understood; but, sir, it is not declared to be so.[27]

Spencer wanted a brighter line drawn between the power of the federal government and the rights of the people. "There ought to be a bill of rights, in order that those in power may not step over the boundary between the powers of government and the rights of the people, which they may do when there is nothing to prevent them.... I look upon it therefore that there ought to be something to confine the power of this government within its proper boundaries."[28]

Spencer concluded that a bill of rights "would keep the states from being swallowed up by a consolidated government."[29]

Another Founder, George Mason, who authored Virginia's Declaration of Rights, specifically referenced the General Welfare Clause while making an argument for adding language protecting the rights of states to the proposed Constitution at Virginia's ratifying convention (where Madison himself was also a delegate). Mason asked, "Is there any thing in this Constitution which secures to the states the powers which are said to be retained? Will powers remain to the states which are not expressly guarded and reserved?"[30]

If the Constitution did not include explicit language limiting Congress to its enumerated powers, Mason feared, Congress could trample on the fundamental rights of citizens.

I will suppose a case. Gentlemen may call it an impossible case, and suppose that Congress will act with wisdom and integrity. Among the enumerated powers, Congress are to lay and collect taxes, duties and imposts, and excises, and to pay the debts, and to provide for the general welfare and common defence; and by that clause (so often called the sweeping clause), they are to make all laws necessary to execute those laws.

Now suppose oppressions should arise under this government and any writer should dare to stand forth and expose to the community at large the abuses of those powers; could not Congress, under the idea of providing for the general welfare, and under their own construction, say that this was destroying the general peace, encouraging sedition, and poisoning the minds of the people? And could they not, in order to provide against this, lay a dangerous restriction on the press? Might they not even bring the trial for this restriction within the ten miles square, when there is no prohibition against it? Might they not thus destroy the trial by jury? Would they not extend their implication? It appears to me that they may and they will. And shall the support of our rights depend on the bounty of men whose interest it may be to oppress us?

That Congress should have power to provide for the general welfare of the Union, I grant. But I wish a clause in the Constitution, with respect to all powers which are not granted, that they are retained by the states. Otherwise, the power of providing for the general welfare may be perverted to its destruction.[31]

Mason took what President Ronald Reagan might later have called a trust-but-verify position.

Many gentlemen whom I respect, take different sides on this question. We wish this amendment [the Tenth Amendment] to be introduced, to remove our apprehensions. In my humble apprehension, unless there be some such clear and finite expression, this clause now under consideration will go to any thing our rulers may think proper. Unless there be some express declaration that every thing not given is retained, it will be carried to any power Congress may please.[32]

Loyola Law School Professor Kurt T. Lash, in a study of the origins of the Tenth Amendment, noted that at the ratifying conventions there was widespread sentiment for adding an amendment to the Constitution to clarify that the federal government would be limited to the specific powers enumerated for it in the document. That sentiment helped lead James Madison, who had originally opposed a bill of rights, to become its sponsor. In the *Notre Dame Law Review*, Lash wrote, "Along with their notice of ratification, most of the state conventions either proposed amendments which would restrict the new Congress to expressly enumerated powers or submitted "declarations" indicating their understanding that this principle already informed the Constitution. Delivering on a promise made to the Virginia convention, James Madison proposed a Bill of Rights, including early drafts of the Ninth and Tenth Amendments."[33]

Lash also noted that the New York convention issued this declaration with its ratification statement: "[E]very Power, Jurisdiction, and Right, which is not by the said Constitution clearly delegated to the Congress of the United States, or the departments of the Government thereof, remains to the People of the several States, or to their respective State Governments to whom they may have granted the same."[34]

In order to meet the concerns raised at the ratifying conventions, as a representative in the first Congress elected under the new Constitution, Madison introduced a set of amendments that would become the Bill of Rights. The Ninth Amendment stipulated that the necessarily limited list of rights enumerated in the Constitution "shall not be construed to deny or disparage others retained by the people." The Tenth Amendment said, "The powers not delegated to the United States by the Constitution, nor prohibited by it to the States, are reserved to the States respectively, or to the people." The Ninth and Tenth amendments should have ended all debate about whether the General Welfare Clause gave Congress unlimited legislative power or, on the contrary, the federal government was restricted to the enumerated powers delegated to it in the Constitution. Clearly, as Madison had written in The Federalist and as the ratification of these two amendments made certain, the Constitution created a federal government that was one of "few and defined" delegated powers.

But owing to the fact that politicians in power are always tempted to try to expand their power, the debate did not end there. The Ninth and Tenth Amendments served to reinforce the understanding of the Constitution that the ratifying states held: that the necessarily limited enumeration of individual rights in the Constitution "shall not be construed to deny or disparage others retained by the people," as the Ninth Amendment stated. And that, according to the Tenth Amendment, "powers not delegated to the United States by the Constitution, nor prohibited by it to the States, are reserved to the States respectively, or to the people."

The argument over the meaning of the Constitution and the powers of the federal government was not settled by the adoption of a Bill of Rights. During the presidency of George Washington, Treasury Secretary Alexander Hamilton ignited a debate about the meaning of the new Constitution when he proposed incorporating a national bank, making the case that a national bank would help the government carry out its specific delegated power to collect taxes and borrow money. Secretary of State Thomas Jefferson, backed by Madison, objected on constitutional grounds, and argued that the federal government did not have the authority to incorporate entities. Hamilton and Jefferson presented Washington with written adversarial opinions on the matter.

Jefferson argued that the constitutional principle of the Tenth Amendment was at the core of the new government. He wrote,

I consider the foundation of the Constitution as laid on this ground: That "all powers not delegated to the United States, by the Constitution, nor prohibited by it to the States, are reserved to the States or to the people." To take a single step beyond the boundaries thus specially drawn around the powers of Congress, is to take possession of a boundless field of power, no longer susceptible of any definition.[35]

He rejected the idea that the General Welfare Clause could be used to justify the federal government incorporating a bank, concluding that the power of Congress to provide for the general welfare was laced "up straitly" by the enumerated powers.

> For the laying of taxes is the power; and the general welfare is the purpose for which the power is to be exercised. They are not to lay taxes ad libitum for any purpose they please; but only to pay the debts or provide for the welfare of the Union. In like manner, they are not to do anything they please to provide for the general welfare but only to lay taxes for that purpose. To consider the latter phrase, not as describing the purpose of the first, but as giving a distinct and independent power to do any act they please, which might be for the good of the Union, would render all the preceding and subsequent enumerations of power completely useless. It would reduce the whole instrument to a single phrase, that of instituting a Congress with power to do whatever would be for the good of the United States; and, as they would be the sole judges of the good or evil, it would be also a power to do whatever else they please.[36]

Jefferson argued that to interpret the General Welfare Clause this way ran counter to common sense.

> It is an established rule of construction where a phrase will bear either of two meanings, to give it that which will allow some

meaning to the other parts of the instrument, and not that which would render all the others useless. Certainly no such universal power was meant to be given them. It was intended to lace them up straitly within the enumerated powers, and those without which, as means, these powers could not be carried into effect.[37]

Even though Jefferson conceded that the Constitution allowed Congress to use means not expressly stated in the document to carry out ends that were, he did not believe incorporating a bank qualified as such a means. In drawing this conclusion, he adopted a very narrow interpretation of what means were acceptable under the Necessary and Proper Clause: If a means was not literally "necessary," said Jefferson, it was not constitutional.

"It has been urged that a bank will give great facility or convenience in the collection of taxes," he wrote. "Suppose this were true: yet the Constitution allows only the means which are 'necessary,' not those which are merely 'convenient' for effecting the enumerated powers." Therefore, Jefferson concluded, in carrying out its specific powers, Congress was restricted to "the necessary means, that is to say, to those means without which the grant of power would be nugatory."[38]

In response, Hamilton did not base his argument for incorporating a national bank on the General Welfare Clause. Nor did he object to Jefferson's view that the government must act in accordance with the principle of the Tenth Amendment. As Hamilton wrote,

> The first of these arguments is, that the foundation of the Constitution is laid on this ground: "That all powers not delegated to the United States by the Constitution, nor prohibited to it by the States, are reserved for the States, or to the people." Whence it is meant to be inferred, that Congress can in no case exercise any power not included in those not enumerated in the Constitution. And it is affirmed that the power of erecting a corporation is not included in any of the enumerated powers.

"The main proposition here laid down, in its true signification is not to be questioned," he conceded. "It is nothing more than a consequence of this republican maxim, that all government is a delegation of power."[39]

But then Hamilton pointed out that Jefferson had accepted the fact that the Constitution created implied powers that could be used as means for carrying out its explicit powers. Where he and Jefferson differed was on the degree of discretion Congress could employ in choosing these means. He conceded that the justification for any means used by Congress had to rest on an enumerated power, but rejected Jefferson's conclusion that the incorporation of a bank did not.

> But the doctrine which is contended for is not chargeable with the consequences imputed to it. It does not affirm that the national government is sovereign in all respects, but that it is sovereign to a certain extent; that is, to the extent of the objects of its specified powers.
>
> It leaves, therefore, a criterion of what is constitutional, and of what is not so. This criterion is the end, to which the measure relates as a mean. If the end be clearly comprehended within any of the specified powers, and if the measure have an obvious relation to that end, and is not forbidden by any particular provision in the Constitution, it may safely be deemed to come within the compass of the national authority.[40]

As a concrete example of what this meant, Hamilton used the police department of Philadelphia, which he believed was beyond the regulatory reach of the federal government. He wrote,

> Thus a corporation may not be erected by Congress for superintending the police of the city of Philadelphia, because they are not authorized to regulate the police of that city. But one may be erected in relation to the collection of taxes, or to the trade with

foreign countries, or to the trade between the States, or with the Indian tribes; because it is the province of the federal government to regulate those objects, and because it is incident to a general sovereign or legislative power to regulate a thing, to employ all means which relate to its regulation to the best and greatest advantage.[41]

Washington sided with Hamilton and signed the bank bill. Then, ten months later, Hamilton presented his Report on Manufactures, which included a proposal that the federal government provide "bounties" to factories and farmers to broaden the base of the national economy. To justify doing this, Hamilton offered a much broader interpretation of federal power than he had in his argument for the national bank. Here he suggested an interpretation of the General Welfare Clause that seemed to move in the direction of creating the open-ended legislative power that, in The Federalist, Madison had argued the Constitution did not allow, and that the Tenth Amendment had been proposed to prevent. Now Hamilton argued:

> The terms "general welfare" were doubtless intended to signify more than was expressed or imported in those which preceded; otherwise, numerous exigencies incident to the affairs of a nation would have been left without a provision. The phrase is as comprehensive as any that could have been used, because it was not fit that the constitutional authority of the Union to appropriate its revenues should have been restricted within narrower limits than the "general welfare," and because this necessarily embraces a vast variety of particulars, which are susceptible neither of specification nor of definition.[42]

He argued that it should be left to Congress to decide what kind of federal spending was in the "general welfare" and therefore constitutionally legitimate. As he wrote in the Report,

It is, therefore of necessity left to the discretion of the National Legislature to pronounce upon the objects which concern the general welfare, and for which, under that description, an appropriation of money is requisite and proper. And there seems to be no room for a doubt that whatever concerns the general interests of learning, of agriculture, of manufactures, and of commerce are within the sphere of the national councils, as far as regards, an application of money.

The only qualification of the generality of the phrase in question, [i.e., "general welfare"] which seems to be admissible, is this: That the object to which an appropriation of money is to be made be general, and not local; its operation extending in fact or by possibility throughout the Union, and not being confined to a particular spot.

No objection ought to arise to this construction, from a supposition that it would imply a power to do whatever else should appear to Congress conducive to the general welfare. A power to appropriate money with this latitude, which is granted, too, in express terms, would not carry a power to do any other thing not authorized in the Constitution either expressly or by fair implication.[43]

Despite Hamilton's argument in the Report on Manufactures, more than 140 years later the nation had still not drifted far from the limited-government interpretation of the General Welfare Clause that had been presented by Madison and Jefferson, and that was consistent with the Tenth Amendment. In *U.S.* v. *Butler*, the court again voted six to three against the government. Hughes and Roberts again joined the four conservatives. Roberts again wrote the majority opinion, and he again said Congress had taken an action beyond the powers delegated to it by the Constitution. "The act invades the reserved rights of the states," he wrote. "It is a statutory plan to regulate and control agricultural production, a matter beyond the powers delegated to the federal government."[44]

But Roberts also made a seemingly contradictory point. He said Alexander Hamilton (as interpreted from his Reports on Manufactures by Justice Joseph Story in his *Commentaries on the Constitution of the United States*[45]) was right in taking an expansive view of the federal spending power under the General Welfare Clause. "It results," wrote Roberts, "that the power of Congress to authorize expenditure of public moneys for public purposes is not limited by the direct grants of legislative power found in the Constitution."[46]

The court would soon exploit Roberts's concession to authorize the sort of federal social insurance Roberts had ruled against in the railroad case.

Switch in Time

In November 1936, Democrats won a sweeping victory in the national elections. Roosevelt was reelected with 60 percent of the vote, taking every state except Vermont and Maine. The Democrats returned to Washington controlling not only the White House but also 334 of the 435 seats in the House and 76 of the 96 seats in the Senate.

Seemingly in solid control of the first and second branches of the federal government, Roosevelt launched a campaign to control the third—a Supreme Court he had viewed as hostile territory.

In February 1937, Roosevelt proposed the Judicial Reorganization Act, popularly known as his "court-packing" plan. The act would allow the president to increase the number of justices on the court from nine to a maximum of fifteen by giving him the power to name an additional justice for each sitting justice who reached the age of seventy and six months and did not retire.

With conservative Justice Butler having turned seventy in 1936, there were now six justices past that age—four conservatives, one swing vote, and one liberal.

In a March 9, 1937 radio broadcast, Roosevelt defended this scheme as a means to secure a Supreme Court that would accept a vast expansion of federal power based on a broad interpretation of the words "general welfare" in the Constitution. Roosevelt cited the phrase as it appeared both in the Preamble and in Article 1, Section 8, Clause 1. He cleverly edited the latter, using a formulation that could more readily be interpreted to support a more powerful government than the true text would.

Where the actual words of Article 1, Section 8, Clause 1 give Congress the authority to "lay and collect taxes, duties, imposts and excises, to pay the debts and provide for the common defence and general welfare of the United States," Roosevelt presented the clause as if it granted a unique power to provide for the general welfare separate and apart from the power to tax. The clause, he said, gave Congress "ample broad powers 'to levy taxes . . . and provide for the common defense and general welfare of the United States.'"[47]

At the same time, he posed as an originalist in his interpretation of the Constitution. The Framers, he argued, had envisioned a future in which the federal government could assume ever changing powers depending on historical circumstances. In his radio address, Roosevelt claimed,

> In its Preamble, the Constitution states that it was intended to form a more perfect union and promote the general welfare; and the powers given to the Congress to carry out those purposes can best be described by saying that they were all the powers needed to meet each and every problem which then had a national character and which could not be met by merely local action.
>
> But the framers of the Constitution went further. Having in mind that in succeeding generations many other problems then undreamed of would become national problems, they gave to the Congress the ample broad powers "to levy taxes . . . and provide for the common defense and general welfare of the United States."
>
> That, my friends, is what I honestly believe to have been the clear and underlying purpose of the patriots who wrote a federal Constitution to create a national government with national power, intended as they said, "to form a more perfect union for ourselves and our posterity."

Mere moments later, Roosevelt dropped the pretense of being an original-ist, saying, "[W]e must have judges who will bring to the courts a present-day sense of the Constitution."[48]

Soon after this radio address, the Supreme Court released a remarkable string of opinions relating to New Deal legislation. Although the mem-bership of the court had not changed, its attitude towards FDR's agenda had, with both Chief Justice Hughes and Justice Roberts now siding with the liberals. In *The Supreme Court Reborn: The Constitutional Revolution in the Age of Roosevelt*, historian William E. Leuchtenburg described it this way:

> On March 29, by 5-4 in the *Parrish* case with Justice Roberts join-ing the majority, the Court upheld a minimum wage statute from the state of Washington that to most people seemed identical to the New York law it had wiped out in *Tipaldo* less than a year before. Two weeks later, Roberts joined in a series of 5-4 decisions finding the National Labor Relations Act constitutional. On May 24, the Court validated the Social Security law. These rulings marked a historic change in constitutional doctrine. The Court was now stating that local and national governments had a whole range of powers that this same tribunal had been saying for the past two years these governments did not have.[49]

The *Parrish* case, argued in December 1936 after the Democratic election landslide, had actually been decided by the court before Roosevelt announced his court-packing plan. But the National Labor Relations Act case and the Social Security cases were argued and decided after Roosevelt announced his court-packing plan.

In Social Security Act opinions, which were released on May 24, 1937, the court voted 5 to 4 for the unemployment insurance payroll tax and 7 to 2 for the compulsory tax-funded pension program. In a stunning reversal to his explicit position on the Railroad Retirement Act, Justice Roberts joined the liberals in both cases. In both cases, liberal Justice Benjamin Cardozo wrote the opinion of the court. In both, he adopted Roosevelt's interpretation of the General Welfare Clause and justified it by pointing to Roberts's defense of Alexander Hamilton's view in *U.S. v. Butler*. Roberts wrote no opinion of his own.

Cardozo did not quote the full context of Article 1, Section 8, Clause 1 in his opinions or present any systematic or scholarly argument about the meaning of the words "general welfare" or the intent of the Framers in writing them.

"It is too late today for the argument to be heard with tolerance that, in a crisis so extreme, the use of the moneys of the nation to relieve the unemployed and their dependents is a use for any purpose narrower than the promotion of the general welfare," he said in *Steward*, and referenced Roberts's interpretation of the General Welfare Clause in *Butler* as precedent.[50]

"Congress may spend money in aid of the 'general welfare.' Constitution, Art. I, section 8," Cardozo wrote in *Helvering*, again citing Butler as precedent. "There have been great statesmen in our history who have stood for other views. We will not resurrect the contest. It is now settled by decision."[51]

In *Helvering*, Cardozo said the court should leave it to Congress to decide what it could legitimately do in the name of the "general welfare."

> The line must still be drawn between one welfare and another, between particular and general. Where this shall be placed cannot be known through a formula in advance of the event. There is a middle ground, or certainly a penumbra, in which discretion is at large. The discretion, however, is not confided to the courts. The discretion belongs to Congress, unless the choice is clearly wrong, a display of arbitrary power, not an exercise of judgment.

Cardozo also declared that the meaning of "general welfare" should be expected to change, depending on the "needs" of the time.

Nor is the concept of the general welfare static. Needs that were
narrow or parochial a century ago may be interwoven in our day
with the wellbeing of the Nation. What is critical or urgent
changes with the times.[52]

What made Justice Roberts flip flop? Why did he endorse Cardozo's opinions in the Social Security cases only two years after overturning the Railroad Retirement Act? Why did the conservatives Sutherland and Van
Devanter—who announced that he would be retiring only six days before
the court published the Social Security Act decisions[53]—also quietly assent
to the Helvering decision?

Roberts's stand against compulsory tax-funded railroad pensions came
before the massive Democratic election victory of November 1936 and
Roosevelt's court-packing proposal of February 1937. The counsel for the
Committee on Economic Security himself believed Justices Roberts and
Hughes may have changed their approach to New Deal legislation to fore-
stall Roosevelt's proposal to pack the court. Years later, Thomas Eliot, when
asked why he thought the court upheld Social Security, reflected,

> What happened in 1937 was that in February the President came
> out with a scheme to "pack" the Court. No one knows, and there
> is some dispute about it, but I think that probably it's fair to say that
> the Court was not unmindful of this attack. Two justices, Hughes
> and Roberts, were very alarmed for the future independence of the
> Court. They were, especially Hughes, anxious to prevent the
> [Court packing] bill from going through. However that may be,
> the fact is that in April the National Labor Relations Act came
> before the Court for decision while the President's plan to pack
> the Court by adding six new justices was still being considered in
> the Senate. Hughes and Roberts joined three liberal justices, who
> had been voting in favor of the New Deal legislation, to uphold
> the National Labor Relations Act—even though in doing so they

seemed to be repudiating their own opinions in earlier cases. Whether they did this in order to save the Court from defeat in the Senate I don't know but it may be so. After that break, it was not altogether unexpected that the old age insurance provisions would likewise be upheld. I think the unemployment compensation provisions were fairly safe all the way along because of the earlier decision. I don't know whether this is right or not. There were nine justices on the Supreme Court; one or two of them had to change their positions pretty fundamentally to thwart the threat of that number of nine being added to by six new justices appointed by the President. The old saying about that particular change of front is that, "A switch in time saved nine."[54]

It also cleared the way for a massive increase in government control over people's lives.

Poster Girl

From the signing the Declaration of Independence in 1776 until 1940, no American received a single penny in Social Security payments from the federal government. Succeeding generations, driven by individual initiative and a desire to improve their own lives, tamed a wilderness and built farms, towns, cities, and suburbs. Each left behind a wealthier country for their children.

Then in 1940—the same year President Roosevelt flouted the two-term-limit tradition instituted by President Washington—the Roosevelt administration doled out the first Social Security checks.

The case of the very first beneficiary illustrates why Social Security was a bad deal for America. It was instantly obvious the program was not so much a government-run pension plan as a system for redistributing wealth. Over time it would become apparent that the system increased government leverage over seniors' lives.

Ida May Fuller, a 65-year-old secretary from Vermont, took the first check. Her contributions to the system were less than meager. From January 1, 1937, when the Social Security tax first took effect, until November 1, 1939, when she retired, she paid a 1 percent payroll tax on her annual salary of approximately $900, and the law firm that employed her paid another 1 percent. Together she and the firm paid a lifetime total of $49.50 in Social Security taxes on her behalf.

On January 31, 1940, the government cut Fuller her first monthly benefit check. It was for $22.54. By March 1940, when the government sent Fuller her third check for $22.54, her cumulative benefits had reached $67.62, outstripping the $49.50 she and her employer had paid in Social Security taxes.[55]

The government kept sending Fuller checks. She kept cashing them. By the time she died at 100 years of age in 1975, she had been receiving regular monthly payments from the government for more than a third of her life. Her total take in Social Security benefits was $22,888.92. That was 460 times what she and her employer had paid in Social Security taxes.[56]

For Fuller, Social Security was a winning lottery ticket. For government officials bent on promoting the welfare state, she was the perfect poster girl. Social Security bureaucrats promoted her so persistently as their model beneficiary that in 1994 Democratic Senator Daniel Patrick Moynihan of New York could give a speech on the Senate floor reminiscently referring to her by first name. "I can remember from my youth," said Moynihan, "the annual photograph of the gentleman from the Social Security Administration presenting Ida May with her first check of the year."[57]

One photo of Fuller printed in a government brochure published during the Johnson administration carried a caption pointing out that she was born on a farm in a family with pioneering ancestors. It read,

> Miss Ida Fuller of Ludlow, Vermont, received the very first monthly social security benefit check in January 1940. The retired

legal secretary, who is now 90 years of age, has received a check every month since. Miss Fuller's family had settled in Vermont in 1635. She was born on a farm a few miles from her present home and was the oldest of four children.[58]

Thus a descendant of pioneers became a celebrity for longevity on the dole.

The plain truth about the $22,888.92 the Social Security system gave Fuller is this: Most of it came out of someone else's pocket.

In a sense, even the first $49.50 the government paid Fuller was not her money in the same way it would have been if she had saved and invested it herself. That is because the government ran deficits in each of the years Fuller paid Social Security taxes.[59] It thus necessarily spent all the Social Security tax revenue it received from her the same year she paid it. The payments the government made to Fuller and other initial beneficiaries in 1940 needed to be funded by new federal borrowing or by money taxed away from younger workers in that year.

Social Security contributed to two major trends in American government that followed from Roosevelt's founding of a welfare state: federal borrowing increased and federal taxing increased. Government's need to make promised benefit payments to people who were not working increased the burden of government on those who were.

Between 1776 and 1940 when Fuller received her first Social Security check, the federal government accumulated a total debt of $43 billion.[60] By 1975, when Fuller received her last Social Security check, the debt had boomed to $533.2 billion.[61] During the intervening decades, the federal government had run an annual budget deficit in all but six years.[62]

Over the years, politicians in Washington increased the benefits doled out to Social Security recipients while hiking the Social Security taxes on those still working. In 1972, Congress finally put benefit increases on autopilot, enacting legislation to provide for annual Cost of Living Adjustments. During the period Ida May Fuller was collecting Social Security benefits, the combined employer-employee tax for "Old Age and Survivors

Insurance" more than quadrupled from 2 percent to 9.9 percent. The maximum annual income subjected to the tax also more than quadrupled from $3,000 to $14,100.[63]

Since Fuller's day, both the Social Security tax rate and amount of taxable income have increased. The tax is now 10.4 percent, and as of 2010, the taxable income was $106,800.

When the Social Security Act was debated on the Senate floor in 1935, Republican Senator Daniel Hastings of Delaware accurately predicted that the system would place an escalating tax burden on younger Americans in order to transfer their wealth to older Americans.

> When the young men of the future ask why they and their employers should have to pay so large a rate, the answer will be that years before their fathers and grandfathers had made promises to each other which they did not have the money to carry out in the full. Therefore, they conveniently decided to pass on the deficiency by assessing a surcharge against their children and grandchildren.[64]

Unlike later generations of beneficiaries, Ida May Fuller had not approached retirement expecting or depending on the government to borrow from the future on her behalf. She had not planned her financial life around Social Security. In fact, she did not even qualify as a beneficiary under the law as originally enacted.

Under that initial version of the law, monthly benefit payments were not scheduled to begin until 1942 and would be paid only to those sixty-five or older who had paid the Social Security tax for at least five years. Retirees who had not paid for five years were to be given a modest lump sum intended to compensate them for the Social Security taxes they had paid. When Fuller retired in 1939, she had been paying the tax for only two years and ten months. But three months before she retired, President Roosevelt signed amendments reducing Social Security's eligibility requirements and moving the starting date for monthly benefit payments from 1942 to 1940.

Fuller first visited a Social Security office — after she had retired — almost on a whim. "It wasn't that I expected anything, mind you, but I knew I'd been paying for something called Social Security and I wanted to ask the people in Rutland [VT] about it," she said.[65]

A 1964 Social Security Administration brochure described Fuller as a vigorous 90-year-old who maintained a separate household and income sources beyond Social Security. "Miss Fuller lives alone in her own home and does her own housework," said the brochure. "She supplements her social security benefits with the rental of an apartment and income from some bank stock she owns."[66] The agency later reported that Fuller lived the last eight years of her life with relatives.[67]

As the Social Security system became a settled fact in American life, recipients who had spent a lifetime paying taxes into it became more dependent on the benefits they received. In 2006, according to the Social Security Administration, 63.5 percent of Social Security beneficiaries 65 or older derived at least half their income from their monthly benefit check. Almost 22 percent derived all their income from the program.[68]

To maintain seniors at this level of government dependence for their income will require higher taxes or more government debt. In 2010, according to the Congressional Budget Office, the Social Security system will pay out more in benefits than it brings in through payroll taxes. Over the next seventy-five years, if Social Security taxes and benefits remain at the same levels, the government will need to borrow an additional $7.7 trillion to maintain the system.[69]

However, as we shall explore in the next chapter, Social Security's fiscal problems may seem like a spring breeze compared the financial hurricane looming over the horizon in the form of government-controlled healthcare.

Almost three decades ago, singer-songwriter Merle Haggard and fellow composer Dean Holloway scored a hit with a song called "Big City." It seemed to call Americans back to the defiant, individualistic spirit of the frontier. "Been working every day since I was twenty," sang Haggard. "Haven't got a thing to show for everything I've done. There's folks who never work and they've got plenty. Think it's time for guys like me to have some fun."

The chorus declared: "Turn me loose, set me free, somewhere in the middle of Montana, and give me all I've got coming to me. And keep your retirement and your so-called Social Security. Big City, turn me loose and let me free."[70]

Historian of the American frontier Frederick Jackson Turner would have appreciated the national spirit that made those lyrics popular. Franklin Roosevelt would have lamented it. Barack Obama may put an end to it.

Chapter 3

"We Have Plenty of Authority"
Liberals Want to Control Your Health Care

"We have plenty of authority."[1]

—Senate Judiciary Chairman Patrick Leahy

"If that is held constitutional—for them to be able to tell us we have to purchase health insurance—then there is literally nothing that the federal government can't force us to do. Nothing."[2]

—Senator Orrin Hatch

"It's easy to get up in front of the cameras and rant against exploding deficits."[3]

—President Barack Obama

T
he reporter asked a good question, but Senator Patrick Leahy did not have a good answer.

    Leahy, a Vermont Democrat, chairs the Judiciary Committee, the panel that approves nominees to the United States Supreme Court. He ought to know constitutional issues as well as anyone on Capitol Hill. Yet, when Congress was debating President Obama's plan to force individuals to buy health insurance, Leahy acted as if this revolutionary proposal raised no constitutional issue at all. When reporter Matt Cover of CNSNews.com asked him about one, he responded with scorn.

"Where, in your opinion, does the Constitution give specific authority for Congress to [enact] an individual mandate for health insurance?" asked Cover.

"We have plenty of authority," Leahy said. "Are you saying there is no authority?"

"I'm asking," said Cover.

"Why would you say there is no authority?" said Leahy. "I mean, there's no question there's authority. Nobody questions that."[4]

Cover put the same question to House Speaker Nancy Pelosi, a California Democrat. "Madame Speaker," he said, "where specifically does the Constitution grant Congress the authority to enact an individual health insurance mandate?"

"Are you serious?" said Pelosi. "Are you serious?"

"Yes, yes I am," said Cover.

Pelosi turned mutely away. Her spokesman told Cover: "You can put this on the record. That is not a serious question."[5]

Had these encounters occurred in a fictional Hollywood movie rather than in the halls of Congress, James Madison might have emerged from a nearby doorway to personally ask Leahy and Pelosi: Which article, section, and clause of the Constitution delegated to Congress the power to force individuals to buy health insurance? Where did the people grant you the authority to control this very personal and consequential decision?

Back in 1994, when Congress also considered proposals that would have forced individuals to buy health insurance, the Congressional Budget Office (CBO) studied the issue. The federal government, it discovered, had never before ordered Americans to buy anything. "A mandate requiring all individuals to buy health insurance would be an unprecedented form of federal action," said CBO. "The government has never required people to buy any good or service as a condition of lawful residence in the United States."

CBO uncovered only one federal mandate on individuals that even remotely resembled forcing individuals to buy health insurance. It was the mandate that young men register for the draft. "Federal mandates that apply to individuals are extremely rare," said CBO. "One example is the requirement that draft-age men register with the Selective Service System. The Congressional Budget Office is not aware of any others imposed by current law."[6]

There is a big difference, however, between Congress forcing young men to register for the draft and Congress forcing all Americans to buy health insurance. Several enumerated powers of Congress can at least arguably justify making men of a certain age register for the Selective Service. These include the powers to "raise and support armies" (Article 1, Section 8, Clause 12), to "provide and maintain a Navy" (Article 1, Section 8, Clause 13), to "make rules for the government and regulation of the land and naval forces" (Article 1, Section 8, Clause 14), and to "provide for organizing, arming, and disciplining the militia" (Article 1, Section 8, Clause 16).

To plausibly argue that forcing people to buy health insurance is the constitutional equivalent of forcing young men to register for the draft, a person would need to point to the specifically enumerated power of Congress that is achieved by means of the health insurance mandate the same way that Congress's specifically enumerated power to "raise and support armies" is achieved by means of the draft-registration mandate. To be consistent with the logic that guided Alexander Hamilton's argument that incorporating a national bank was a legitimate means for carrying out Congress's specifically enumerated powers to tax and borrow, they would also need to show that forcing individuals to buy health insurance was not immoral and did not trample on the inalienable rights of citizens.

During the debate over the health care bill, Senator Jack Reed, a Rhode Island Democrat, did try to draw a constitutional analogy between forcing people to register for the draft and forcing them to buy health insurance. He could not say, however, what specific enumerated power of Congress justified this insurance mandate in the same way Congress's power to raise an army could arguably justify the draft-registration mandate.

"Specifically where in the Constitution does Congress get its authority to mandate that individuals purchase health insurance?" CNSNews.com reporter Edwin Mora asked Reed. He replied,

> Let me see. I would have to check the specific sections. So, I'll have to get back to you on the specific section. But it is not unusual that Congress has required individuals to do things, like sign up for the draft, and do many other things, too, which I don't think are specifically contained [in the Constitution]. It gives Congress the right to raise an army, but it doesn't say you can take people and draft them. But since that was something necessary for the functioning of the government over the past several years, the practice on the books, it's been recognized, the authority to do that.[7]

Leahy, Pelosi, and Reed were far from the only members of Congress who dodged or dismissed the question of where the Constitution authorized them to enact a law forcing individuals to buy health insurance. In a series of interviews on Capitol Hill, CNSNews.com reporters encountered numerous senators and representatives who supported forcing individuals to buy health insurance but had no clue where the Constitution authorized Congress to exercise that sort of power.

Some admitted they could point to no constitutional language justifying the mandate. "Does the United States Constitution give the United States Congress the authority to mandate individuals to have health insurance, to carry health insurance?" reporter Nicholas Ballasy asked Senator Daniel Akaka of Hawaii.

"I am not aware of that," said Akaka. "Let me put it that way."

Ballasy tried again. "Is there any specific area of the Constitution that would give Congress the authority to be able to mandate individuals to have to purchase health insurance?" he asked.

"Not in particular with health insurance," said Akaka. "It's not covered in that respect."[8]

Senator Bob Casey of Pennsylvania had a similar answer. "Well, I don't know if there is a specific constitutional provision," he said.[9]

Senator Ben Nelson of Nebraska suggested that only a constitutional scholar was qualified to say where the Constitution authorized Congress to force citizens to buy health insurance. "Well, you know, I don't know that I'm a constitutional scholar," he said. "So, I, I'm not going to be able to answer that question."[10]

Other senators said staff lawyers could answer for them. "Well, we're very lucky as members of the Senate to have constitutional lawyers on our staff, so I'll let them answer that," said Senator Mary Landrieu of Louisiana.[11]

Senate Budget Chairman Kent Conrad of North Dakota guessed it was the Commerce Clause, but left it to the Senate's legal counsel to say for sure. "Could you specifically say where in the Constitution does Congress get the authority to mandate that individuals get health insurance?" CNSNews.com's Mora asked.

"No," said Conrad, "but I'll refer you to legal counsel for the Senate, and they're the ones that lead there, as the full legal basis for the individual mandate—and I assume it's in the Commerce Clause."[12]

Some members adopted a slippery slope theory of constitutional interpretation. Rather than cite a specific article and clause, they pointed out that Congress had already created Medicare, forcing elderly people into a government run health-insurance system.

"Where in the Constitution does Congress get the authority for an individual health care mandate?" CNSNews.com's Cover asked Senator Sherrod Brown of Ohio.

"The same part of the Constitution that allows us to have Medicare," said Brown. "When I hear people think this is a constitutional issue, my first suggestion to them is, 'Do you want to repeal Medicare?' And some people, politically, are so extreme in this country that they want to repeal Medicare, and I think they are dead wrong."[13]

Senator Bernard Sanders of Vermont, a self-professed socialist, added Medicaid, the Children's Health Insurance Program, and veteran's entitlements to the slippery slope theory. "Where in the Constitution?" said Sanders. "Probably the same place that comes Medicare and Medicaid and the CHIP program and the Veterans Administration and health care programs that we've been doing for many, many decades."[14]

Senator Mark Warner of Virginia not only used Medicare and Medicaid as examples of why he believed there must be language somewhere in the Constitution that empowered Congress to force people to buy health insurance, but also cited state driver's license laws.

"Does the Constitution give Congress the authority to mandate whether individuals should purchase health insurance?" CNSNews.com's Ballasy asked Warner.

"The United States Congress passed laws regarding Medicare and Medicaid that became de facto mandatory programs," said Warner. "States all the time require people to have driver's licenses. I think that this is a bit of a spurious argument that's being made by some folks."[15]

Apparently, Warner's reasoning is that if the particular state constitutions include language that authorizes the legislatures of those states to require people in those states to secure driver's licenses before they can drive a car, then the federal constitution must include language that authorizes the federal Congress to require people everywhere in the Union to buy health insurance if they happen to be alive.

Senator Claire McCaskill of Missouri made a similar argument based on state-mandated auto insurance. But she then quickly surrendered the issue to the Supreme Court. "In most states, the government mandates the buying of car insurance," she said, "and I can assure everyone that if anything in this bill is unconstitutional, the Supreme Court will weigh in."[16]

Two senators who did cite specific constitutional clauses that they claimed authorized the Congress to force people to buy health insurance disagreed on which clause it was. Senator Jeff Merkley, picking up where Justice Benjamin Cardozo left off in his decision on Social Security in *Helvering* v. *Davis*, cited the General Welfare Clause. "The very first enumerated power is power to provide for the common defense and general welfare," he said. "So it's right on, right on the front end."[17]

Senator Dianne Feinstein of California cited a clause control freaks often use to justify greater federal intrusion into our lives. "Well, I would assume it would be in the Commerce Clause of the Constitution," said Feinstein. "That's how Congress legislates all kinds of various programs."[18]

Then there were two members who cited non-existent constitutional language. One of them was House Judiciary Chairman John Conyers, the Michigan Democrat who runs the House panel most responsible for constitutional issues. "Under several clauses, the good and welfare clause and a couple others," said Conyers. "All the scholars, the constitutional scholars that I know—I'm chairman of the Judiciary Committee, as you know—they all say there's nothing unconstitutional in this bill and if there were, I would have tried to correct it if I thought there were."[19] Presumably, the chairman meant the General Welfare Clause when he said the "good and welfare clause."

"What does the Constitution say?" said Senator Roland Burris, the Illinois Democrat. "To provide for the health, welfare and the defense of the country."[20]

The word "health" does not appear in the Constitution.

The day before President Obama signed the health care bill, as several states were preparing to file suit against it, reporters pressed White House

Spokesman Robert Gibbs to explain why the White House thought the individual mandate was constitutionally justified.

"I think there's pretty longstanding precedent on the constitutionality of this," Gibbs told one reporter.[21]

Another pressed him for a more specific answer. "You say there's established law, established precedent," said the reporter. "On what, what is it? What is the established precedent?"

"On the regulation of interstate commerce," said Gibbs.

The reporter then asked how mandating an individual to buy health insurance was part of interstate commerce.

"Well, that's—I think, again—look, I'm not a lawyer, right," said Gibbs.[22]

Unlike Gibbs, Virginia Attorney General Ken Cuccinelli was not confused by the question. Acting under power it believed the Constitution reserved to the states, the Virginia legislature had enacted a law stating that Virginians could not be forced to buy health insurance. The same day President Obama signed his health insurance mandate, Cuccinelli moved to protect his state's law and the liberty of Virginians by suing in federal court to have Obama's mandate overturned. Cuccinelli grasped a self-evident truth: choosing not to buy health insurance is not an act of interstate commerce. Because the state of simply being alive while not owning insurance is not an act of interstate commerce, it cannot be regulated by the federal government. Cuccinelli said,

> Just being alive is not interstate commerce. If it were, there would be no limit to the U.S. Constitution's commerce clause and to Congress's authority to regulate everything we do. There has never been a point in our history where the federal government has been given the authority to require citizens to buy goods or services.[23]

The Commerce Clause is written in plain English. It gives Congress the power to "regulate Commerce with foreign nations, and among the several States, and with the Indian Tribes." In other words, it authorizes Congress to regulate "commerce" that takes place across the borders of the United States, or across the borders of the states, or with Indian tribes.

The extent of this authority can be illustrated by following an imaginary orange from producer to consumer. Say, for example, a grocery store chain in New York buys oranges from a farm in Mexico. That is an act of commerce "with a foreign nation." Congress, therefore, can regulate that transaction.

Now, say, the grocery store chain buys oranges from a farm in Florida. That is an act of commerce "among the several States." Congress, therefore, can regulate that transaction, too.

Then, suppose a person is sitting on his porch on Long Island. He decides he would like some oranges. So, he goes down to the local outlet of the grocery store chain to buy some. This New Yorker may discover that when he gets to the grocery store, he does not like the impact that one or another federal regulation has had on the quality or the cost of the oranges on sale. He may even think the lawmakers in Congress were fools to enact those regulations. Even so, he cannot plausibly contest Congress's constitutional authority to regulate the commerce that brought those oranges from Mexico or Florida to this store in his Long Island town. The Constitution gave Congress that authority in specific terms.

Now, suppose this New Yorker decides he does not want oranges after all. He momentarily ponders buying a carton of orange juice instead. Then he decides to take the money he was about to spend at the store and put it in his savings account. He is hoping to take his children to Disney World next winter and thinks that would be a far better use of his money than buying any of the overripe oranges in this lousy store.

Under our Constitution, the federal government has no power to overrule this man's decision.

President Barack Obama, all nine members of the U.S. Supreme Court, all 100 U.S. senators, and all 435 members of the U.S. House of Representatives may unanimously agree that this New York man was a fool when he decided to save his money for a trip to Disney World rather than investing it in the Florida oranges offered for sale at this grocery store chain. These officials can use their freedom of speech, if they wish, to loudly state their personal opinions that eating oranges is good for people, and that all Americans ought to eat them. However, under the Constitution of the United States, they have no power whatsoever to enact a law or issue an order requiring that this man—or anyone else—buy an orange.

The American people did not delegate this kind of power to Congress. The New York man, like all other Americans, remains a free person. If he does not want to buy oranges, no one in the federal government can force him to buy oranges. They no more have the power to tell him he must eat citrus fruit, than they have the power to tell him he must take his children to Disney World. Nor can Congress tell him what car to buy, or what newspaper to read, or what television network to watch, or what church to attend. Our Constitution was designed to protect these freedoms. It did not give the president, Congress, or federal judges the power to annihilate them.

Liberal control freaks in Congress and the Supreme Court have been working for decades to stretch the Commerce Clause beyond its true meaning, and thus increase federal control over our lives. In the 1942 case of *Wickard* v. *Filburn*, for example, the court ruled that the Commerce Clause authorized the federal government to prohibit an Ohio farmer from growing more than eleven acres of wheat on his own land, even though the additional wheat he grew would never leave his farm and was intended for consumption by his family and his livestock. Yet, even here, the court did not rule the government could order this farmer to buy someone else's wheat. It only ruled that the government could limit the amount of wheat he grew.

Senator Orrin Hatch, the senior Republican on the Senate Judiciary, is a man of measured rhetoric. Yet even he issued a startling judgment about the implications for American freedom if the Commerce Clause is falsely interpreted to give Congress the power to force individuals to buy health insurance. "If that is held constitutional—for them to be able to tell us we have to purchase health insurance—then there is literally nothing that the federal government can't force us to do," he said. "Nothing."[24]

President Obama's socialization of the health care industry is a control freak's dream, not only because of the new mandates it imposes on individuals, health care providers, and businesses, but because of the opportunity it creates for further expansion of government power. By establishing the precedent that the federal government can mandate what we buy, it gives the federal government the power to control what we own.

And, as we shall see in a later chapter, there are control freaks who think government should control our very souls.

The Coming Crash

Control freaks have now succeeded in building a welfare state in which large segments of the population are dependent on the federal government for large parts of their lives. But this welfare state has put federal spending on a collision course with the income and savings of the middle class.

Rather than apply the brakes, President Obama has put the pedal to the metal. He is recklessly racing the nation toward disaster. When the emergency crews come to clean up the mess, they will likely see socialized medicine as the last milestone before the scene of the crash.

Obama's unconstitutional health care law requires all Americans to purchase a government-approved health insurance policy by 2014. Those earning less than 400 percent of the federal poverty level—$88,200 for a family of four in 2010—will receive a federal subsidy to help them buy this insurance, which they can only purchase in a government-regulated exchange. The amount of this subsidy will decrease to zero as an individual's or family's income rises toward the 400-percent-of-poverty threshold. Those earning more than that will get no subsidy. Unless they have an employer who chooses to help them, they must pay the entire cost themselves.[25]

By 2016, the CBO estimated, insurance plans satisfying the minimum requirements for government-mandated coverage will cost $4,500 to $5,000 for individuals and $12,000 to $12,500 for families.[26] On average it will cost more than $15,000 for a family.[27]

These government-mandated health insurance expenditures will not be counted in the federal budget, despite a clear warning from the Congressional Budget Office in 1994 that failure to count it would set the stage for a fully state-controlled economy.

> An individual mandate . . . would transform the purchase of health insurance from an essentially voluntary private transaction into a compulsory activity mandated by federal law. Failure to record the cost of this compulsory activity in the budget would open the door to a mandate-issuing government taking control of virtually any resource allocation decision that would otherwise be left to the private sector, without the federal budget recording any increase in the size of the government. In the extreme, a command economy, in which the President and Congress dictated how much each individual and family spent on all goods and services, could be instituted without any change in total federal receipts and outlays.[28]

Even if this spending is not counted in the federal budget, it certainly will be felt in business and family budgets.

To pay the promised subsidies to those earning less than 400 percent of poverty, the government will need to redistribute wealth from those earning more than that. They will also need to redistribute wealth from future generations. They will do this through new taxes and new borrowing, adding to the national debt and to the interest payments that service the debt. This new borrowing will come on top of the already enormous load of future federal borrowing needed to pay promised Medicare and Social Security benefits.

The bottom line is this: The control freaks' welfare state is an oversized house financed with an adjustable rate mortgage. Obamacare is an extravagant new wing added just before the monthly payments balloon. The financial day of reckoning we face will make the housing bubble look like a modest cash flow problem.

With customary audacity and hypocrisy, President Obama sold his health care plan as a fiscally responsible act. He even insisted it would save money for the private sector. "This legislation will also lower costs for families and for businesses and for the federal government, reducing our deficit by over $1 trillion in the next two decades," he said as he signed the bill.[29] But this is not true.

The Congressional Budget Office (CBO), which did the official financial analysis of Obamacare, never said it would reduce the deficit by $1 trillion over two decades. It focused on the program's first decade.[30]

When the CBO looked at only part of the plan in isolation, it is true it showed a modest reduction in the deficit. However, when the full scope of the plan was considered, and when accounting "gimmicks"—pointed out by Representative Paul Ryan of Wisconsin—were uncovered, the plan added to the deficit.

Responding to an inquiry from Representative Ryan, the CBO published a tell-tale letter just a few days before the House voted to approve the health care bill. This letter looked at the combined budget impact of three pieces of legislation. These included: 1) the Senate health-care bill that President Obama signed; 2) the "reconciliation" bill that included the amendments to the Senate bill that House Democrats demanded as a condition for passing the Senate version of the bill instead of their own; and 3) a bill known as the "doc fix" designed to make sure Medicare payments to doctors did not suddenly plunge by 21 percent in April 2010.[31]

This "doc fix" bill was needed because of a budget trick Congress had played on voters. The trick made it appear that budget bills Congress had approved in the past caused smaller deficits than they actually did. It did this by having the budgets operate on the phony assumption that on some future date Medicare payments to doctors would be dramatically slashed. If the payments were in fact slashed, it would save the federal government billions and reduce the deficit. But the congressional leadership never had any intention of slashing the payments. It always intended to restore them at the last minute to avert a crisis in the Medicare system.

Congressional Democrats initially included the "doc fix" in the health-care reform legislation, which was a logical place for it. They had removed it—in fitting irony—to make the cost of the bill appear smaller than it truly was. Nonetheless, congressional leaders were committed to enacting the "doc fix" separately—just as, for example, they passed the "reconciliation" bill separately, hiding the true impact.

Representative Ryan asked the CBO to estimate the budget impact of all three bills together. The CBO reported that the Senate bill and the reconciliation bill, analyzed together, cut the deficit by $138 billion over ten years. When the "doc fix" was added, the deficit increased by $59 billion over ten years.[32]

Nor was separating the "doc fix" from the main bill the only gimmick the Democratic leadership used to hide its full cost. The CBO also estimated that after enacting the health care package, Congress would still need to approve "at least $50 billion" in additional spending over ten years to make sure the federal bureaucracies were in place to handle the administrative needs of the new system. Also, because the individual mandate and the federal subsidies to help people pay for it were not scheduled to start until 2014, while new taxes started immediately, the accounting for the first decade of the plan included ten years of new revenues to cover only six years of new spending.[33]

Even these factors do not put Obamacare in full fiscal perspective, however. That requires stepping back and looking at it in the context of both Obama's overall budget and the fiscal realities of the welfare state.

Just as he tried to defend his health insurance entitlement as a measure that would save money for private citizens as well as for the government, President Obama tries to mask his overall fiscal recklessness with fiscally conservative rhetoric. So it was in February 2009 that he attacked politicians who say one thing and do another when it comes to amassing federal debt—just

after he had signed a bill authorizing the Treasury to borrow another $1.9 tril-
lion in the name of American taxpayers. "After a decade of profligacy, the
American people are tired of politicians who talk the talk but don't walk the
walk when it comes to fiscal responsibility," he said. "It's easy to get up in front
of the cameras and rant against exploding deficits. What's hard is actually getting deficits under control. But that's what we must do. Like families across
the country, we have to take responsibility for every dollar we spend."[34]

Obama is right. But he should have been looking in the mirror when he
spoke these words.

According to data published by the Office of Management and Budget
(OMB) in Obama's own White House, he is the biggest-spending president
since 1930, the earliest year reported on OMB's chart of federal receipts
and outlays as a percentage of Gross Domestic Product (GDP). OMB also
puts him on a track to borrow more than any president since Franklin
Delano Roosevelt.[35]

When measured as a percentage of GDP, no president since 1930 can
match Obama's projected expenditures.

FDR was responsible for the twelve fiscal years from 1934 to 1945,
which included part of the Great Depression and all of World War II. His
average annual spending was 19.35 percent of GDP. George W. Bush,
responsible for the eight fiscal years from 2002 to 2009, ran up average
annual spending of 20.43 percent of GDP. In the four fiscal years from
2010 to 2013, according to OMB, Obama will spend an annual average of
24.13 percent of GDP. That is 18 percent more than Bush and almost 25
percent more than Roosevelt.

From 1934 to 1941, the eight fiscal years FDR served before the start of
World War II, annual federal spending averaged only 9.85 percent of GDP.
Obama's projected average annual spending of 24.13 percent of GDP is
almost two-and-a-half times that much. His spending today dwarfs FDR's
in the midst of the Great Depression.

Obama is not projected to beat FDR for borrowing money, but that is
only because of the tremendous debt the federal government incurred

fighting World War II. According to OMB, Obama will run average annual deficits of 7.05 percent of GDP from 2010 to 2013 compared to Roosevelt's average annual deficits of 9.76 percent of GDP. However, in the pre-war years of 1934 to 1941, FDR ran average annual deficits of 3.56 percent of GDP. Obama, according to OMB, will borrow at about twice that rate. Obama is also the first president since the end of World War II to run a double-digit annual deficit. In 2010, he borrowed 10.6 percent of GDP.[36]

The CBO's analysis of Obama's fiscal 2011 budget also depicts a president launching America on a borrowing and spending spree unprecedented among post-World War II administrations. Obama's budget plan, CBO estimates, will add $9.8 trillion in new debt between 2011 and 2020, with $3.7 trillion of that debt attributable to new policies proposed by Obama. Annual federal interest payments will more than quadruple, reaching $916 billion per year by 2020. The annual deficit will bottom out at $724 billion in 2014—compared to $458 billion in 2008, President Bush's last year in office. But then it will head ever upward, hitting $793 billion in 2015, $894 billion in 2016, $940 billion in 2017, $996 billion in 2018, $1.152 trillion in 2019, and $1.254 trillion in 2020.[37]

The longer-term trend is not wholly Obama's fault. It is the inevitable consequence of a welfare state the control freaks built on the supposition that wealth could be endlessly redistributed from future generations to the present generation through endless taxing and borrowing. But the bill is coming due. The generations alive today will have to make the payments.

In 1965, three decades after FDR signed the Social Security Act, President Johnson signed legislation creating Medicare and Medicaid, dramatically increasing the federal social-welfare system that had started with the New Deal. LBJ sold the programs very much like FDR sold Social Security before him, and like Barack Obama would sell a nationalized health care system after him. Government dependency was the new "frontier," Johnson told Americans. A modest new tax would readily pay for it. The day the House approved Medicare, Johnson said, "In 1935 the passage of the original Social Security Act opened up a new era of expanding income security for our older citizens. Now, in 1965, we are moving once again to open still another frontier: that of health security."[38]

When he signed the Medicare bill, Johnson vowed it would protect the savings of older Americans and save the younger generation from being economically devastated by the cost of caring for their elders.

> No longer will older Americans be denied the healing miracle of modern medicine. No longer will illness crush and destroy the savings that they have so carefully put away over a lifetime so that they might enjoy dignity in their later years. No longer will young families see their own incomes, and their own hopes, eaten away simply because they are carrying out their deep moral obligations to their parents, and to their uncles, and their aunts.

All of this, Johnson said, would be covered with a tiny little tax.

> During your working years, the people of America—you—will contribute through your social security program a small amount each payday for hospital insurance protection. For example, the average worker in 1966 will contribute about $1.50 per month. The employer will contribute a similar amount. And this will provide the funds to pay up to 90 days of hospital care for each illness, plus diagnostic care, and up to 100 home health visits after you are 65. And beginning in 1967, you will also be covered for up to 100 days of care in a skilled nursing home after a period of hospital care.
>
> And under a separate plan, when you are 65—that the Congress originated itself, in its own good judgment—you may be covered for medical and surgical fees whether you are in or out of the hospital. You will pay $3 per month after you are 65 and your government will contribute an equal amount.[39]

This was too good to be true, of course. By 2003, when "compassionate conservative" George W. Bush pushed a Republican Congress to add a prescription drug entitlement to Medicare, the system was already heading toward collapse. Instead of the $1.50 per month per worker price tag LBJ advertised, the system now faces a $38.2 trillion long-term gap between promised benefits and expected revenues.

The Financial Report of the United States Government for 2009, quietly published in 2010, revealed the hard numbers behind America's fiscal situation. Using those numbers, the non-partisan Peter G. Peterson Foundation reported that, as of September 30, 2009, the federal government faced a total $61.9 trillion in unfunded liabilities.[40] These included debts the government has already amassed as well as welfare-state entitlement benefits it has promised to pay over the next seventy-five years that are not covered by the tax revenue the government is currently expecting to take in.

This $61.9 trillion shortfall includes $14.5 trillion in public debt and unfunded promised benefits to veterans, military personnel, and civilian government employees; $2 trillion for federally guaranteed programs such as student loans and deposit insurance; $7.7 trillion for Social Security; and the $38.2 trillion for Medicare.[41]

The Treasury Department itself conceded the nation cannot continue in the financial direction it is heading. "As currently structured, the Government's fiscal path cannot be sustained indefinitely and would, over time, dramatically increase the Government's budget deficit and debt," said the opening section of the 2009 Financial Report of the U.S. Government.[42]

The Government Accountability Office, the auditing agency for Congress, took its own look at the numbers. Without policy changes, it predicted in a statement from the comptroller general of the United States, "the interest costs on the growing debt together with spending on major entitlement programs could absorb 92 cents of every dollar of federal revenue in 2019."[43] That would leave almost no money for carrying out the core constitutional functions of the federal government, such as defending the nation against foreign enemies and securing our borders.

"Clearly," said the comptroller general, "this is not sustainable."[44]

The Peterson Foundation put the issue in perspective for taxpayers. The $61.9 trillion in unfunded liabilities, it calculated, equaled more than $200,000 for every person in the United States. That means $200,000 for every newborn baby as well as $200,000 for every baby's grandfather and grandmother.[45] A couple's combined share would be enough to buy a nice home in virtually any region of the country.

FDR and LBJ sold Social Security and Medicare on the premise that these programs would spare children the burden of having to care for their elderly parents. Now, these programs threaten the financial security of everyone's children.

Because Americans have grown accustomed to government controlling a significant part of their retirement-age health care and income—and because Americans of a certain age have paid taxes their entire lives on the expectation of receiving Social Security and Medicare benefits—the programs cannot be terminated. They must be reformed. The best reforms would nudge the nation back toward its heritage of individualism and self-reliance, and eventually liberate Americans from government dependency.

A Social Security reform sponsored by Representative Paul Ryan and former Senator John Sununu of New Hampshire, for example, would have done just that by allowing people to set aside part of their Social Security tax in individual retirement accounts.[46] A person who decided to start one of these accounts, rather than stay in the current Social Security system, would have been required to purchase an annuity when he retired that would pay him a monthly amount equal to a Social Security check. If the person's individual account did not contain enough money at retirement to purchase an annuity of sufficient value, the government would make up the difference. If the person's retirement account had more money than was needed to buy the annuity, he could keep the surplus. If the person still had some of this money when he died, he could give it to his children and grandchildren—instead of adding to the tax burden of future generations as the current system does.

The actuary for the Social Security Administration, determined the Ryan-Sununu plan, would have made Social Security solvent in the long run.[47] Yet liberals bitterly opposed it. Why? Perhaps because it could set many people free from government dependency.

If liberals will not support programs that liberate people from dependency as a means of closing the federal government's $200,000 per person shortfall, they will need to raise taxes instead. This is the path President Obama is taking. At his request, the health care law included a new tax that is theoretically dedicated to paying Medicare benefits. It is a 3.8 percent charge against income earned from interest, dividends, annuities, royalties, and rent by individuals making more than $200,000 per year and married couples making more than $250,000 per year.

House Speaker Nancy Pelosi called this a tax on "unearned income, whatever category that is."[48] In reality, it is a new tax on savings. It is a tax on the house that is paid off, the insurance policy dutifully kept, the little extra that members of a family decided not to spend today so they could invest in a business that would profit in the long run. It is a tax on people who believed in the American dream and acted on it, on people who worked hard and made plans to take care of themselves and their own. It is a tax on Americans who still think and act like pioneers.

It is a pipeline, laid down by control freaks, to drain the lifesavings of the provident into the $61.9 trillion pit of the welfare state. It is a tax they can use to help finance a mortgage-style bailout for the house of big government.

Now that this tax is in place, watch as they try to increase the rate and decrease the income threshold for those required to pay it.

Chapter 4

Coveting Thy Neighbor's House

Liberals Want to Control Your Property

"Thou shalt not covet thy neighbor's house."[1]

—**Exodus, 20:17**

"Where an excess of power prevails, property of no sort is duly respected."[2]

—**James Madison**
Essay in the *National Gazette*, March 27, 1792

"Redistribution of wealth both within and among nations is absolutely essential, if a decent life is to be provided for every human being."[3]

—**Paul R. Ehrlich, Anne H. Ehrlich, and John P. Holdren**
Human Ecology: Problems and Solutions, 1973

Not long after the Bill of Rights was ratified, James Madison, its principal author, published a series of newspaper columns making the case for limited government under the nation's new Constitution. One of these columns explained his belief that all individual rights could be considered a form of property and that when government grew too powerful, no form of property was safe.

A person's property, Madison argued, included "everything to which a man may attach a value and have a right; and which leaves to every one else the like advantage." He continued,

> In the former sense, a man's land, or merchandize, or money is called his property. In the latter sense, a man has a property in his opinions and the free communication of them. He has a property of peculiar value in his religious opinions, and in the profession and practice dictated by them. He has a property very dear to him in the safety and liberty of his person. He has an equal property in the free use of his faculties and free choice of the objects on which to employ them. In a word, as a man is said to have a right to his property, he may be equally said to have a property in his rights.
>
> Where an excess of power prevails, property of no sort is duly respected. No man is safe in his opinions, his person, his faculties, or his possessions.[4]

Madison's words were prophetic.

A Man's Castle

What happens when liberals in government covet your house? In the first years of the twenty-first century, residents of the Fort Trumbull neighborhood of New London, Connecticut, unhappily found out when the municipal development agency condemned their homes. For these Americans, government ceased being the protector of their property and became a thief.

Fort Trumbull exemplified the middle-class American neighborhood. Its homes embodied the hard work, memories, and aspiration of their own-ers. What happened to these homes symbolizes one of the fundamental struggles Americans now face to preserve their liberty—the struggle to pre-serve the constitutional protection for private property. In this particular case, the struggle pitted liberals in control of a municipal government against homeowners whose interests they should have protected.

Respect for private property, as Madison argued, is indispensible to a free society. The moral principle behind it lies at the heart of two of the Ten Commandments—"Thou shalt not steal" and "Thou shalt not covet thy neighbor's house." It also sits at the heart of the Bill of Rights, in the Tak-ings Clause of the Fifth Amendment: "Nor shall private property be taken for public use without just compensation."

Like most words in the Constitution, the words of the Takings Clause appear to convey an obvious meaning: The government can take "private property" in those instances when it is needed for a "public use"—such as to build a courthouse or a road—but only if the government pays "just com-pensation" to the owner for doing so.

The Founders did not intend to create a government that had the power to take private property for private use—to redistribute it from one person to another. Indeed, they believed redistributing property was beyond the legitimate scope of any government. In 1798, Supreme Court Justice Samuel Chase, a signer of the Declaration of Independence, made exactly this point in the case of *Calder* v. *Bull*. "There are acts which the Federal, or State, Legislature cannot do, without exceeding their authority," wrote Chase. These include acts that "take away that security for personal liberty, or private property, for the protection whereof the government was estab-lished." He continued,

A few instances will suffice to explain what I mean. A law that punished a citizen for an innocent action, or, in other words, for an act, which, when done, was in violation of no existing law; a law that destroys, or impairs, the lawful private contracts of citizens; a law that makes a man a Judge in his own cause; or a law that takes property from A and gives it to B: It is against all reason and justice, for a people to entrust a Legislature with such powers; and, therefore, it cannot be presumed that they have done it.[5]

President Franklin Roosevelt, as we have seen, rejected this principle when he began constructing a welfare state that required government to take from A and give to B. As we shall see, taking from A and giving to B is precisely what the City of New London wanted to do with the homes of Fort Trumbull—in order to achieve their particular vision for remaking that town. And, as we shall also see, liberals believe they must be able to take from A and give to B if they are going to achieve even grander visions for remaking American society and preserving the entire planet against environmental catastrophe.

In pursuit of visions grand and small, liberals would turn upside down the Founding Fathers' understanding of the purpose of the state. Rather than measure the legitimacy of government by the degree to which it protects the rights of individuals—including the right to private property—they would measure the legitimacy of an individual's property rights by the degree to which they advance the government's agenda.

In New London, Connecticut, city officials looked at the homes in the Fort Trumbull neighborhood and decided that letting the owners continue to possess them would not yield the tax revenue the city wanted. So they decided to use the power of eminent domain to seize the homes and give them to a new owner who appeared capable of paying higher taxes. The city's development agency would technically maintain possession of the seized properties, but the agency would lease the properties to a private developer who would bulldoze the condemned homes and use the cleared land to build office buildings, a hotel, and new residences. City officials believed this would enrich the local government. They also argued that seizing and destroying the middle-class homes and erecting new buildings where they had stood would improve the local environment and create jobs.[6]

Some homeowners, however, refused to cooperate. They would not sell out to the city. In 2000, the city condemned their properties and the case went to court. The holdouts included at least one remarkable extended family. The mother and father lived in a century-old home where the mother had been born in 1918. The son and daughter-in-law lived next door in a house the parents had given them as a wedding present. The son explained in the local newspaper why he, his wife, his mother, and his father were fighting city hall. "Quite frankly, most things don't matter enough to me to expend the energy required to resist," he said. "However in this case, the only thing that I truly hold dear in the world is being targeted: my family."[7]

Another holdout homeowner was Susette Kelo, who is now immortalized in the Supreme Court case that bears her name. Kelo's Fort Trumbull home was a long-sought dream. She, too, fought the city government to keep it. "I've always loved New London," she told the local newspaper. "I wanted to come back and live by the water. So, for me, it's not about the money. It's about a person being able to live where they want to live. It's about a person buying a home and being able to stay in it. And this is where I want to live."[8]

Like George III in the years after the French and Indian War, or contemporary politicians in the state of Oregon, development officials in New London drew a line on the map in order to unreasonably regulate property ownership. But while the lines that the British crown and Oregon drew were designed to restrict the ability of people to acquire and develop land, New London drew a line designed to take land away from its current owners and give it to someone else to develop.[9]

In 2005, the Kelo case arrived in the U.S. Supreme Court. The court split five to four in favor of the little King Georges of New London. Justices John Paul Stevens, Stephen Breyer, Ruth Bader Ginsburg, David Souter, and Anthony Kennedy said the city could take land from unwilling sellers and hand it over to a private developer. Chief Justice William Rehnquist, and Justices Sandra Day O'Connor, Antonin Scalia, and Clarence Thomas, said the city could not do this.[10]

Justice Stevens, writing the majority opinion, did not pretend New London was seizing homes to convert them to a "public use" as traditionally interpreted. The city, he conceded, was going to turn over use of the confiscated land to a new owner who would engage in private activities that were preferred by the government and that were anticipated to yield greater tax revenue. He conceded, in other words, that the government could take property from one person and give it to another so the government could control what the new owner did with the property. In the majority opinion, Stevens wrote,

> The City has carefully formulated an economic development plan that it believes will provide appreciable benefits to the community, including—but by no means limited to—new jobs and increased tax revenue. As with other exercises in urban planning and development, the City is endeavoring to coordinate a variety of commercial, residential, and recreational uses of land, with the hope that they will form a whole greater than the sum of its parts. To effectuate this plan, the City has invoked a state statute that specifically authorizes the use of eminent domain to promote economic development.

Stevens noted that Americans had once believed government could take private property only for a "public use," meaning literally for "use by the public." This, he argued, was an antiquated view.

"On the other hand, this is not a case in which the City is planning to open the condemned land—at least not in its entirety—to use by the general public. Nor will the private lessees of the land in any sense be required to operate like common carriers, making their services available to all comers. But although such a projected use would be sufficient to satisfy the public use requirement, this 'Court long ago rejected any literal requirement that condemned property be put into use for the general public.' Indeed, while many state courts in the mid-19th century endorsed 'use by the public' as the proper definition of public use, that narrow view steadily eroded over time."[11]

Thanks to a series of Supreme Court decisions, Stevens said, the term "public use" in the Fifth Amendment of James Madison's Bill of Rights should henceforth be interpreted to mean "public purpose"—as if the Framers could not have used the words "public purpose" rather than "public use" if that had been what they meant.

Stevens did not bother to define or place specific limits on what "public use" might mean. He left that to legislative bodies to determine as they expropriated private property in the future. The court, Stevens essentially argued, should not let the actual words of the Constitution become an obstacle to the liberals' "evolving" vision of government. "Not only was the 'use by the public' test difficult to administer," he wrote, "... but it proved to be impractical given the diverse and always evolving needs of society."[12]

O'Connor, who often sided with the liberals on the court, wrote this time for the conservative dissenters. In her argument, she specifically pointed to Madison's defense of property rights in the *National Gazette* and Justice Chase's declaration in *Calder* v. *Bull* that government had no power to take property from one person and give it to another. She wrote,

> Today the Court abandons this long-held, basic limitation on government power. Under the banner of economic development, all private property is now vulnerable to being taken and transferred to another private owner, so long as it might be upgraded—*i.e.*, given to an owner who will use it in a way that the legislature deems more beneficial to the public—in the process.

O'Connor warned that the court's decision would "wash out any distinction between private and public use of property—and thereby effectively delete the words 'for public use' from the Takings Clause of the Fifth Amendment."[13]

The public dissented from the court's decision in *Kelo* v. *New London*, too. A Quinnipiac University poll conducted a month after the ruling asked Connecticut voters whether they agreed or disagreed with the court's opinion that "government can use eminent domain to buy a person's property and transfer it to private developers whose commercial projects could benefit the local economy." Eighty-eight percent said they disagreed.[14]

Yet the damage was done. In approving New London's plan to bulldoze the homes of Fort Trumbull, the Supreme Court bulldozed the constitutional barrier that had blocked government in the United States from taking the property of A and giving it to B.

Building Windmills

Before he became president, Barack Obama looked across America and decided people were not using their money the way he wanted them to use it. Among other things, they were not buying enough windmills. He intended to do something about it.

Just before his inauguration, Obama delivered a speech at a factory that made bolts used in windmills. The speech, Obama boasted, was attended by "representatives from the biggest wind power companies in America." He promised these executives that the "recovery" bill he was developing with Congress would be a windfall for them. The nation's long-term success, he said, depended on government "investing" in industries like theirs.

> Think of what's happening in countries like Spain, Germany and Japan, where they're making real investments in renewable energy. They're surging ahead of us, poised to take the lead in this new industry. This isn't because they're smarter than us, or work harder than us, or are more innovative than we are. It's because their governments have harnessed their people's hard work and ingenuity with bold investments—investments that are paying off in good, high-wage jobs, jobs they won't lose to other countries.[15]

As was his habit, Obama used the word "investment" not to describe individuals freely deciding to use their own money as they deemed fit, but to describe the government deciding to tax money from individuals and spend it as the government deemed fit. In this case, Obama wanted the government to "invest" other people's money to create "green" jobs.

Just after Inauguration Day, a reporter reminded White House Spokesman Robert Gibbs that the president had been promising to create a million of these so-called "green" jobs. "Could you define what that is?" the reporter asked.

"Sure," said Gibbs. "The president visited in this campaign a windmill manufacturer that produces—it wouldn't even fit in this room—turbine blades for windmills. Those are green jobs."

"How is he going to create a million of them?" the reporter asked. "The question is a million."

"Well," said Gibbs, "hopefully we're going to build more windmills."[16]

Within three weeks, Obama had signed the $787 billion American Recovery and Reinvestment Act. It included his promised "investment" in the windmill-building industry. One provision said people would receive a tax credit to cover 30 percent of the cost of erecting a windmill to power their house, farm, or small business. Another extended the time limit for an existing tax credit that goes to businesses that produce electricity with windmills.

Clearly, these tax credits were not for all Americans, but only for those willing and able to use their property the way President Obama wanted them to use their property. If you lived or operated your business in a neighborhood where it was impractical to erect a windmill, or if you simply did not want to build a windmill in your backyard, you were among those targeted to pay for the credit, not receive it. As Justice Chase might have put it, you were the A whose property (in the form of tax revenues) the government would unjustly take and give to B.

The Joint Committee on Taxation of the U.S. Congress has neatly described what targeted tax credits like these do: they allow the government to control how people use their property. A committee report said:

Targeted tax policies are generally unfair because they do not apply equal treatment to similarly situated taxpayers. In other words, households with the same ability to pay taxes may be taxed differently depending on their composition or consumption choices. In essence, targeting is a way of using tax incentives to get Americans to do what the government wants them to do—those who do not comply do not receive the tax break.[17]

The committee's insight was not a new one. James Madison made precisely the same point in his essay on property rights for the *National Gazette*. "A just security to property," he wrote, "is not afforded by that government, under which unequal taxes oppress one species of property and reward another species."[18]

Earlier, arguing for ratification of the Constitution, Madison had pointed to another evil that arises when government use taxes and regulations to control how people use their property: the laws become so extensive and complicated that few comprehend them, allowing the rich and well-connected to gain an unfair advantage over the common man. In *The Federalist Papers*, Madison wrote,

It will be of little avail to the people, that the laws are made by men of their own choice, if the laws be so voluminous that they cannot be read, or so incoherent that they cannot be understood; if they be repealed or revised before they are promulgated, or undergo such incessant changes that no man, who knows what the law is to-day, can guess what it will be tomorrow. Law is defined to be a rule of action; but how can that be a rule, which is little known, and less fixed?

Another effect of public instability is the unreasonable advantage it gives to the sagacious, the enterprising, and the moneyed few over the industrious and uniformed mass of the people. Every new regulation concerning commerce or revenue, or in any way affecting the value of the different species of property, presents a new harvest to those who watch the change, and can trace its consequences; a harvest, reared not by themselves, but by the toils and cares of the great body of their fellow-citizens. This is a state of things in which it may be said with some truth that laws are made for the *few*, not for the *many*.[19]

President Obama's $787 billion recovery act exemplified Madison's idea of bad government. It added more than a hundred pages of new tax provisions to an already ridiculously complex and voluminous Internal Revenue Code.

Nor would Madison have been surprised to learn that one of America's most powerful families tried to use its influence to protect its own interests from federal wind-power tax subsidies.

Since 2001, an energy company had been trying to build a wind farm on a shoal in Nantucket Sound, a body of water that sits between the island of Martha's Vineyard and the Cape Cod region of the Massachusetts mainland. This was an ideal location for windmills, with shallow waters, strong winds, and no private land that needed to be condemned to make way for the project.

The contemplated wind mills would not block shipping lanes or the path of airliners descending into Boston's airport. They would create "green jobs" and generate electricity while leaving a small carbon footprint. However, they would also feature massive turbines rising more than 400 feet above the sound, marring the view from nearby shores.

Along those shores stood the Kennedy family's famed Hyannisport beach retreat. The late Senator Ted Kennedy, otherwise an environmentalist of passion and conviction, conspicuously opposed the proposed wind mills.[20] Robert F. Kennedy, Jr., the senator's nephew and an environmentalist lawyer, wrote an op-ed for the *New York Times* explaining why wind mill farms should be encouraged, just not near Cape Cod. He wrote,

As an environmentalist, I support wind power, including wind power on the high seas. I am also involved in siting wind farms in appropriate landscapes, of which there are many. But I do believe that some places should be off limits to any sort of industrial development.

The quality of life would be ruined in the region, Kennedy argued, if the wind mill project near his family's retreat was approved. "Hundreds of flashing lights to warn airplanes away from the turbines will steal the stars and nighttime views," he said. "The noise of the turbines will be audible onshore."[21]

A green energy project designed to create green jobs in a state run by green politicians was stalled for nine years because greens objected to it. When the U.S. Department of the Interior finally did approve it in 2010, environmentalists immediately announced they would sue to stop the project. [22] Using the tax code to target special benefits to entrepreneurs who produced light and noise pollution creating "green" jobs was fine in someone else's backyard, but not in Kennedy country.

James Madison and other Founding Fathers knew people would act this way, which is why they wrote a Constitution designed to protect the property rights of all and prevent the rich and powerful from abusing those of the common man.

Polar Bears vs. People

Environmentalists have often claimed that one or another species of animal needed government protection under the federal Endangered Species Act (ESA) as a means of restricting the use of private property in whatever region of the country that species happened to inhabit.

Spotted owls, kangaroo rats, fairy shrimp, and many others have been touted as threatened or endangered creatures whose future well-being justified government regulations that restricted property rights and threatened the livelihoods of American human beings.

The polar bear, however, probably had greater potential than any other creature to threaten property rights if the federal government decided to formally list it as "threatened" or "endangered" under the ESA.

During the Bush administration, environmentalists started a campaign to force the Department of Interior to do just that. But protecting the bear was only their intermediate aim. Their ultimate goal was to limit human energy production and consumption along with emissions of the so-called greenhouse gases that theoretically cause global warming. They justified this by contending that human activities far from the bear's Arctic domain were causing global warming that melted the sea ice that formed the bear's indispensible habitat.

If government policymakers heeded the environmentalists' argument, they might or might not make life better for the bear, but they would certainly make life more difficult for man. Costs would go up for everything from listening to the radio, to watching a television, to heating a home, to fueling a car.[23] Virtually all businesses, large and small, would see their overhead escalate and their profit margins diminish.

Curiously, the environmentalists pushing for the government to declare the bear threatened were not especially concerned about what the evidence said about the actual trend in the bear's population. In fact, this trend could not be definitively discerned, because no truly global and systematic survey of the bear's population had ever been conducted. Scientists did not know how many bears there were or how many there once had been.

In 1965, scientists from the five nations with Arctic territories—the United States, Canada, Norway, Denmark, and the Soviet Union—met in Fairbanks, Alaska, for the first international conference on polar bears. These scientists concluded that they did not know how many bears existed.[24]

Edward Carlson, a researcher for the Interior Department who chaired the conference, opened the event by quoting from a speech delivered earlier that year by Democratic Senator Bob Bartlett of Alaska. In that speech, Bartlett said,

I am informed that at the present time there are no accurate or reliable figures available on the total world polar bear population or on the size of the annual kill. Scientists know very little about the habits or habitat of the polar bear. They know very little about polar bear movements, reproduction, longevity, or population structure. They do not even know the answer to the basic question whether there is but one population of polar bears moving from nation to nation on the slowly revolving ice pack, or whether there are two or more populations.[25]

The Canadian delegates provided a summary of "current scientific knowledge" on the polar bear. They cited three sketchy population estimates that, taken together, set the bear's total population at somewhere between 5,000 and 19,000 animals. "Scott (1959) and others concluded that about 2,000 to 2,500 polar bears existed near the Alaskan coast. By extrapolation they arrived at a total polar bear population of 17,000 to 19,000 animals," the Canadians reported. "Uspensky (1961) estimated the world polar bear population at 5,000 to 8,000 animals. Harington (1964) has given an estimate of 6,000 to 7,000 polar bears in the Canadian Arctic and believes the world polar bear population is well over 10,000."[26]

The American delegates said Alaska's polar bears had never been systematically surveyed. "While estimates of the number of polar bears occurring in areas adjacent to Alaska's coasts have been made, all have been based on tenuous assumptions and extrapolations of fragmentary data," they said. "Certainly they do not provide a confident basis for guiding management efforts."[27]

In the end, the scientists from the five countries reached this consensus:

It is the mutual opinion that each nation should conduct to the best of its ability a research program on the polar bear within its territory or adjacent international waters to obtain adequate scientific information for effective management of the species.[28]

Four decades later, the Fourteenth International Polar Bear Conference convened in Seattle, Washington. Scientists had significantly more information than they had in 1965. Yet, they still could not estimate the polar bear population based strictly on scientific observation. The bears, they had come to believe, lived in nineteen distinct subpopulations. But for some of these subpopulations, scientists had collected little or no data.

"No subpopulation inventories have been conducted in East Greenland and therefore the size of the subpopulation is unknown," said their report. "The subpopulation size is unknown and no population surveys have been conducted in the Kara Sea," it said. In the Barents Sea, it concluded, "there has probably been an increase in the subpopulation size after 1973 until recently, but current subpopulation growth trend is unknown."[29]

In some places, scientists estimated the polar bear population by using anecdotal information provided by people living in the bear's habitat. They called this "traditional ecological knowledge"—or TEK. Some scientists worried that using these observations might artificially inflate the bear population—and, indeed, in some regions people said they were seeing more bears.

"There was some concern expressed about the use of traditional knowledge to increase subpopulation estimates where, at best, there is no new scientific data and in some cases there are strong data available that do not support the increases," said the polar bear conference report. "There was no disagreement with the accuracy of local knowledge and there was no one doubting that hunters were seeing more bears. What was questioned was that an increasing subpopulation is the only explanation for seeing more bears."[30]

In the end, the conference estimated the world polar bear population was between 20,000 to 25,000 animals. That means that scientists reckoned in 2005 that the minimum number of polar bears in the world was at least 1,000 more than the maximum of 19,000 they had reckoned existed in 1965.[31]

This did not diminish the efforts of those seeking ESA protection for the bear. The same year that the Fourteenth International Polar Bear

Conference estimated there were at least 20,000 polar bears in the world, an environmentalist group called the Center for Biological Diversity filed a petition with the Department of Interior asking the department to list the bear as "threatened." Greenpeace and the Natural Resources Defense Council quickly joined in the petition.[32]

These environmentalist groups did not argue that the polar bear population was declining. ESA, they said, required the government to examine the status of a species according to multiple criteria, including whether there is "present or threatened destruction, modification, or curtailment of its habitat range." Another criterion, they said, was whether there was an "inadequacy of existing regulatory mechanisms" to protect the species from harm. If one of these factors was putting a species "in danger of extinction throughout all or a significant portion of its range," the government must list the species as endangered. If one was making it "likely" a species will "become an endangered species within the foreseeable future throughout all or a significant portion of its range," the government must list the species as "threatened."[33]

When the government lists a species as "threatened" or "endangered," it normally becomes illegal to engage in activities that "take" members of that species. To "take" in the law means to "harass, harm, pursue, hunt, shoot, wound, kill, trap, capture, or collect, or attempt to engage in such conduct." The Supreme Court ruled in 1995 that the Department of Interior could interpret the word "harm" in this context to include "significant habitat modification or degradation that actually kills or injures wildlife."[34]

Similarly, when the government lists a species as threatened or endangered, federal agencies are required to make certain that government actions—including providing licenses and permits to individuals and corporations—do not harm the habitat of the listed species or hurt its chances for survival.

In the case of the polar bear, the environmentalists asked the government to conclude that even though the animal currently enjoyed a healthy population, its future decline was inevitable as a result of global warming caused by greenhouse gas emissions that would melt the Arctic sea ice where the bears hunted and lived. Inadequate regulation of greenhouse gas emissions in the United States as well as around the world, they argued, was the ultimate cause of the "harm" done to the bear's sea ice habitat. Computer models, they said, indicated that manmade global warming would ultimately destroy this habitat and drive the bear to extinction.

"Most polar bear populations, as well as the global species, are not currently endangered," the Center for Biological Diversity conceded in its petition.

> However, ESA listing criteria, and particularly the definition of "Threatened," are prospective and forward looking. Evidence of past or current population declines is not necessary before a species is listed as Threatened under the ESA. Therefore, even polar bear populations that are stable or increasing still meet the definition of a Threatened species because the best available science indicates that they are likely to become endangered in the foreseeable future by global warming, disappearance of their sea-ice habitat, and other factors, as detailed below.[35]

How deep into the "foreseeable future" did Interior need to look to see if the polar bear would become extinct? Noting that dealing with global warming would be a "long-term process," the Center for Biological Diversity's petition to the Interior Department said, "Petitioners suggest consideration of 200 years as the 'foreseeable future' for analyzing the threats to the continued survival of the polar bear."[36]

On the other hand, the environmentalists argued that the government needed to act immediately to cut greenhouse gas emissions. "Because the United States is responsible for approximately 24 percent of worldwide carbon dioxide emissions, regulation of United States greenhouse gas emissions is essential to saving polar bears from extinction," they said.[37]

The Center sued the Interior Department to force action on their petition. Their argument was bolstered by satellite images of the polar region that indicated that late-summer sea ice had diminished significantly since 1979. But this was countered by the fact that the polar bear had survived other periods when temperatures warmed and the ice retreated. A report from the Congressional Research Service explained,

> Some scientists also point out that, since polar bears have survived at least two major warming periods over the last 10,000 years, including the intense warming event that ended the Last Glacial Maximum about 8,000 to 9,000 years ago (when temperatures were believed to have been much warmer than now), polar bears and other Arctic mammals could be capable of adjusting, adapting, and coping with the current climatic change. At the end of the last Ice Age, the Northern Hemisphere entered an extended period of rapid warming, with temperatures in Arctic regions eventually reaching levels several degrees warmer than today. At that time, the sea ice above North America is known to have retreated substantially, allowing Arctic species such as bowhead whales and walrus to move northward into areas of the Canadian Arctic that they cannot reach today.[38]

At the very least, the case for declaring the polar bear "threatened" rested on debatable predictions. These included the prediction that global temperatures would rise over the coming decades as a result of human activity, that when the temperatures rose the Arctic sea ice would substantially disappear in summertime, and that when that happened the bears would be unable to adapt and would disappear from the planet.

Yet even if you conceded that all these predictions could come true, accepting the environmentalists' case for curtailing human action on behalf of the polar bear nonetheless would require a value judgment. It would require judging that saving the bear's habitat justified giving government—not only in the United States, but globally—sweeping power to control how humans used their own habitat. It would mean accepting the notion that keeping polar bears on intact summer sea ice justifies governments around the world restricting the way humans roam their own land and warm and cool their own dens. Grant the environmentalists not only their predictions but also their value judgments, and the inevitable conclusion is this: government must put human freedom on thinner ice so a few bears can have thicker ice.

Facing a court-ordered deadline to make a decision on the environmentalists' polar bear petition, Interior Secretary Dirk Kempthorne announced in May 2008 that he would accept the environmentalists' predictions. Accordingly, he listed the bear as threatened. But he did not accept their values. So, using an escape clause written into the law, he published a special rule that prevented the listing of the bear from being used to restrict human activities within the United States that were far from the bear's habitat. "Listing the polar bear as threatened can reduce avoidable losses of polar bears," he said. "But it should not open the door to use the ESA to regulate greenhouse gas emissions from automobiles, power plants and other sources."[39]

There is currently great debate and controversy over the soundness of the science behind the theory that human activity is causing global warming. Phil Jones, who headed the Climate Research Unit at the University of East Anglia and who is one of the world's most prominent advocates of the theory that man is causing global warming conceded to the BBC in February 2010 that there had been no statistically significant warming since 1995.[40] If the science behind the theory were definitively debunked, nothing would be left for the polar bear protectionists. They would be pushing a cause founded on faulty science and flawed values.

It is important not only to examine the potential impact of listing any given creature as threatened or endangered, but also the process by which it is done. As exemplified by the case of the polar bear, the battle over listing species as threatened or endangered does not take place in Congress (whose elected representatives can be held accountable at election time if they make decisions contrary to the public will) it takes place in the courts and in the bureaucracy, where unelected judges and bureaucrats make the decisions. Congress structured the Endangered Species Act to remove itself from the decision-making process, thus protecting its own members from being threatened at the polls.

Who is in control here? Not the individual. Not the local or state government. Not even the U.S. Congress. Officials who do not face a direct vote of the people are in control.

Environmentalists are still seeking to restrict humans on behalf of bears. As we shall see, this effort may be only a minor front in a comprehensive crusade.

"A World of Zero Net Physical Growth"

John P. Holdren, President Barack Obama's top science adviser and director of the White House Office of Science and Technology Policy, is one of the environmental movement's most venerated leaders.

He brought unmatched academic credentials to the White House staff, including a doctorate in physics from Stanford and a career spent teaching at some of the nation's most prestigious institutions of higher learning, among them the University of California at Berkeley and Harvard's John F. Kennedy School of Government, where he was the Theresa and John Heinz Professor of Environmental Policy.[41]

Obama clearly knew of Holdren's illustrious record when he named him to the White House staff. Announcing Holdren's appointment, Obama said,

> A physicist renowned for his work on climate and energy, he's received numerous honors and awards for his contributions and has been one of the most passionate and persistent voices of our time about the growing threat of climate change. I look forward to his wise counsel in the years ahead."[42]

What Obama did not mention was that Holdren had argued in his writings that mankind faced a potential ecological catastrophe that required limiting population and redistributing wealth on a global basis.

In 1973, Holdren co-authored *Human Ecology: Problems and Solutions* with Stanford University ecologists Paul R. Ehrlich and Anne H. Ehrlich. Paul Ehrlich was already famous by then for his 1968 bestseller, *The Population Bomb*, which opened with this declaration: "The battle to feed all of humanity is over. In the 1970s and 1980s hundreds of millions of people will starve to death in spite of any crash program embarked upon now."[43]

Ehrlich further wrote,

> Nothing could be more misleading to our children than our present affluent society. They will inherit a totally different world in which the standards, politics, and economics of the past decade are dead. As the most influential nation in the world today, and its largest consumer, the United States cannot stand isolated. We are today involved in events leading to famine and ecocatastrophe; tomorrow, we may be destroyed by them. Our position requires that we take immediate action at home and promote effective action worldwide. We must have population control at home, hopefully through changes in our value system, but by compulsion if voluntary methods fail. Americans must also change their way of living so as to minimize their impact on the world's resources and environment."[44]

Holdren had made a similar argument in a 1973 paper published by the California Institute of Technology. "Is even the present U.S. population of 210 million too large? Should there be zero economic growth as well as zero population growth?" he asked. "I will argue here that 210 million now is too many and 280 million in 2040 is likely to be much too many; that, accordingly, a continued decline in fertility to well below replacement should be encouraged, with the aim of achieving ZPG [Zero Population Growth] before the year 2000 and a gradually declining population for some time thereafter; and that redirecting economic growth and technological change (*not* stopping either) is an essential concomitant to but not a substitute for these demographic goals."[45]

Holdren and Ehrlich's views on population were derived from Thomas Robert Malthus, a British economist of the late eighteenth and early nineteenth centuries. Malthus believed that human population tended to grow exponentially while food production grew only arithmetically. As a result, he concluded that the number of people on the planet was inevitably and repeatedly outstripping the available food supply only to be brought back into balance by a phalanx of inevitable evils including pestilence, famine, and war.[46]

In *Human Ecology*, which was listed prominently on Holdren's curriculum vitae at the time he became Obama's top science adviser, Holdren and the Ehrlichs advanced an updated theory of over-population even more dismal than Malthus's original. Where Malthus saw food production as the ultimate limiting factor on human beings, Holdren and the Ehrlichs saw the generalized use of finite natural resources by an increasing number of humans as threatening to the planet's fragile ecological balance and thus its ability to sustain life.[47]

In the book and elsewhere, they expressed their vision in an equation (popularized under the acronym "I-PAT") that utilized the three factors they believed were exerting a negative impact ("I") on the environment that could ultimately, if left unchecked, drive the human race toward misery and possible extinction. These factors were the number of people ("P") on the planet, the amount of affluence ("A") these people amassed, and the impact of the technology ("T") they used to amass it.[48] In the view of Holdren and the Ehrlichs, creating more of any of these things—people, affluence, or technology—was problematic. They summed up their theory as follows:

> The relation can be written as a mathematical equation: total environmental damage equals population, times the level of material affluence per person, times the environmental damage done

by the technology we use to supply each bit of affluence.[49]

According to this equation, a husband and wife who have a large family, or who work hard to create and acquire more and better goods, are committing acts that accelerate the destruction of the planet. Holdren and the Ehrlichs wrote,

> Halting population growth must be done, but that alone would not be enough. Stabilizing or reducing the per capita resources in the United States is necessary, but not sufficient. Attempts to reduce technology's impact on the environment are essential, but ultimately will be futile if population and affluence grow unchecked. Clearly, if there is to be any chance of success, simultaneous attacks must be mounted on *all* the components of the problem. Such a coordinated effort may be unlikely, but nothing less will do the job.[50]

They specifically rejected the notion that freely acting human beings, through their intellect and industry, could devise new technologies that reduced or reversed environmental damage while increasing per capita wealth. The only solution, they believed, was to control all three factors in their formula of environmental doom. They wrote, "The most dramatic improvements in technology will ultimately be cancelled out by rising population and consumption levels. At the same time, control of population will be of no avail if technology and consumption are not controlled as well."[51]

There was no time to waste, they concluded. "Considering present technology and patterns of human behavior, our planet is grossly overpopulated.... The limits of human capability to produce food by conventional means have very nearly been reached."[52]

Without remedial action, man might not be driven to extinction but he could be reduced to a brutish state.

There is good reason to believe that population growth increases the probability of a lethal worldwide plague and of thermonuclear war. Either could provide a catastrophic "death-rate solution" to the population problem; each is potentially capable of destroying civilization and even of driving Homo sapiens to extinction....

Perhaps more likely than extinction is the possibility that man will survive only to endure an existence barely recognizable as human—malnourished, beset by chronic disease, physically and emotionally impoverished, surrounded by the devastation wrought by an industrial civilization that could not cope with the results of its own biological and social folly.[53]

Given the dire circumstances they believed man confronted, they understandably recommended dramatic solutions. To explain what they had in mind, they pointed to the work of economist Kenneth Boulding, who had written in the 1960s that the human race needed to realize it now lived on "Spaceship Earth." Earlier generations, Boulding argued, had engaged in a "cowboy" economy that exploited nature and pursued economic expansion as if resources were infinite and growth could go on forever. In reality, he believed, the planet was a closed system like a spaceship where resources were limited and economic growth must stop. He proposed establishing a "spaceman economy" that recognized these facts.[54]

Holdren and the Ehrlichs agreed and outlined a sweeping plan for moving the planet into the "spaceman economy." "What is actually required is nothing less than a transformation of human society," they wrote.[55]

This transformation would start with population control, which might eventually require involuntary measures if voluntary ones failed. "Several coercive proposals deserve discussion, mainly because societies may ultimately have to resort to them unless current trends in birth rates are rapidly reversed by other means," they said.

Political pressure must be applied immediately to induce the United States government to assume its responsibility to halt the growth of the American population. Once growth is halted, the government should undertake to influence the birth rate so that the population is reduced to an optimum size and maintained there.[56]

They also advocated "de-developing" the United States.

A massive campaign must be launched to restore a high-quality environment in North America and to de-develop the United States. De-development means bringing our economic system (especially patterns of consumption) into line with the realities of ecology and the global resource situation. Resources and energy must be diverted from frivolous and wasteful uses in overdeveloped countries to filling the genuine needs of underdeveloped countries.[57]

Taking property from A and giving it to B was at the core of their plan. But rather than limiting themselves, say, to taking property from automobile owners and giving it to bicycle riders, or taking it from one group of people in New London and giving it to another group of people in New London, or taking it from one age group in America and giving it to another age group, they would go so far as to take wealth from Americans generally and give it to people elsewhere.

"Redistribution of wealth both within and among nations is absolutely essential, if a decent life is to be provided for every human being," they wrote.[58] Transition to the spaceman economy could not go forward on any other basis. "Otherwise," they said, "fixing the quantity of physical goods in use would 'freeze' the majority of human beings in a state of poverty."[59]

As part of the campaign to de-develop the United States, Holdren and the Ehrlichs envisioned the government redirecting industries. Three decades before the federal government would take majority ownership of General Motors, they argued that de-development of the United States should start with the automobile industry.

> We believe a Federal task force should be established to do the planning and lay the groundwork for dealing with the automobile problem without great disruption of the national economy. Such a task force might be part of a larger institution with the responsibility to devise policies for making the transition to a stable, ecologically sound economy. This task is enormous, but it is both possible and necessary. In the short term, alternative activities must be found for various industries, including those related to the automobile.[60]

They also pointed approvingly to a proposal by economist Herman Daly who called for imposing restrictions, or "depletion quotas," on the volume of natural resources (including fossil fuels) that could be developed so that the price of these resources would be inflated making it harder for consumers to use them. "With resources scarce (and thus expensive), a premium would be placed on the durability of goods, recycling, and the restriction of effluents (which often contain 'resources' not now economically recoverable)," they wrote. "Limiting the amount of energy available would, of course, also tend to limit the size and number of automobiles, encourage the use of mass transit, and promote the substitution of efficient high-speed trains for energetically wasteful and medium-haul jet airplanes."[61]

Their program, they acknowledged, would cause "temporary unemployment," but they had an answer for that, too: restrict the amount of time people could work, and cut their pay.

> In the longer term, it may be that the solution to the unemployment problem will require a reduction in the amount of work

done by each worker in order to create more jobs. Gradually shortening the work week (ultimately to 20 hours or less) or decreasing the number of work weeks per year (companies could have different spring-summer and fall-winter shifts) would accomplish this.[62]

As people became more enlightened, they would realize that restrictions on their right to work and prosper were good for them.

There would be few but positive consequences from such a reduction in working time. Pay would perhaps be reduced, but so would many expenses if material goods were built to endure and there was no longer social pressure to consume for the sake of consuming. If people could be diverted from the speedy, mechanized forms of leisure activity now promoted by advertising, the pace of life would undoubtedly slow down, with attendant psychological and physical benefits.[63]

Holdren and the Ehrlichs also believed laws should be enacted to restrict freedom of speech.

Advertising now functions in large part to keep the economy growing by creating demand for a wide variety of often useless, dangerous, or environmentally destructive products. Its most dangerous abuses might be halted immediately by legislative actions. For instance, it could be made illegal for any utility to advertise in such a way as to promote greater demand for power. Also, references to size, power or sexual potency (direct or implied) could be banned from automobile advertising. Certainly, every effort should be made to expunge from advertising the idea that the quality of life is closely related to the rate at which new products are purchased or energy is consumed.[64]

The neo-Malthusian rationale that drove Holdren and the Ehrlichs to advocate an economy in which government would restrain human work, reproduction, and speech was successfully challenged, however, by Julian
Simon, a professor of economics at the University of Illinois.[65]

Simon came up with a practical way to test the theory that a growing
human population was rapidly depleting natural resources found on the
planet in limited supply. He simply examined how much human labor it
cost to purchase a particular resource as time passed: as population
increased, did the real cost rise or fall? The truth was startling: the long-
term trends indicated more people meant cheaper resources.[66] Simon even
discovered that per-capita food production had increased as the global population grew.[67] Malthus got it wrong.

What could account for this? Simon reasoned that as population
increased, the rising demand for a given resource caused temporary shortages that, in turn, increased the incentive for people to find new stocks and
develop better retrieval methods.[68] More importantly, Simon believed history demonstrated that increasing demand for a resource also created an
incentive for people to find substitutes that could provide human beings
with the same service that the original resource provided.[69] For example, if
a growing population increased demand for coal as a source of energy,
entrepreneurs might find new sources for coal and better ways to mine it,
while also turning to oil as a substitute for coal. In Simon's view, this process
would continue as men found it ever more efficient to harness the energy
of the sun, which, after all, is what they were indirectly doing by burning
coal or oil. "Of course the sun may eventually run down," said Simon. "But
even if our sun were not as vast as it is, there may well be other suns elsewhere."[70]

Solving resource-related problems, Simon argued, increased the stock
of human knowledge. The speculative ventures of one generation became
the intellectual capital of the next.[71] Policymakers, however, needed to recognize that two indispensible engines drove this wealth-creating train: the
human mind and human freedom.[72] Creating fewer babies today would

mean fewer bright ideas tomorrow, when those babies were grown and educated. Restricting freedom now would mean restraining the creative energy of human beings that leads to a better tomorrow.

Looking at the universe around him, Simon saw no practical reason to believe that man in any meaningful time frame would run up against physical limitations on the number of people who could be allowed to live or the economic growth those people could sustain.

"There is no physical or economic reason why human resourcefulness and enterprise cannot forever continue to respond to impending shortages and existing problems with new expedients that, after an adjustment period, leave us better off than before the problems arose," he wrote. "Adding more people will cause us more such problems, but at the same time there will be more people to solve these problems and leave us with the bonus of lower costs and less scarcity in the long run."[73]

Simon's essential insight was simple. People were the most valuable thing on the planet. They were net producers, not net consumers. "The ultimate resource," he said, "is people—skilled, spirited, and hopeful people who will exert their wills and imaginations for their own benefit, and so, inevitably, for the benefit of all."[74]

Simon was willing to put his own money on the line to back up this theory. In 1980, he offered a wager to anyone willing to challenge his conviction "that the cost of non-government-controlled raw materials (including grain and oil) will not rise in the long run."[75] He agreed to let whoever accepted the challenge choose the raw materials they would bet on and the future date when the bet would end. If on that date the raw materials in question cost more in inflation-adjusted dollars than they had on the date the bet began, Simon would lose.

Paul Ehrlich and John Holdren took up Simon's challenge. They joined with John Harte, a scientist at the Lawrence Berkeley Laboratory, to bet that quantities of copper, chrome, nickel, tin, and tungsten worth $200 each (for a total value of $1,000) on September 29, 1980, would be worth more than that on September 29, 1990.

The neo-Malthusians bought the five metals. They waited the ten years. Then they had to pay up.

"Each of the five metals chosen by Ehrlich's group, when adjusted for inflation since 1980, had declined in price," the *New York Times* reported when the wager was settled. "The drop was so sharp, in fact, that Simon would have come out slightly ahead overall even without the inflation adjustment called for in the bet. Prices fell for the same Cornucopian reasons they had fallen in previous decades—entrepreneurship and continuing technological improvements."[76]

The *New York Times* asked Ehrlich if Simon's victory held any lessons for the future. "Absolutely not," he said.[77] Five years after losing the bet, he and Holdren would join Gretchen Daily of Stanford's Center for Conservation Biology in writing an essay published by the World Bank in a book entitled *The Meaning of Sustainability*. Almost three decades after Ehrlich's *Population Bomb* had erroneously predicted that hundreds of millions of people would starve to death in the 1970s and 1980s, he and Holdren were still preaching a gospel of doom.

The Meaning of Sustainability was not as strident as *Human Ecology*. It did not call for all the draconian measures suggested in that earlier work. But it did persist in depicting both population and economic growth as the enemies of man. In the more than two decades that passed between the two publications, Ehrlich and Holdren had updated their I-PAT equation while maintaining its essential point. Now their formula defined "damage," as "reduced length or quality of life for the present generation or future generations."[78] The updated version of their equation said: "Damage = population x economic activity per person (affluence) x resource use per economic activity (resources) x stress on the environment per resource use (technology) x damage per stress (susceptibility)."[79]

Simply put, they believed that each additional human being who was born threatened the length or quality of life of the people already here, as well as people yet to be born. The more people worked to improve their circumstances, the more they imperiled the lives and wellbeing of others.

Believing their equation described the world as it really is, Ehrlich, Holdren, and Daily concluded in the World Bank essay that growth and population needed to be limited. They wrote,

> We know for certain, for example, that:
> - No form of material growth (including population growth) other than asymptotic growth, is sustainable;
> - Many of the practices inadequately supporting today's population of 5.5 billion people are unsustainable;
> - At the sustainability limit, there will be a tradeoff between population and energy-matter throughput per person, hence, ultimately between economic activity per person and well-being per person.
>
> This is enough to say quite a lot about what needs to be faced up to eventually (a world of zero net physical growth), what should be done now (change unsustainable practices, reduce excessive material consumption, slow down population growth), and what the penalty will be for postponing attention to population limitation (lower well-being per person).[80]

The co-author of these words now sits at the left hand of President Obama.

A Man Who Walks on Water

After Obama nominated Holdren to run the Office of Science and Technology Policy, the venerated environmentalist appeared in the Senate Commerce, Science, and Transportation Committee for a confirmation hearing. No one at that hearing asked Holdren about his and Ehrlich's 1973 book that argued for de-developing the United States. No one asked him about his, Ehrlich's, and Daily's 1995 warning that the human race must resign itself to a "world of zero net physical growth."

One senator did ask Holdren about past statements he had made about population control and global warming. On population control, Holdren retreated from one of his most dramatic prior assertions. On global warming, he did not back down as far.

"In 1973," asked Senator David Vitter of Louisiana, referring to Holdren's Cal Tech essay, "you encouraged a 'decline in fertility to well below replacement' in the United States because '280 million in 2040 is likely to be too many.' What would your number for the right population in the U.S. be today?"

"I no longer think it's productive, senator, to focus on the optimum population for the United States," said Holdren. "I don't think any of us know what the right answer is. When I wrote those lines in 1973, I was preoccupied with the fact that many problems the United States faced appeared to be being made more difficult by the rate of population growth that then prevailed. I think everyone who studies these matters understand that population growth brings some benefits and some liabilities. It is a tough question to determine which will prevail in a given time period. But I think the key thing today is that we need to work to improve the conditions that all of our citizens face economically, environmentally and in other respects and we need to aim for something that I have for years been calling sustainable prosperity."

Vitter pressed for a more definitive answer. "Well, since we are at 304 million, I am certainly heartened that you are not sticking to the 280 million figure," he said. "But, much more recently, namely a couple of weeks ago, in response to my written questions, you did say on this matter: 'Balancing costs and benefits of population growth is a complex business, of course, and reasonable people can disagree about where it comes out.' I'll be quite honest with you: I am not concerned about where you or I might come out. I am scared to death that you think this is a proper function of government, which is what that sentence clearly implies. Do you think determining optimal population is a proper role of government?"

"No, senator, I do not," said Holdren. "And I did not certainly intend that to be the implication of that sentence. The sentence means only what it says, which is that people who have thought about these matters come out in different places. I think the proper role of government is to develop and deploy the policies with respect to economy, environment, security that will ensure the well-being of the citizens we have. I also believe that many of those policies will have the effect, and have had the effect in the past, of lowering birth rates because when you provide health care for women, opportunities for women, education, people tend to have smaller families on average and it ends up being easier to solve some of our other problems when that occurs."

Holdren did not retreat as far from another dire prediction. "In 1986, you predicted that global warming could cause the deaths of 1 billion people by 2020," Vitter asked. "Would you stick to that statement today?"

"Well, again, I wouldn't have called it a prediction then and I wouldn't call it a prediction now," said Holdren. "I think it is unlikely to happen. But it is—"

"You think it could happen?" asked Vitter.

"I think it could happen, and the way it could happen is climate crosses a tipping point in which a catastrophic degree of climate change has severe impacts on global agriculture," said Holdren. "A lot of people—"

"So, you would stick to that statement?" asked the senator.

"I don't think it's likely," said Holdren. "I think we should invest effort, considerable effort, to reduce the likelihood further."

"But you would stick to the statement that it could happen," pressed the senator.

"It could happen," said Holdren.

"One billion by 2020," said the senator.

"It could," said Holdren.

Before the end of his exchange with Holdren, the senator returned to the issue. "You would still say, I think you did, that 1 billion people lost by 2020 is still a possibility?" he asked.

"It is a possibility, and one we should work energetically to avoid," said Holdren.[81]

In 1973, liberal environmentalists saw over-population as the agent of doom. In 2009, it was global warming. Yet over the years, their prescription has not varied: increase government control over people's lives and property.

The full Senate confirmed John P. Holdren by unanimous consent. When he returned to the Commerce, Science, and Transportation Committee for a hearing several months after his confirmation, Senator Jay Rockefeller, the committee chairman, expressed his admiration for the president's science adviser in terms that were apt for the role liberal environmentalists believe government officials ought to play in our lives.

"Dr. Holdren, I don't want to embarrass you," said Rockefeller, "but I sometimes refer to you as walking on water."[82]

Chapter 5

Ban This Book
Liberals Want to Control Your Speech

"Not true."[1]

—Justice Samuel Alito
January 27, 2010

"The government urges us in this case to uphold a direct prohibition on political speech."[2]

—Chief Justice John Roberts
Citizens United v. *FEC*

"For my part, I would merely say to the licensee, 'You may speak.'"[3]

—FCC Commissioner Robert Jones
1949

I t was like the classic act of a schoolyard bully, punching another student in the ribs as an accomplice held the victim's arms back. Only this was not a schoolyard, it was the chamber of the U.S. House of Representatives—and the bully was the president of the United States.

About forty-six minutes into his 2010 State of the Union Address, President Barack Obama looked down pompously from the speaker's podium. Directly below him—in the first two rows of the chamber—sat six of the nine justices of the United States Supreme Court.

These six justices had been gracious enough to show up and listen to the president's long, boring and, until this moment, thoroughly predictable speech. In keeping with their status as members of the third branch of the federal government, they had persevered in polite silence. They had neither cheered nor applauded, in contrast to members of the president's political party, who rose again and again in raucous celebration every time he said something with which they remotely agreed.

But now, the president had something he wanted to say directly to the justices. And given that they appeared properly restrained, he must have thought it was safe to deliver his blow.

> With all due deference to the separation of powers, last week the Supreme Court reversed a century of law that I believe will open the floodgates for special interests—including foreign corporations—to spend without limit in our elections. I don't think American elections should be bankrolled by America's most powerful interests, or worse, foreign entities. They should be decided by the American people. And I'd urge Democrats and Republicans to pass a bill that helps to correct some of these problems.[4]

As Obama said these words, the Democratic members of Congress, sitting immediately behind the justices, spasmodically stood and delivered another ovation. Sitting calmly in the second row, Justice Samuel Alito had a different reaction. He delivered a swift, unexpected and devastating counter-punch.

He shook his head and silently mouthed, "Not true."[5]

These will be the only words long remembered from that night. The president did not utter them. They were not even uttered aloud. But they spoke truth to power. And the scene they immortalized ought to be forever understood to symbolize the threat that liberal control freaks pose to freedom of speech: they want government to lecture us, while limiting our ability to speak back. They want us to sit down and shut up.

The Supreme Court decision Obama criticized that night—*Citizens United* v. *Federal Election Commission*—illustrates the point. Was this decision really about letting powerful—or even foreign—interests "bankroll" our elections? Or was Justice Alito right? Were the president's words not true?

The Supreme Court decision in question was not about foreign interests "bankrolling" American political campaigns. It was about fourteen simple words in the Constitution: "Congress shall make no law...abridging the freedom of speech, or of the press."

These words are not obscure. Members of Congress should be able to understand them without consulting constitutional scholars. The First Amendment does not say: "Congress shall make *some* laws...abridging the freedom of speech, or of the press." It does not say: "Congress shall make no law...abridging the freedom of speech, or of the press—unless it applies to individuals and organizations the majority party in Congress disagrees with." It says: "Congress shall make *no* law..."

Because we have a federal government of delegated powers—that, as James Madison said, are "few and defined"[6]—any act of Congress abridging the freedom of speech is a double offense against the Constitution. It not only assumes a power not delegated by the Constitution, it assumes a power expressly denied by the Constitution.

Patrick Henry argued in the Virginia ratifying convention that the Constitution needed a bill of rights to explicitly protect freedom of the press and freedom of religion.

I trust that gentlemen, on this occasion, will see the great objects of religion, liberty of the press, trial by jury, interdiction of cruel punishments, and every other sacred right, secure, before they agree to that paper. These most important human rights are not protected by that section, which is the only safeguard in the Constitution. My mind will not be quieted till I see something substantial come forth in the shape of a bill of rights.[7]

Edmund Randolph, however, considered Patrick's concerns overwrought, and countered that these freedoms did not need to be explicitly protected because the Constitution did not give Congress any power to touch them. Randolph said,

Then, sir, the freedom of the press is said to be insecure. God forbid that I should give my voice against the freedom of the press. But I ask, (and with confidence that it cannot be answered,) Where is the page where it is restrained? If there had been any regulation about it, leaving it insecure, then there might have been reason for clamors. But this is not the case. If it be, I again ask for the particular clause which gives liberty to destroy the freedom of the press.

He said of Patrick Henry,

He has added religion to the objects endangered, in his conception. Is there any power given over it? Let it be pointed out. Will he not be contented with the answer that has been frequently given to the objection? The variety of sects which abounds in the United States is the best security for freedom of religion. No part of the Constitution, even if strictly construed, will justify a conclusion that the general government can take away or impair the freedom of religion.[8]

The concerns voiced by delegates like Patrick Henry inspired swift ratification of the Bill of Rights, placing an additional fortification around the freedoms of speech and religion that men like Randolph were convinced had already been protected by the federal Constitution because it gave Congress no power over them at all.

Americans of the Founding era were quite familiar with a disputatious press. They argued their own causes in rival newspapers, and understood freedom of speech to be an indispensible check on the power of government.

But in his unprecedented State-of-the-Union attack on the Supreme Court for its decision in the *Citizens United* case, President Obama implicitly defended abridging not just the freedom of speech, but the freedom of political speech.

The *Citizens United* case was prompted by a 90-minute documentary movie shown in theatres in a number of cities around the country and made available for sale in DVD form. Its producers had also made a deal to distribute it through an on-demand cable television service and to alert potential viewers of its availability in that venue though 10-second and 30-second advertisements that would run on regular cable channels. People who saw these ads and decided they wanted to watch the movie could order it electronically and view it at their leisure. People who did not want to watch it did not have to order it. Unless they ordered it, it would never appear on their television sets.

The question for the Supreme Court was whether the federal government could make it a crime for the producers of this movie to distribute it through the on-demand cable service—which facilitated a bilateral act in which both parties participated freely. It was this free act that liberal control freaks wanted to stop.

Now, had this movie been pornography, liberals would not have objected. Nor would they have objected if it had promoted some social or environmental cause they favored—such as, say, saving the planet from over-population or global warming. But the movie was not pornographic, and it was not about the purported perils of over-population or climate change. It was about a powerful politician, a member of a class whose special interests, liberals believed, needed protection from the potential effects of one group of Americans communicating with another. It only made matters more difficult that the specific group that made the movie—Citizens United, a non-profit corporation—was a conservative organization, and the subject of the movie, Hillary Clinton, was decidedly not.

Lawyers from Citizens United told the Supreme Court,

> In mid-2007, Citizens United began production of *Hillary: The Movie*, a biographical documentary about Senator Hillary Clinton, who was then a candidate to become the Democratic Party's nominee for President. Although Senator Clinton's candidacy was the backdrop for the 90-minute documentary, neither the movie's narrator nor any of the individuals interviewed during the movie expressly advocated her election or defeat as President. The movie instead presents a critical assessment of Senator Clinton's record as a U.S. Senator and as First Lady in order to educate viewers about her political background.[9]

For more than a century, Congress has maintained a ban on corporations making direct contributions—or bankrolling—federal election campaigns. The justification for this ban is that a corporate contribution could appear to be, or could actually constitute, a bribe. By banning corporate contributions, it is argued, Congress prevents corruption and the appearance of it and preserves public faith in the democratic process.

In recent decades, however, Congress has gone beyond merely barring corporations from directly contributing to federal candidates. In the 1970s, in a section of law known as 441b, it banned corporations from making their own independent expenditures to expressly advocate the election or defeat of a candidate for federal office. In 2002, the McCain-Feingold campaign finance law—known as the Bipartisan Campaign Reform Act

(BCRA)—expanded this provision to include a ban on corporations engaging in what it called "electioneering communications." This was defined as "any broadcast, cable or satellite communication which refers to a clearly identified candidate for federal office" during the thirty days before a primary and the sixty days before a general election. So-called "media corporations"—those corporations that own and operate traditional news organizations, such as television stations that broadcast regular news programs—were exempted from this prohibition on political speech. They remained free to spend money discussing, analyzing, criticizing, endorsing, and opposing federal candidates. But all other corporations, including nonprofits like Citizens United, were prohibited from doing so.

Citizens United planned to offer *Hillary: The Movie* to on-demand cable viewers in early 2008, during the time Senator Clinton would be competing in the Democratic presidential primaries. In December 2007, the group asked the federal district court in the District of Columbia to prevent the Federal Election Commission from using the law that prohibited corporations from "electioneering communications" to stop distribution of the movie via cable on-demand. The court ruled against Citizens United. The case went to the Supreme Court.

When President George W. Bush signed BCRA in 2002, he confessed he believed some of its "provisions present serious constitutional concerns."[10] He told Americans, in other words, that he suspected the law he was signing violated their rights. When the case challenging the application of BCRA to *Hillary: The Movie* arrived in the high court in 2009, however, the Obama administration was not worried about violating citizens' rights. They fully backed not only BCRA's prohibition on corporate-funded speech that merely mentioned a federal candidate in broadcast, cable, or satellite media; they also backed the broader 441b provision barring corporations from spending money in any media whatsoever on speech that supported or opposed a candidate for federal office. As they interpreted the First Amendment, the government could impose sweeping restrictions on political speech.

Deputy Solicitor General Malcolm Stewart delivered the oral argument when the court heard the case in March 2009. Unlike the House chamber during the State of the Union, this was a forum where Justice Alito could talk back—and talk back he did. He was joined by Justice Anthony Kennedy and Chief Justice John Roberts in cross-examining Stewart.

The revelations started when Stewart tried to explain the meaning of the congressional prohibition on corporate "electioneering communication."

> I think the real key to ascertaining Congress's intent is to look to the definition of electioneering communication that Congress enacted into the statute, and that definition requires that the communication be a broadcast, cable or satellite communication, and that it be aired within a certain proximity to a federal election.

Chief Justice Roberts took the first crack.

"So," asked Roberts, "if Wal-Mart airs an advertisement that says we have candidate action figures for sale, come buy them, that counts as an electioneering communication?"

"If it's aired in the right place at the right time, that would be covered," said Stewart.

Then Justice Alito pushed Stewart to reveal whether the Obama administration believed the government had the constitutional authority to impose a similar speech ban on the Internet, or even in old-fashioned book publishing.

"Do you think the Constitution required Congress to draw the line where it did, limiting this to broadcast and cable and so forth?" asked Alito. Was there any "constitutional difference between the distribution of this movie on video demand, and providing access on the Internet, providing DVDs, either through a commercial service or maybe in a public library, providing the same thing in a book? Would the Constitution permit restriction of all those things as well?"

Stewart answered that the restrictions "could have been applied to addi-tional media as well."

"That's pretty incredible," said Alito. "You think that if a book was pub-lished, a campaign biography that was the functional equivalent of express advocacy, that could be banned?"

Stewart essentially said it depended on what the meaning of "banned" was.

"I'm not saying it could be banned," he said. "I'm saying that Congress could prohibit the use of corporate treasury funds and could require a cor-poration to publish it using its—"

He was most likely about to say "Political Action Committee," which is an entirely different organization from the corporation itself, but Justice Alito cut him off.

"Well, most publishers are corporations," said Alito. "And a publisher that is a corporation could be prohibited from selling a book?"

Stewart now tried to explain the administration's belief that the "institu-tional press"—that is, the largely liberal press—has a greater right to free-dom of speech than everyone else.

"Well, of course," said Stewart, "the statute contains its own media exemption or media—"

Alito cut him off again.

"I'm not asking what the statute says," said Alito. "The government's position is that the First Amendment allows the banning of a book if it's published by a corporation?"

Stewart then expressly stated the administration's view that corporations that run the "institutional press" have a greater right to free speech.

"Because the First Amendment refers both to freedom of speech and the press, there would be a potential argument that media corporations, the institutional press, would have a greater First Amendment right," he said.

Justice Kennedy now intervened.

"Well, suppose it were an advocacy organization that had a book," said Kennedy. "Your position is that under the Constitution, the advertising for this book or the sale for the book itself could be prohibited within the sixty... the thirty day period?"

Stewart admitted as much. "If the book contained the functional equivalent of express advocacy," he said.

Then Kennedy asked if the government could ban the book if it was distributed on Kindle. "And I suppose it could even, is it the Kindle where you can read a book?" said Kennedy. "I take it that's from a satellite. So the existing statute would probably prohibit that under your view?"

"Well," said Stewart, "the statute applies to cable, satellite and broadcast communications."

But Kennedy wanted more than the administration's view of what the statute allowed, he wanted the administration's view of what the Constitution allowed. "Just to make clear," he asked, "it's the government's position that under the statute, if this Kindle device where you can read a book which is campaign advocacy, with the sixty to thirty day period, if it comes from a satellite, it's under, it can be prohibited under the Constitution and perhaps under this statute?"

This time Stewart's answer depended on what the meaning of "prohibited" is.

"It can't be prohibited, but a corporation could be barred from using its general treasury fund to publish the book and could be required to use— to raise funds to publish the book using its PAC," he said.

Here Chief Justice Roberts stepped back into the discussion.

"If it has one name, one use of the candidate's name, it would be covered, correct?" asked Roberts.

"That's correct," said Stewart.

"It's a 500-page book," said the chief justice, "and at the end it says: And so vote for X. The government can ban that?"

"Well," said Stewart, "if it says vote for X, it would be express advocacy and it would be covered by the pre-existing Federal Election Campaign Act provision."

Like Kennedy, Chief Justice Roberts wanted more than the Obama administration's view of what the statute allowed; he wanted the administration's view of what the Constitution allowed.

"No, I'm talking about under the Constitution, what we've been discussing, if it's a book?" asked Roberts.

Stewart finally started circling toward a definitive answer.

"If you had Citizens United or General Motors using general treasury funds to publish a book that said at the outset, for instance, Hillary Clinton's election would be a disaster for this—"

"Take my hypothetical," interrupted Roberts. "It doesn't say at the outset .... This [book] is a discussion of the American political system, and at the end it says: Vote for X."

"Yes," said Stewart, "our position would be that the corporation would be required to use PAC funds rather than general treasury funds."

"And if they didn't, you could ban it?" asked Roberts.

"If they didn't," Stewart said, "we could prohibit the publication of the book using corporate treasury funds."

Justice Alito then wanted to know if the administration's understanding of the First Amendment meant Congress could enact legislation preventing a corporation from publishing a book or a movie on the Internet—perhaps on YouTube—if it advocated election or defeat of a federal candidate.

"If Congress in the next act covered that in light of advances in the Internet, would the Constitution permit that?" asked Alito.

"Yes," said Stewart, pointing to some of the court's previous decisions on corporate speech that he believed established the precedent that such a restriction would be constitutional.

Justice Antonin Scalia intervened with some sarcasm. "I'm a little disoriented here, Mr. Stewart," said Scalia. "We are dealing with a constitutional provision, are we not, the one that I remember which says Congress shall make no law abridging the freedom of the press? That's what we're interpreting here?"

"That's correct," said Stewart.[11]

Having heard the administration's argument for abridging freedom of speech—based on the court's own precedents upholding abridgements of corporate speech—the court decided it had to use *Citizens United* v. *FEC* to revisit those precedents. It delayed a decision in the case and called for a second round of oral arguments in September 2009.

This time Solicitor General Elena Kagan, whom President Obama would later nominate to the Supreme Court, made the argument for Obama's Justice Department. She came prepared to say that the administration had altered its position on book banning.

"May I ask you one question that was highlighted in the prior argument, and that was if Congress could say no TV and radio ads, could it also say no newspapers ads, no campaign biographies?" asked Justice Ruth Bader Ginsburg. "Last time the answer was, yes, Congress could, but it didn't. Is that still the government's answer?"

"The government's answer has changed, Justice Ginsburg," said Kagan.

But then she did not say that the law or the Constitution simply would not allow the government to ban books because of their political content. She only conceded that if the government did expand the law controlling political speech by corporations to include banning corporations from publishing books that expressly advocate the election or defeat of politicians, the publishers might have grounds for a narrow constitutional challenge of that particular application of the law.

"We went back, we considered the matter carefully," said Kagan, "and the government's view is that although 441b does cover full-length books, that there would be quite a good as-applied challenge to any attempt to apply 441b in that context."

Chief Justice Roberts again wanted a precise declaration of how far the administration believed the government could go in restricting speech. "And if you say that you are not going to apply it to a book," he said, "what about a pamphlet."

"I think a pamphlet would be different," said Kagan. "A pamphlet is pretty classic electioneering, so there is no attempt to say that 441b only applies to video and not to print."[12]

Justice Alito could not have known at that moment that four months later, he would be sitting in front of the president of the United States who would look down on him as he declared to the world that this case was about allowing foreign interests to bankroll American elections.

It was Justice Kennedy, the ultimate swing vote on the contemporary court, who wrote the majority opinion in *Citizens United* v. *FEC*, throwing out federal legal restrictions on the type of speech corporations can fund about federal candidates. Kennedy said that the court did not need to address the question of what the government could or could not do about a largely foreign-owned corporation engaging in speech about American political campaigns, because the law went far beyond abridging that speech. He wrote,

> Section 441b is not limited to corporations or associations that were created in foreign countries or funded predominately by foreign shareholders. Section 441b therefore would be overbroad even if we assumed, *arguendo,* that the Government has a compelling interest in limiting foreign influence over our political process.

It was Chief Justice Roberts, however, who in a concurring opinion most powerfully summarized the Obama administration's contempt for freedom of speech.

> The government urges us in this case to uphold a direct prohibition on political speech. It asks us to embrace a theory of the First Amendment that would allow censorship not only of television and radio broadcasts, but of pamphlets, posters, the Internet, and

virtually any other medium that corporations and unions might find useful in expressing their views on matters of public concern.

Consistently applied and carried through to its logical conclusion, the control freak's view of the First Amendment could annihilate freedom of the press. The chief justice wrote,

> [The Administration's] theory, if accepted, would empower the government to prohibit newspapers from running editorials or opinion pieces supporting or opposing candidates for office, so long as the newspapers are owned by corporations—as the major ones are.[13]

The court decided this case five to four.[14] Freedom of speech has a one-vote margin.

"No Power at All"

The legislators who enacted the first comprehensive law regulating America's broadcasting airwaves understood the meaning of the First Amendment. They believed a federal statute was needed to ensure the technical workability of commercial radio. But they did not believe Congress had the power to tell broadcasters what they could and could not say on the air.

These legislators had a practical problem to solve. As radio outlets proliferated in the 1920s, stations broadcasting on the same wave length often interfered with one another. Because broadcast signals crossed state lines, some sort of nationwide order needed to be established to allow the radio industry to grow and prosper. In 1925, then-Commerce Secretary Herbert Hoover sponsored a conference of people involved in the industry to discuss solutions. It recommended that Congress create a federal authority to approve and regulate broadcast licenses.[15]

Representative Wallace White, a Republican from Maine who would eventually cap his political career as Senate majority leader, sponsored a House bill based on the recommendations of the conference. Senator Clarence Dill, a Democrat from Washington, sponsored a similar bill in the Senate. Both sought to maintain two principles: free speech and free markets.

When White offered his bill in March 1926, he cited the guiding principles the radio conference had recommended. They included: "That the doctrine of free speech be held inviolate."[16]

White urged Congress not to over-regulate an emerging technology. The new medium of radio, he said, must be left free to compete in an open market that included other modes of electronic communication.

> We are now dealing with a new means of communication. It is fighting to develop its usefulness in a field in which telephones, telegraphs, and cables are now entrenched. We should exercise every care in the public interest, but there exists a reasonable doubt whether we are justified in applying to this industry different and more drastic rules than the other forms of communication are subjected to.

White viewed radio as a pioneering industry. He wanted government to build as few fences as possible on the frontier it was opening. "Laws, narrow, restrictive, destructive of a new industry serve no public good," he said. "We should avoid them."[17]

Representative Fiorello LaGuardia, the future mayor of New York—who was a Republican, but no conservative—wanted to reinforce the freedom-of-speech issue at the outset of debate on White's bill.

"The gentleman stated the recommendations among which was a guaranty of free speech over the radio," said LaGuardia. "What provision does the bill make to carry that out?"

White believed in the plain meaning of the amendment that "Congress shall make no law...abridging the freedom of speech."

"It does not touch that matter specifically," he told LaGuardia. "Personally I felt that we could go no further than the Federal Constitution in that respect. The pending bill gives the secretary no power of interfering with freedom of speech in any degree."

LaGuardia wanted the record to show that there was no ambiguity in White's answer.

"It is the belief of the gentleman and the intent of Congress in passing this bill not to give the secretary any power whatever in that respect in considering a license or the revocation of a license," said LaGuardia.

"No power at all," said White.[18]

Senator Dill would later be remembered for working with FDR to push through federal funding for the Grand Coulee Dam on the Columbia River. But when it came to regulating radio, Dill shared White's belief in freedom of speech, and he wanted to limit government involvement in the medium as much as possible. In his mind, the rapid rise of broadcasting in America could be directly attributed to the nation's exceptional tradition of freedom. When his bill came up in the Senate, Dill said,

> First, and most important of all, radio in the United States is free. It is so free to the listener-in that anybody anywhere may listen to any broadcasting whatsoever, whether it be by amateurs who are experimenting or by telegraphers who are sending wireless messages in code or by broadcasters who are giving programs to amuse, entertain and instruct, without any restraint or hindrance whatsoever by the government....
>
> The other condition regarding radio in the United States that is different from conditions in other countries relates to broadcasting. In practically all other countries the government either owns or directly controls all broadcasting stations. In this country there has been practically no control exercised by the government,

except to the assignment of wave lengths and regulations as to the amount of power to be used.

Freedom worked, Dill believed. He asked,

> What has been the result of this policy of freedom for radio broadcasting and radio reception? The result is that American initiative and American business ingenuity have developed radio broadcasting in the United States far beyond anything known in other parts of the world. With only 6 percent of the world's population living in the United States, we have more than 80 percent of the receiving sets on earth and five times as many broadcasting stations as all the rest of the world combined.[19]

He wanted to keep America first.

Wallace succeeded in putting his bill through the House without any amendments limiting the political speech of broadcasters. But this perturbed some liberals in the chamber. The House committee that reviewed the bill published a minority report lamenting that it would allow a radio station, if it wished, to relentlessly advocate one candidate, one political party, or one point of view. It could freely act as a partisan.

> The broadcasting field holds untold potentialities in a political and propaganda way; its future use in this respect will undoubtedly be extensive and effective. There is nothing in this bill to prevent a broadcasting station from permitting one party or one candidate or the advocate of a measure or a program or the opponent thereof, to employ its service and refusing to accord the same right to the opposing side; the broadcasting station might even contract to permit one candidate or one side of a controversy to broadcast exclusively upon the agreement that the opposing side should not be accorded a like privilege.[20]

In the Senate, a formidable movement wanted stringent government controls on broadcasters. To get the bill out of committee, Dill was forced to agree to language mandating that if a radio station allowed itself to be used by any candidate for office or allowed discussion of any public issue, the station would be deemed a "common carrier" and required to accept for broadcast any message from anybody who wanted to use its airwaves.

When the bill came to the floor, Dill offered an amendment to remove this language. The amendment required broadcasters to offer "equal opportunities" to opposing candidates for public office if it offered any candidate time at all, but it did not require broadcasters to air opposing views on public issues.[21]

Senator Robert Howell, a liberal Republican from Nebraska, adamantly opposed Dill's amendment. The government should require every broadcaster, he believed, to give equal opportunities not only to all candidates but also to all issues discussed on its air.

"If all candidates cannot be heard, none should be heard," said Howell. "If both sides of a question cannot be heard over a particular radio station, none should be heard. I cannot emphasize this too strongly."

If the government did not adopt this doctrine, Howell feared, private broadcasters would formulate the views of America's youth.

> The discussion of public questions by radio is reaching the youth of this country, and will have tremendous effect in the formation of their views. The youth of the country are listening in constantly. In fact, the larger proportion of the radio audience is the youth of the country. Give me control of the character of the matter that goes out over broadcasting stations and I will mold the views of the next generation.[22]

Even if there was merit to Howell's views about the potential influence of electronic media, it is notable that he was not talking about the broadcasting of obscenity and indecency here—which the bill did ban in a provision that raised no controversy at all in either the House or the Senate. He was talking about political speech, and there remained only two parties potentially capable of controlling political speech on the radio: the station owners or the government. Howell wanted the government in control.

Dill told Howell he sympathized with his concerns. But he predicted Howell's proposed regulation would stifle all discussion of public issues on the radio. Under Howell's proposal, Dill said, broadcasters "would have to give all their time to that kind of discussion or no public question could be discussed."[23]

The Senate sided with Dill, not Howell. It passed a radio bill requiring stations to give political candidates "equal opportunities" if it gave them any opportunities at all, but it did not require equal opportunities for opposing sides of public issues.[24] The House acquiesced to the Senate's equal-opportunity rule for candidates, and the conference committee produced a final bill that otherwise left political speech on the radio wholly unregulated.[25] President Coolidge signed the bill, and the Radio Act of 1927 created a Federal Radio Commission that would issue broadcast licenses and oversee the law, but that was specifically barred from censoring speech.

"Nothing in this act," said the law, "shall be understood or construed to give the licensing authority the power of censorship over radio communications or signals transmitted by any radio station, and no regulation or condition shall be promulgated or fixed by the licensing authority which shall interfere with the right of free speech by means of radio communications."[26]

When the radio commission came into being, the commissioners seemed to understand that their mandate was to protect free speech, not to prevent it, and that it would be up to consumers to determine which radio stations prospered and which ones did not.

Two months after President Coolidge signed the Radio Act, Federal Radio Commissioner Henry Bellows spoke at a dinner sponsored by the League of Women Voters.

> Very rightly, Congress has held that the broadcaster shall not be subject to governmental dictation as to the character of the material he sends out; the Federal Radio Commission under present

law cannot and will not interfere with any broadcaster's right to control and censor his own programs. In that matter his relations are not with the government, not with the commission, but with you. It is for you, the listeners, not for us, to censor his programs. It is for you to tell him when he is rendering, or failing to render, real service to the public, and you may be sure that he will listen to your voices.[27]

In 1934, President Roosevelt asked Congress to revamp the Radio Act of 1927 to convert the Federal Radio Commission into a Federal Communications Commission, empowered to regulate all interstate and international radio and wire communications.[28] Congress responded with the Communications Act of 1934. During consideration of this Act, Congress again engaged the issue of political speech on the radio. Like the 1927 Act, the version of the new bill that passed the Senate authorized the FCC to require broadcasters to provide competing candidates with equal opportunities if it provided them any opportunities at all. But it also included language that would have authorized the FCC to require broadcasters "to permit equal opportunity for the presentation of both sides of public questions."[29] The Senate report on the bill said, "This section extends the requirement of equality of treatment of political candidates to supporters and opponents of candidates, and public questions before the people for a vote."[30]

But the House rejected this language, and the final bill did not include it. The Communications Act of 1934 signed by President Roosevelt featured precisely the same equal-opportunities-for-candidates language as the Radio Act of 1927. It did not require broadcasters to provide equal opportunities for the airing of opposing views on public issues. Like the 1927 Act, it prohibited censorship of radio speech. It did not abridge the First Amendment rights of broadcasters.

But the federal commissioners found a loophole in the act to take them through the First Amendment. Both the 1927 and 1934 laws included language directing the commissioners to consider the "public interest, convenience, or necessity" in determining whether to grant or renew broadcast licenses. The language said: "If upon examination of any application for a station license or for a renewal of a station license the licensing authority shall determine that the public interest, convenience or necessity would be served by the granting thereof, it shall authorize the issuance, renewal or modification thereof, in accordance with said finding."[31] The commissioners used this general "public interest, convenience or necessity" standard to justify imposing on broadcasters the specific sort of speech restrictions Congress had unmistakably rejected when it considered the 1927 and 1934 laws.

In its 1929 ruling on the application of *Great Lakes Broadcasting*, the Federal Radio Commission adopted the policy that radio stations must air opposing views on public issues. The commission concluded,

> It would not be fair, indeed it would not be good service, to the public to allow a one-sided presentation of the political questions of a campaign. Insofar as a program consists of discussion of public questions, public interest requires ample play for the free and fair competition of opposing views, and the commission believes that the principle applies not only to addresses by political candidates but to all discussion of issues of importance to the public.

In the same opinion, the commissioners said broadcasters must air programming that appealed to all sectors of their local community.

> This does not mean that every individual is entitled to his exact preference in program items. It does mean, in the opinion of the commission, that the tastes, needs and desires of all substantial groups among the listening public should be met, in some fair proportion, by a well-rounded program, in which, entertainment, consisting of music of both classical and lighter grades, religion,

education and instruction, important public events, discussions of public questions, weather, market reports, and news, and matters of interest to all members of the family find a place.

The commission stopped short of plotting the exact timing in the day when it expected a broadcaster to provide each of these programming genres, but it did expect broadcasters to generally conform to its suggested scheme.

> The commission does not propose to erect a rigid schedule specifying hours or minutes that may be devoted to one kind of program or another. What it wishes to emphasize is the general character which it believes must be conformed to by a station in order to best serve the public.[32]

Based on this view of the "public interest," and the necessarily limited number of broadcast licenses that could be distributed, the commission said it did not favor providing additional licenses to what it called "propaganda stations." Addressing the fact that there were religiously oriented stations already well-established, the commission said it would not remove their licenses but would discriminate against them by granting them inferior technical capabilities. The commission even seemed to draw a distinction between what it considered ordinary religious radio and what it called "high class religious stations."

> Unfortunately, under the law in force prior to the radio act of 1927, the secretary of commerce had no power to distinguish between kinds of applicants and it was not possible to foresee the present situation and its problems. Consequently, there are and have been for a long time in existence a number of stations operated by religious or similar organizations. Certain enterprising organizations, quick to see the possibilities of radio and anxious to present their creeds to the public, availed themselves of license privileges from the earlier

days of broadcasting, and now have good records and a certain degree of popularity among listeners. The commission feels this must be dealt with on a common-sense basis. It does not seem just to deprive such stations of all right to operation and the question must be solved on a comparative basis. While the commission is of the opinion that a broadcasting station engaged in general public service has, ordinarily, a claim to preference over a propaganda station, it will apply this principle as to existing stations by giving preferential facilities to the former and assigning less desirable facilities to the latter to the extent that engineering principles permit. In rare cases it is possible to combine a general public-service station and a high-class religious station in a division of time which will approximate a well-rounded program. In other cases religious stations must accept part time on inferior channels or on daylight assignments where they are still able to transmit during the hours when religious services are usually expected by the listening public.[33]

Thus the commissioners struck a double blow against the First Amendment, hitting freedom of speech and the free exercise of religion in a single decree.

In 1940, when Social Security payments were starting to flow, President Roosevelt was running for an unprecedented third term, and Democrats had controlled both houses of Congress for eight years, the Federal Communications Commission moved decisively against opinionated radio. The Yankee Network applied for renewal of its broadcast license for station WAAB in Massachusetts. Another applicant, Mayflower Broadcasting, wanted the same license. Yankee had openly editorialized on WAAB. It had taken stands for and against candidates and on public issues. The FCC agreed to renew Yankee's license, but only after the network certified it had ceased editorializing and would never do it again.[34]

The FCC ruling in the Mayflower case explicitly stripped broadcasters of the right to advocate, and turned the meaning of "free" upside down.

"A truly free radio cannot be used to advocate the causes of the licensee," said the FCC. "It cannot be used to support the candidacies of his friends. It cannot be devoted to the support of principles he happens to regard most favorably. In brief, the broadcaster cannot be an advocate."[35]

The commission essentially repealed the First Amendment for broadcasters.

"Radio's biggest guns," *Time* Magazine reported, "began hammering away at the decision as an unwarranted shackling of freedom of speech."[36]

In 1949, the FCC revisited its Mayflower decision in a ruling on "Editorializing by Broadcast Licensees." This ruling scaled back the FCC ban on editorializing, but formalized the regulation that broadcasters were required to both present programming on public issues and provide reasonable opportunities for contrasting views to be heard. This policy, which became known as the Fairness Doctrine,[37] was by no means the work of a united FCC. Two of the seven commissioners, including the chairman, did not participate in the ruling. Two others assented to it but filed separate opinions.[38] One commissioner, Frieda Hennock, a liberal New York lawyer who had been appointed by President Truman,[39] opposed the doctrine of "fairness" promulgated by the majority because she thought it was unenforceable. Under the circumstances, she wanted all editorializing to remain completely banned.

"In the absence of some method of policing and enforcing the requirement that the public trust granted a licensee be exercised in an impartial manner, it seems foolhardy to permit editorializing by licensees themselves," she said.[40]

The statement of policy by the commission's majority in the ruling on "Editorializing by Broadcasters" lacked clarity and left much room for interpretation. It said, for example, that in the "presentation of news and comment, the public interest requires that the licensee must operate on a basis of overall fairness, making his facilities available for expression of the contrasting views of all responsible elements in the community on the various issues that arise." But it did not define how a broadcaster—or the government—would decide who the "responsible elements in the community" were.

"Only where the licensee's discretion in the choice of the particular programs to be broadcast over his facilities is exercised so as to afford a reasonable opportunity for the presentation of all responsible positions on matters of sufficient importance to be afforded radio time can radio be maintained as a medium of freedom of speech for the people as a whole," said the FCC ruling. But it did not say how a broadcaster—or the government—would determine a "responsible position," or what was of "sufficient importance" to be discussed on the radio.

Finally, the FCC declared it had "come to the conclusion that overt licensee editorialization, within reasonable limits and subject to the general requirements of fairness detailed above, is not contrary to the public interest."[41]

How was a broadcaster to deal with this new federal regulation on speech in the actual practice of his business? In a separate opinion Commissioner Edward M. Webster, a Truman appointee who had previously served as the chief communications officer of the U.S. Coast Guard,[42] agreed with the commission's ruling that broadcasters could editorialize, but criticized the majority's explanation of this ruling because it "still leaves the licensee in a quandary and a state of confusion in that he must follow with his own interpretation of an involved academic legal treatise to determine what he can or cannot do in his day-to-day operations." A broadcaster, Webster said, was "entitled to know from the Commission just that—'what he can or cannot do'—in as concise and unequivocal language as possible."[43]

Commissioner Robert Jones a Truman appointee who was a former Republican member of Congress,[44] also agreed with the ruling that broadcasters could editorialize, but criticized the commission's explanation of it. He argued that the Mayflower decision had been flatly unconstitutional and should be fully and unambiguously repudiated. "I, therefore, rest my decision that editorializing by licensees is in the public interest not on any policy requirement created by the Commission but upon the inviolate terms of the First Amendment." Jones offered a simple alternative vision:

> I cannot subscribe to the action of the Commission in expressly imposing prospective conditions on the exercise of the licensee's right to use the facilities of a station for purposes of editorialization. I would not say to the licensee as does the Commission's decision, "You may speak but only on the prospective conditions laid down in your report." For my part, I would merely say to the licensee, "You may speak."[45]

A decade after the FCC published its ruling formalizing the Fairness Doctrine, Congress passed an amendment to the Communications Act of 1934, retroactively recognizing a discretionary authority in the commission to enforce it, but not mandating that the commission do so. A decade after that, citing the scarcity of broadcast wavelengths, the Supreme Court ruled that the Fairness Doctrine was a constitutionally acceptable limitation on freedom of speech. For almost four decades, the FCC maintained the policy, thus inhibiting, rather than encouraging, energetic debate of public policy on the radio. Broadcasters who feared running aground on the Fairness Doctrine simply steered clear of controversial issues.

In his 1976 book, *The Good Guys, the Bad Guys and the First Amendment*, former CBS News President Fred Friendly described a strategy carried out by the Democratic Party during the 1964 presidential campaign that exploited the Fairness Doctrine to limit the impact of "right-wing" radio. Bill Ruder, a former assistant secretary of commerce in the Kennedy administration who was involved in executing the strategy, explained it to Friendly this way:

"Our massive strategy was to use the Fairness Doctrine to challenge and harass right-wing broadcasters and hope that the challenges would be so costly to them that they would be inhibited and decide it was too expensive to continue."[46]

At the end of the 1964 campaign, one of the lawyers involved in executing the Democrats' Fairness Doctrine strategy sent a confidential memo to the Democratic National Committee pointing to the strategy's long-term potential beyond the campaign season. The memo, as quoted by Friendly, said:

> The right-wingers operate on a strictly cash basis and it is for this reason that they are carried on so many small stations. Were our efforts to be continued on a year-round basis, we would find that many of these stations would consider the broadcasts of these programs bothersome and burdensome (especially if they are ultimately required to give us free time) and would start dropping the programs from their broadcast schedule.[47]

During the Reagan administration in the 1980s, the FCC studied the impact of the Fairness Doctrine on radio programming and decided it was not doing what it was intended to do, and that its constitutionality was questionable. In 1987, the commission unanimously repealed the regulation. "In sum," the commissioners said, "the fairness doctrine in operation disserves both the public's right to diverse sources of information and the broadcaster's interest in free expression." It "contravenes the First Amendment."[48]

The U.S. Court of Appeals for the District of Columbia upheld the FCC's decision. Liberals nonetheless struggled to maintain federal power to regulate political speech on the radio. The same year the FCC repealed the Fairness Doctrine, a Democrat-controlled Congress passed legislation to reinstate it. President Reagan vetoed the bill on First Amendment grounds. "History has shown that the dangers of an overly timid or biased press cannot be averted through bureaucratic regulation," he said in his veto message, "but only through the freedom and competition that the First Amendment sought to guarantee." [49]

The repeal of the FCC regulation abridging freedom of political speech on the radio opened a new era of communications in America. Led by

Rush Limbaugh, conservative voices proliferated on talk radio. Across the nation, conservative hosts attracted large audiences by providing listeners with information, analysis, and commentary unavailable in an establishment media long dominated by liberals. Unlike the establishment media, which often acted as big government's best friend, conservative talk radio performed a vital function in our society: it was a check on the power of the state.

Two decades after the repeal of the FCC's political-speech regulation, liberals were still trying to resurrect it. In 2005, Democratic Representative Louise Slaughter of New York introduced "The Fairness and Accountability in Broadcasting Act," which would have explicitly reinstated the Fairness Doctrine as statutory law. It was directly targeted at talk shows whose point of view Representative Slaughter did not like.

"Since the rescission of the Fairness Doctrine," the bill said, "the country has experienced a proliferation of highly partisan networks, news outlets, and ownership groups that disseminate unbalanced news coverage and broadcast content."[50]

At a *Christian Science Monitor* breakfast in 2008, House Speaker Nancy Pelosi applauded Slaughter for her efforts on the Fairness Doctrine and told John Gizzi of *Human Events* that she favored reinstating it.[51]

Senate Energy and Natural Resources Chairman Jeff Bingaman, a New Mexico Democrat, took the same position in a 2008 interview with host Jim Villanucci on KKOB in Albuquerque.

"Do you think there will be a push to reinstate the Fairness Doctrine?" asked Villanucci.

"I don't know. I certainly hope so," said Bingaman. He then stated that he supported the doctrine.[52]

Bingaman's colleague, Senate Democratic Whip Dick Durbin of Illinois, believes the radio industry cannot be trusted to the free market.

In 2007, Republican Senator Norm Coleman of Minnesota tried to offer an amendment to prohibit the FCC from reinstating the Fairness Doctrine. Senate Democratic leaders blocked it from consideration. Nonetheless, Durbin rose to debate Coleman on the issue. Eighty years before, on the same Senate floor, the Democratic sponsor of the Radio Act had urged his colleagues to recognize that radio was thriving in America because—like nowhere else on earth—Americans let the free market work. Now, Durbin said, it did not work.

I want all sides to be heard," said Coleman. "What I don't want—and the fundamental disagreement is—for the regulatory power of government to sit in judgment as Big Brother, to oversee and take stock with pencil and pad and take notes: Well, we had Sean Hannity over here. Now we have to get somebody on the left over there." He continued,

> Balance should be heard, but we have a marketplace that provides that opportunity. We have folks who support the perspective of the senator from Illinois, and we have folks who support my perspective. Sometimes we are the same. But for government to dictate, that is the concern. That is why the FCC got rid of the fairness doctrine in 1987. It is why the Supreme Court raised questions about the necessity of the fairness doctrine. I don't think it is constitutional.[53]

Durbin scoffed at Coleman's faith in the market.

> But the Senator is arguing that the marketplace can provide. What is the Senator's response if the marketplace fails to provide? What if it doesn't provide the opportunity to hear both points of view? Since people who are seeking the licenses are using America's airwaves, does the government, speaking for the people of this country, have any interest at that point to step in and make sure there is a fair and balanced approach to the information given to the American people?[54]

Perhaps Durbin's problem with a free market in radio is precisely that it does provide fairness and balance. In a nation where the major media are dominated by editorial decision-makers who share Durbin's ideological perspective, free market radio gave Rush Limbaugh, Sean Hannity, Mark Levin, Laura Ingraham, Bill Bennett, and many other conservatives a means to reach the ears of America. And worse—from the control freak's perspective—America liked what it heard.

But don't look for congressional control freaks like Pelosi, Bingaman, and Durbin to push now for a bill like Representative Slaughter's to reinstate the Fairness Doctrine. They likely sense such a move would cause a market reaction—at the polls. In 2007, when Republican Representative Mike Pence of Indiana offered an amendment to prevent the FCC from spending any money in fiscal 2008 on reinstating the Fairness Doctrine, it won 309 to 115.[55] Although this Fairness Doctrine funding ban was temporary, the vote was a good test of the political viability of any overt effort to censor talk radio.

If liberals launch another attack on the freedom of speech of broadcasters, it will not target the programming broadcasters put on their stations; it will target the broadcasters themselves. It will try to redistribute their stations to new owners who liberals believe will be more likely to schedule the kind of programming the liberals want. Like so many other control-freak programs, it will take from A and give to B.

About the same time the House was voting 309 to 115 for Mike Pence's anti-Fairness Doctrine amendment, the liberal Center for American Progress was publishing a report entitled, "Structural Imbalance of Talk Radio."[56] It concluded that the five top owners of news-talk radio stations around the country carried far more conservative programming than "progressive" programming, and that they also tended to carry nationally syndicated programs.

"This analysis suggests that any effort to encourage more responsive and balanced radio programming will first require steps to increase localism and diversify radio station ownership to better meet local and community needs," said the report. To change the ownership of stations and increase localism, the report recommended placing national and local caps on the number of stations one owner could possess, shortening the lifespan of broadcast licenses from eight years to three, and charging broadcasters who did not live up to their "public interest obligations to pay a fee to support public broadcasting."[57]

In other words, it called for making private-sector broadcasters subsidize government-sector radio. This is the liberal answer to the market-based success of conservative radio: tax successful broadcasters to pay for more government radio, so liberal radio hosts can talk at us from government-funded pulpits the way President Obama talked at Justice Alito from the podium of the U.S. House of Representatives. Only unlike Alito in the House chamber, we would at least retain the freedom to shut the radio off.

The Center for American Progress report was co-authored by Mark Lloyd—who went on to become the "chief diversity officer" at the Federal Communications Commission.

What is happening in communications in our time is another vindication of economist Julian Simon's argument that man, with his ingenuity and entrepreneurial spirit, is the ultimate resource.[58] Faced with the limited capacity of television and radio airwaves, people came up with new resources to provide the same service. Instead of watching CBS, we download Netflix. Instead of listening to AM signals beamed from towers, we carry devices in our pockets that can pick up signals bounced off platforms in space.

The capital investment needed today to start a Web site that people can read around the globe is miniscule compared to what was needed yesterday to start a newspaper for distribution in one small town.

The communications frontier we face today is like the territorial frontier Americans faced four centuries ago. Open spaces of almost unimaginable potential stretch out before us. Just as the pioneers preserved their freedom by moving West, beyond the reach of Old World tyrants, we can preserve our freedom by moving deeper into electronic communications, beyond the reach of those who want government to regulate our political discussions.

They are trying to hold the line at the Appalachians. We have crossed the Mississippi and are moving on.

Chapter 6

"Above My Pay Grade"
Liberals Want to Control Whether You Live or Die

"We hold these truths to be self-evident, that all men are created equal, that they are endowed by their Creator with certain inalienable rights."[1]

—Thomas Jefferson

"The sacred rights of mankind are not to be rummaged for among old parchments or musty records. They are written, as with a sunbeam, in the whole volume of human nature, by the hand of the Divinity itself, and can never be erased or obscured by mortal power."[2]

—Alexander Hamilton

"I think that whether you're looking at it from a theological perspective or a scientific perspective, answering that question with specificity, you know, is above my pay grade."[3]

—Barack Obama

T he nurse carried a premature baby boy, born at about twenty-two weeks, down a hallway in the labor-and-delivery ward at Christ Hospital in Oak Lawn, Illinois. She was taking him to the soiled utility room, where she intended to leave him to die alone and uncomforted among the dirty sheets and pillowcases.

The little boy had Down Syndrome. His mother, who did not want him, had come to the hospital that day to terminate his life. The hospital had used a procedure known as induced labor abortion.[4] But something went wrong. The boy survived.

Jill Stanek, another nurse in Christ's labor-and-delivery ward, heard what was happening and saw the little boy pass by in the hall. In the spirit of the Prince of Peace who was the hospital's namesake—but not its role model— she decided to be her brother's keeper.[5]

"I could not bear the thought of this suffering child dying alone in a soiled utility room, so I cradled and rocked him for the 45 minutes that he lived," Stanek later told the U.S. House Judiciary Subcommittee on the Constitution. "He was too weak to move very much, expending any energy that he had trying to breathe. Toward the end of his life he was so quiet that I couldn't tell if he was still alive unless I held him up to the light to see if his little heart was still beating through his chest wall. After he was pronounced dead, we folded his little arms across his chest, tied his hands together with a string, wrapped him in a tiny shroud, and carried him to the hospital morgue where all of our other dead patients go."[6]

Allison Baker, another nurse in Christ's labor-and-delivery ward, saw three babies in one year who survived induced labor abortions. She was shocked one day when she walked into the soiled utility room to discover a naked newborn squirming and struggling for air. She, too, told her story to the House Subcommittee on the Constitution.

The little boy was "lying on the metal counter, a fetus, naked, exposed and breathing, moving its arms and legs," Baker told the panel. "The fetus was visibly alive, and was gasping for breath. I left to find the nurse who was caring for the patient and this fetus. When I asked her about the fetus, she said that she was so busy with the mother that she didn't have time to wrap and place the fetus in the warmer, and she asked if I would do that for her. Later I found out that the fetus was 22-weeks-old, and had undergone a therapeutic abortion because it had been diagnosed with Down Syndrome. I did wrap the fetus and place him in a warmer and for 2-and-a-half hours he maintained a heartbeat, and then finally expired."[7]

On another occasion, Baker assisted a nurse caring for a woman whose Down Syndrome baby had been subjected to an induced labor abortion in the sixteenth week of pregnancy. For a second time, she made a gruesome discovery. "Again, I walked into the soiled utility room and the fetus was fully exposed, lying on the baby scale," she said. "I went to find the nurse who was caring for this mother and fetus, and she asked if I could help her by measuring and weighing the fetus for the charting and death certificate. When I went back into the soiled utility room, the fetus was moving its arms and legs. I then listened for a heartbeat, and found that the fetus still was alive. I wrapped the fetus and in 45 minutes the fetus finally expired."[8]

Doctors generally cannot detect Down Syndrome or spina bifida until the second trimester of pregnancy.[9] Neither defect is fatal. Down Syndrome is caused by an extra chromosome in the baby's cells. "In 1929, the average life span of a person with Down Syndrome was nine years," reports the National Institutes of Health. "Today, it is common for a person with Down Syndrome to live to age fifty and beyond. In addition to living longer, people with Down Syndrome are now living fuller, richer lives than ever before as family members and contributors to their community."[10]

Spina bifida is caused when a baby's spinal cord fails to completely fuse as he develops in the womb. The resulting nerve damage can cause various types of paralysis.[11] "Children with spina bifida can lead relatively active lives," says the NIH. "Prognosis depends on the number and severity of abnormalities and associated complications. Most children with the disorder have normal intelligence and can walk, usually with assistive devices."[12]

Aborting a child because he has Down Syndrome or spina bifida is not only a murderous act, but also an act of eugenics. The baby is killed because he has a characteristic that someone has decided makes him less worthy of life.

At Christ Hospital, according to Jill Stanek, induced labor abortions were sometimes used to terminate pregnancies in which the unborn child had already reached the age where he or she might survive outside the womb if given good care.[13] "I was recently told about a situation by a nurse who said, 'I can't stop thinking about it,'" Stanek told the subcommittee. "She had a patient who was 23-plus weeks pregnant, and it did not look as if her baby would continue to be able to live inside of her. The baby was healthy and had up to a 39 percent chance of survival, according to our national statistics. But the patient chose to abort.

"The baby was born alive," Stanek said. "If the mother had wanted everything done for her baby at Christ Hospital, there would have been a neonatologist, a pediatric resident, a neonatal nurse, and respiratory therapist present for the delivery, and the baby would have been taken to our Neonatal Intensive Care Unit for specialized care. Instead, the only personnel present for this delivery were an obstetrical resident and my co-working friend. After delivery, the baby, who showed early signs of thriving—her Apgars improved—was merely wrapped in a blanket and kept in the Labor and Delivery Department until she died two and a half hours later."[14]

The induced-labor abortions that Stanek and Baker testified about in Congress were a gruesome reminder of the fundamental question raised by every abortion: Who has the right to control whether another innocent person lives or dies? Who has the right to play God?

Stanek initially appealed to the hospital to do something about the practices there. When the induced-labor abortions continued, she went public with her complaints.[15] The office of then-Illinois Attorney General Jim Ryan, who was pro-life, determined there was "no basis for legal action" arising from the practices of the hospital.[16] Pro-lifers in the Illinois legislature then began an effort to change the law so the barbaric practice of treating born babies as if they were less than human would be stopped.

As a result of this effort, an Illinois state senator by the name of Barack Obama had three opportunities to support granting full legal protection to the constitutional rights of all babies from the moment of birth forward. Three times he declined.

In 2001, the Illinois state senate Judiciary Committee, on which then-state Senator Barack Obama served, heard testimony about this type of abortion.[17] That year, and again in 2002 and 2003, Obama opposed legislation that would have defined any baby born alive — including a little boy or girl who survived an abortion — as a "human being," "child," "person," and "individual" under Illinois state law.[18]

When the bill first came up on the Illinois senate floor on March 30, 2001, Obama was the only senator to speak against it. He made two key points: He knew the bill addressed the status of babies who were born alive, and he did not support giving equal protection of the law to born babies who survived abortions, as he made clear in a colloquy with the bill's sponsor on the floor of the Illinois Senate.

"I do want to just make sure that everybody in the Senate knows what this bill is about, as I understand it," said Obama. "Senator O'Malley, the testimony during the committee indicated that one of the key concerns was, is that there was a method of abortion, an induced abortion, where the, the fetus, or child — as some might describe it, is still temporarily alive outside the womb. And one of the concerns that came out in the testimony was the fact that they were not being properly cared for during that brief period of time that they were still living. Is that correct? Is that an accurate sort of description of one of the key concerns in the bill?"[19]

Senator O'Malley, the bill's sponsor, stated that what his bill did was ensure that babies who survived induced-labor abortions in Illinois were given the same protection under the U.S. Constitution as any other living person.

"Senator Obama, it is certainly a key concern that...the way children are treated following their birth under these circumstances has been reported to be, without question, in my opinion, less than humane," said O'Malley, "and so this bill suggests that appropriate steps be taken to treat that baby as . . . a citizen of the United States and afforded all the rights and protections it deserves under the Constitution of the United States."[20]

By calling all born babies "persons," O'Malley's bill would have guaranteed that every living baby in the state was protected by the Fourteenth Amendment of the United States Constitution, which says: "Nor shall any state deprive any person of life, liberty, or property without due process of law; nor deny to any person within its jurisdiction the equal protection of the laws."

Obama, the Harvard Law graduate, understood exactly what it meant to call every born baby a person, and he found it unacceptable. He would not agree to protect the constitutional rights of babies who survived an induced-labor abortion. "Number one, whenever we define a previable fetus as a person that is protected by the Equal Protection Clause or the other elements of the Constitution, what we're really saying is, in fact, that they are persons that are entitled to the kinds of protections that would be provided to a— child, a nine-month old—child that was delivered to term," Obama said. "That determination then, essentially, if it was accepted by a court, would forbid abortions to take place. I mean, it—it would essentially bar abortions, because the Equal Protection Clause does not allow someone to kill a child, and if this is a child, then this would be an anti-abortion statute."[21]

There was a certain diabolical ad hoc logic to Obama's position. He understood that if he conceded that an abortion-surviving baby was a person with inalienable rights outside the womb, it would be absurd for him to argue that the same baby was not a person with inalienable rights inside the womb. Yet rather than concede that a baby has rights no matter where he is located relative to his mother's womb, Obama decided, in this instance, he needed to deny that babies have rights no matter where they happen to be located relative to their mother's wombs. In order to make it appear as if this position was not a rationalization for infanticide—which on its face it was—Obama was careful in this 2001 speech on the Illinois Senate floor to speak of abortion-surviving babies as "previable fetuses," as if "viability"—the point during development when current medical technology can maintain a premature baby's life outside the womb—ought to be the determining factor in whether a baby is accorded the constitutional rights of a "person."

To follow through on the logic of this 2001 speech, Obama would have needed to oppose all post-viability abortions. Because, according to his own logic, a viable baby, no matter what space he occupies relative to his mother's womb, is a person who has rights. But Obama had no intention of following through on the unavoidable implications of his 2001 argument about who does and who does not have a constitutionally protected right to life. He made the argument only because it was expedient then. A few years later, he would make clear that he opposed the Supreme Court's ruling in *Gonzales* v. *Carhart* that upheld the federal ban on partial birth abortion,[22] meaning that he believed the court should have nullified the ban and thus allowed partial-birth abortions to continue through all nine months of pregnancy. He also vowed to Planned Parenthood that he would sign the Freedom of Choice Act, which would prohibit the states from restricting abortion on demand at any point in pregnancy.[23] In both these instances, Obama would deny the constitutional personhood of all unborn babies—viable or not.

Obama's position on the fundamental duty of the state to protect human life is not only unprincipled and incoherent, it is absurd. It only makes sense when it is assumed his ultimate goal is not to protect the God-given right to life of all human beings, but to preserve the power of some human beings to control whether others live or die.

This was perhaps never more obvious than on August 16, 2008, when Pastor Rick Warren of the Saddleback Church in Lake Forest, California, asked then-presidential candidate Obama a tellingly simple question: "At what point does a baby get human rights, in your view?"

Obama professed not to know. "Well, you know," he said, "I think that whether you're looking at it from a theological perspective or a scientific perspective, answering that question with specificity, you know, is above my pay grade."[24]

The Berlin Wall of Life

When he became president, however, Barack Obama apparently did not consider it above his pay grade to determine that human embryos have no rights. Though Obama often presents himself as a defender of the weak against the strong, just six weeks into his presidency, he issued an Executive Order directing that tax dollars be spent on stem cell research that requires the killing of human embryos[25]—on the theory that a sort of therapeutic cannibalism might be established through which some might see their health improved based on the deliberate and fatal dismemberment others.

Obama signed this order at a White House ceremony that gathered together many of the most powerful figures in Washington, D.C., including House Speaker Nancy Pelosi and House Majority Leader Steny Hoyer. Representatives from several of the nation's most prestigious universities attended the event, as well as numerous Nobel laureates.[26]

These elites stood and cheered when Obama strode into the room to begin the ceremony. Many held up cameras and took snapshots to memorialize the event.[27] As the world's most powerful man ordered taxpayers to fund research that kills the world's most vulnerable humans, the crowd acted as if it was participating in a victory celebration. But, if that were the case, who had triumphed? What principle had been vindicated?

In a fraudulent show of magnanimity in victory, President Obama claimed as he gave his brief address that day that he understood the point of view of those who objected to funding research that kills human embryos. "Many thoughtful and decent people are conflicted about, or strongly oppose, this research," he said. "I understand their concerns, and I believe that we must respect their point of view."[28]

But he never stated what their objections were. And if he truly understood them, respected them, and was serious about protecting human rights, he could not have continued with the ceremony and signed his order forcing taxpayers to pay for this deadly research.

People do not need Harvard Law degrees or Nobel Prizes to understand why killing a human embryo is a moral outrage. The simple *biological fact* is that a unique human life begins at conception. At the time a human sperm fertilizes a human ovum, a new person is created, who is no less a human being than a politician or a Nobel Laureate.

President Obama, Nancy Pelosi, Steny Hoyer, and each of the Nobel Laureates who attended the president's embryo-killing-research-funding-executive-order-signing ceremony are all human individuals, who started their individual human lives at fertilization. They were all human embryos, human fetuses, human infants, human toddlers, and human adolescents. At every step, they retained both their humanity and their individuality.

The argument against homicide at any stage of human development is based on a basic principle at the foundation of America's historical understanding of legitimate government: all men have certain God-given rights. Most fundamental is the right to life, which it is the purpose of government to protect.

Given that a human embryo is indisputably a human individual, someone trying to justify deliberately killing an embryo must reject the principle of natural law our Founding Fathers believed all legitimate government must recognize and obey: "We hold these truths to be self-evident, that all men are created equal, that they are endowed by their Creator with certain inalienable Rights, that among these are Life, Liberty, and the pursuit of Happiness. That to secure these rights, Governments are instituted among Men, deriving their just powers from the consent of the governed."[29]

Almost a half-century after Thomas Jefferson wrote these words, he sent a letter to fellow Virginian Henry Lee explaining why he had written them.

"This was the object of the Declaration of Independence," Jefferson said. "Not to find out new principles, or new arguments, never before thought of, not merely to say things which had never been said before; but to place before mankind the common sense of the subject, in terms so plain and firm as to command their assent, and to justify ourselves in the independent stand we are compelled to take. Neither aiming at originality of principle or sentiment, nor yet copied from any particular previous writing, it was intended to be an expression of the American mind, and to give to that expression the proper tone and spirit called for by the occasion."[30]

The truth of Jefferson's assertion that the Declaration gave voice to the "American mind" is demonstrated by the passionate and logically argued pamphlet that had been written more than a year before the Declaration by 18-year-old[31] Alexander Hamilton, who later became Jefferson's great rival in the early years of the Republic. Although Hamilton and Jefferson would end up on the opposite ends of partisan politics, they shared the view, as all the Founding Fathers did, that God's unchanging moral law was the sole legitimate foundation for the laws of the state.

Hamilton wrote his pamphlet in response to a loyalist clergyman who had published "A Letter from a Westchester Farmer," defending the alleged right of the British Parliament to legislate for the colonies, the issue at the heart of the revolutionary movement in America.[32] Hamilton's rejoinder, "The Farmer Refuted," defended the right of the colonists to govern themselves and to preserve their God-given rights.

Hamilton argued that there was no such thing as a state of nature where man was free from the law. God's rules, the foundation of all law, governed everywhere and at all times.

> To grant that there is a Supreme Intelligence who rules the world and has established laws to regulate the actions of His creatures, and still to assert that man, in a state of nature, may be considered as perfectly free from all restraints of law and government, appears, to a common understanding, altogether irreconcilable. Good and wise men, in all ages, have embraced a very dissimilar theory. They have supposed that the Deity, from the relations we stand in to Himself and to each other, has constituted an eternal and immutable law, which is indispensably obligatory upon all mankind prior to any human institution whatever.[33]

This law, Hamilton said, was the natural law. The rights of man derived from it.

> Upon this law depend the natural rights of mankind: the Supreme Being gave existence to man, together with the means of preserving and beautifying that existence. He endowed him with rational faculties, by the help of which to discern and pursue such things as were consistent with his duty and interest; and invested him with an inviolable right to personal liberty and personal safety.[34]

Individuals and nations alike, Hamilton said, were obligated by the natural law to respect and protect man's basic rights. "Hence, in a state of nature, no man had any moral power to deprive another of his life, limbs, property, or liberty; nor the least authority to command or exact obedience from him, except that which arose from ties of consanguinity. . . . To usurp dominion over a people in their own despite, or to grasp a more extensive power than they are willing to intrust, is to violate that law of nature which gives every man a right to his personal liberty, and can therefore confer no obligation to obedience."[35]

Hamilton saw plainly that the God-given rights the American colonists sought to vindicate in 1775 belonged not only to them but to all men. They could not be justly taken from anyone.

> The sacred rights of mankind are not to be rummaged for among old parchments or musty records. They are written, as with a sunbeam, in the whole volume of human nature, by the hand of the divinity itself, and can never be erased or obscured by mortal power. The nations of Turkey, Russia, France, Spain and all other despotic kingdoms in the world, have an inherent right, whenever they please, to shake off the yoke of servitude (though sanctioned by the immemorial usage of their ancestors), and to model their government upon the principles of civil liberty.[36]

Both Jefferson and Hamilton were influenced in their views by Marcus Tullius Cicero.[37]

"Directly or indirectly," the great conservative Russell Kirk wrote in *The Roots of American Order*, "the mind and life of Cicero are bound up with the American understanding of order more than are the thought and action of any other man of classical times."[38] Historian Clinton Rossiter noted that the tendency of Americans of the Founding era to reference Cicero and a "heroic line" of likeminded political philosophers is evidence that they were "conscious conservatives."[39]

Cicero told his fellow Romans half a century before the birth of Christ that the "moral power of law, is not only far more ancient than these legal institutions of states and peoples, but it is coeval with God himself, who beholds and governs both heaven and earth."[40] He insisted that God had authored unchanging moral rules that all nations and all men must obey at all times.

> There is a true law, a right reason, conformable to nature, universal, unchangeable, eternal, whose commands urge us to duty, and whose prohibitions restrain us from evil. Whether it enjoins or forbids, the good respect its injunctions, and the wicked treat them with indifference. This law cannot be contradicted by any other law, and is not liable either to derogation or abrogation. Neither the senate nor the people can give us any dispensation for not obeying this universal law of justice.[41]

Cicero believed that men, whether they like it or not, know this law in their hearts. "It needs no other expositor and interpreter than our own conscience," said Cicero. "It is not one thing at Rome and another at Athens; one thing today and another tomorrow; but in all times and nations this universal law must for ever reign, eternal and imperishable. It is the sovereign master and emperor of all beings. God himself is its author—its promulgator—its enforcer. He who obeys it not, flies from himself, and does violence to the very nature of man."[42]

This permanent law—the law that forms the foundation of the Declaration and the Constitution, and thus the foundation of the American understanding of justice—cannot be reconciled with legalizing the killing of innocents. Tellingly, Cicero himself used the example of fraudulent medical practitioners, who poison their patients rather than provide them with proper medicines, as a metaphor for unjust laws generally.[43]

To justify killing human embryos or human beings at any other stage of development, American politicians, whether they admit it or not, must turn away from the principle that all men are endowed by their Creator with inalienable rights. They must pull up the roots of American law from the 2,000-year moral tradition in which the Founding Fathers planted it.

In atheistic societies—such as the People's Republic of China or the old Soviet Union—which do not pretend to recognize natural law, the governing elite determines whether a particular individual or class of individuals should live or die, speak or not speak, or exercise their religion, depending on whether allowing that individual or class to live, speak, or worship, aids or hinders the governing elite in the pursuit of its goals.

In America, however, no one in national elective office openly embraces the atheistic position. All at least pretend to recognize the natural law, and claim allegiance to the principle that human beings have inalienable God-given rights, including the right to life.

But all American politicians who advocate embryonic stem cell research or legalized abortion build their own version of the Berlin Wall. On one side are the human beings whose God-given rights they acknowledge and want the state to protect. On the other are human beings whose God-given rights they do not acknowledge and whom they do not want the state to protect.

You will not very often see liberal politicians publicly acknowledging they have built such a wall or explaining exactly why they located it where they did. Often this is because they realize they cannot adequately defend the rationale for their wall; and sometimes it is because they want to leave open the option of moving it.

"Cloning for Human Reproduction"

Obama's defense for using tax dollars to fund embryo-killing research was ultimately as irrational as his defense of denying personhood to born babies.

"But after much discussion, debate and reflection, the proper course has become clear," he said at his order-signing ceremony. "The majority of Americans—from across the political spectrum, and from all backgrounds and beliefs—have come to a consensus that we should pursue this research. That the potential it offers is great, and with proper guidelines and strict oversight the perils can be avoided. That is a conclusion with which I agree."[44]

He might as well have said that a majority of Americans have come to a consensus that the reporters and editors at the *New York Times* should not have a right to free speech and that he was ordering that tax dollars be used to shut the paper down. Assuming there were in fact a popular consensus in favor of federal funding of embryo-killing research, Obama would still be unjustified in ordering federal funding of an action that violates a fundamental human right. It would not matter if 95 percent of Americans decided the government should spend funds to shut up the reporters at the *New York Times*. The majority has no more right to deprive journalists of freedom of speech than they have to deprive embryos of their right to life.

Obama also suggested that funding embryo-killing research was justified because "the potential it offers is great."[45] This is simply to say the end justifies the means. There are many good people in this country who are valuable contributors to their communities who might benefit from, say, a heart transplant. But that does not justify the government paying doctors to round up people off the streets—focusing, perhaps, on those who arguably have contributed less to their communities—and forcing them to surrender their hearts. Such a scheme might have great "potential" for the recipients of stolen hearts, but it violates the God-given right to life of those whose hearts are stolen. For the same reason, killing a human embryo to develop stem cells cannot be justified by the prospect that it could improve another human's health.

Obama argued that "with proper guidelines and strict oversight the perils" of promoting embryo-killing research "can be avoided."[46] In other words, careful regulation of the way an evil is done can somehow make the evil itself disappear. This is as if the government said: "We think people ought to be able to kill their parents when they reach the age of eighty-nine. Families can reap potential benefits from doing this (and the government can save money on Medicare). So, we are going to provide euthanasia grants to the next of kin of all Americans at that age or older. But, rest assured, we will make certain that whenever the post-productive elderly are removed from the population, it is done within proper guidelines and with strict oversight."

Some may object that killing a 2-week-old embryo is different than killing an 89-year-old grandmother. But how so? Both are human beings. Both are endowed by God with an inalienable right to life. And, if human cloning is permitted to proceed, someday the 89-year-old grandmother and the 2-week-old embryo may even share the same DNA. To justify killing one but not the other is to build one of those Berlin Walls across the span of human life, granting human rights to those on one side but not the other. In other words, the power of life and death is seized from God and handed to a control freak, in this case, perhaps, a Nobel laureate in a starched white coat who relies on tax dollars taken from working Americans to conduct lethal research in a high-powered university laboratory.

Speaking of Cloning

In announcing his decision to allow federal funding for embryo-killing stem cell research, Obama also deftly left open the door to research that clones human embryos. He did so even as he seemed to claim he was closing the door to cloning.

"And we will ensure that our government never opens the door to the use of cloning for human reproduction," he said. "It is dangerous, profoundly wrong, and has no place in our society, or any society."[47]

To the unsuspecting ear this might have sounded like a definitive rejection of cloning. No sooner had Obama said it, in fact, than the Associated Press put out a story headlined, "Obama calls cloning 'dangerous, profoundly wrong.'"[48] Anyone who had closely followed the debate over human cloning, however, would have instantly recognized that Obama was not declaring that the government should completely close the door to human cloning. He was only saying that the government should never open the door to the "use" of human cloning for a particular purpose—namely, "for human reproduction."[49] He was not saying the government should never open the door to human cloning for other purposes.

Now, in the ordinary use of the English language (as opposed to the political abuse of the English language), closing the door to the "use" of cloning for "human reproduction" would indeed close the door to human cloning because cloning a human being means quite literally "reproducing" one. But in congressional debates on the issue, legislators who favored cloning human embryos and killing them for their stems cells had developed a lexicon for publicly discussing the issue that was designed to obscure the essential nature of what they advocated. "Reproductive cloning" and "therapeutic cloning" were key terms in this lexicon.

"Reproductive cloning" means creating an embryonic clone of a human being and then implanting it in a woman's womb—or an artificial womb—and keeping the cloned human being alive until he or she develops into a viable infant. "Therapeutic cloning" means creating an embryonic clone of a human being and then killing the clone to derive stem cells that might be used in medical therapies on the person who has been cloned.[50] Critics of "therapeutic cloning" call it "clone and kill."[51]

Somatic cell nuclear transfer (SCNT), the technical procedure that would be used to create a cloned human embryo, is the same technical procedure that was used to clone Dolly the sheep. The fact that this procedure, when used on human cells, would create a cloned human embryo was spelled out in a 2004 Congressional Research Service report on stem cell research.

"Another potential source of embryonic stem cells is somatic cell nuclear transfer (SCNT), also referred to as cloning," said the CRS report. "In SCNT the nucleus of an egg is removed and replaced by the nucleus from a mature body cell, such as a skin cell. The cell created via SCNT is allowed to develop for a week and then the stem cells are removed. In 1996, scientists in Scotland used the SCNT procedure to produce Dolly the sheep, the first mammalian clone."[52]

The CRS report explained why scientists who were interested in doing embryonic stem cell research were also interested in cloning human embryos. If stem cells derived from one person were used in therapy on another, that other person's immune system would be prone to reject those stem cells. But if the person needing therapy could be genetically reproduced in a cloned embryo, and the cloned embryo was then destroyed for his or her stem cells, the resulting stem cells might not be rejected by the recipient's immune system.[53]

Representative Diana DeGette, a Democrat from Colorado, was in the audience at the White House when President Obama signed his stem-cell Executive Order and said he would "ensure that our government never opens the door to the use of cloning for human reproduction." In 2007, DeGette sponsored the Orwellian entitled "Human Cloning Prohibition Act," which did not prohibit human cloning, but instead redefined human "cloning" to mean when a cloned human embryo was implanted in a womb. Under this bill, researchers would be allowed to clone human embryos all they wanted so long as they never implanted a cloned human embryo in a woman's uterus — or in a machine that did the work of a woman's uterus. "The term 'human cloning,'" said the bill, "means the implantation of the product of human somatic cell nuclear transfer technology into a uterus or the functional equivalent of a uterus."[54]

In 2001, when a similar bill was debated in the House, DeGette explained why she supported cloning human embryos and destroying them for their stem cells, but not cloning human embryos and implanting them in a womb. Cloning, she believed, was one of the great questions of the age.

"Cloning is one of the most important and far-reaching issues we will examine in our public service," she said. "Its impact may be incalculable. Cloning will alter our world."[55]

But she wanted to contain cloning's world-altering power to the act of creating embryos for pre-planned destruction in formulating medical therapies. She did not want to unleash the world-altering power of having fully grown people who were genetic replicas of each other. DeGette supported the 2001 bill, which, she said, "bans reproductive cloning, but allows strictly regulated, privately funded therapeutic cloning."

"Reproductive cloning practices which must be banned are an attempt to create a new human being and, as we heard in hearings throughout the spring, there are fringe groups who would like to clone humans. This is wrong, and must be stopped," DeGette said. "Conversely, somatic cell nuclear transfer, or so-called 'therapeutic cloning,' is a way to take stem cell research and all of its promise from the lab to the patient who has diabetes, Parkinson's Disease, Alzheimer's, spinal cord injury, and other health problems."[56]

Making the same point the Congressional Research Service would later make, DeGette explained that it might be necessary to clone human embryos to solve the problem of immune rejection in stem cell therapies. "Stem cell research helps us take a stem cell, a cell that is a building block to be made into any other cell, and turn that cell into a variety of different tissues for the body," she said. "But medical experts tell us that that stem cell, because the DNA differs from the DNA of the individual that the new tissue is to be donated to, will often be rejected, because the genetic makeup of that tissue is different. Somatic cell nuclear transfer gets around that problem of rejection, because stem cells that create the organ or tissue are from the patient. As a result the patient's body will not recognize the organ or tissue as a foreign object."[57]

In plain English, it will not be from a foreign object, because it will be from his killed clone.

Opening the door to federal funding of embryonic stem cell research, as President Obama did, without opening the door to human cloning to derive stem cells for potential therapies, would have been like opening a door that leads to a wall. It would have made little sense. That is why President Obama was careful not to rule out all "uses" of human cloning.

When DeGette's bill was debated on the House floor in 2007, Representative Joe Pitts, a Pennsylvania Republican, accurately explained what it would do. "In fact, the bill allows for unlimited cloning of human embryos but prevents women and doctors from trying to implant one of these embryos to initiate a pregnancy," said Pitts. "In practice, this means that embryos will be cloned, used for experimentation, harvesting, research, then assigned a death sentence. So, cloned embryos would be required by law to die. Not only does this bill allow the practice of cloning to move forward, it also mandates the killing of those human embryos."[58]

On March 10, 2010, following up on President Obama's executive order allowing federal funding of embryo-killing stem cell research, DeGette introduced legislation directing the secretary of health and human services to "conduct and support research that utilizes human stem cells, including human embryonic stem cells."[59] The bill would limit federal funding to research that uses stem cells derived from embryos unused by in vitro fertilization clinics. It would also prohibit the secretary of health and human services from using federal funds to support research involving "human cloning." But it inaccurately defines "human cloning" as the implantation of a cloned human embryo in a uterus or a gestation machine.[60]

The bill would not outlaw cloning a human embryo, or implanting one in a womb, it would only prohibit the use of federal funding for research that implants cloned human embryos in real or artificial wombs.

The "therapeutic cloning" DeGette envisions—and that President Obama does not rule out—is a form of human slavery. It gives one human being total control over another. A scientist doing "therapeutic cloning" will decide what a cloned human being's identity will be, when he or she will come to life, to what end his or her life will be used, and when he or she will die. In the control freak's world, human beings may be cloned, but all clones must reside on tyranny's side of the Berlin Wall, never conceded a right to life, their destinies controlled by scientists who aspire to be gods, while lacking the true love and mercy of the God who gives us all a right to life.

So much for defending the weak against the strong.

Chapter 7

"Culture Wars Are Just So Nineties"
Liberals Want to Control Your Conscience

"In other words, if we turned our back on the basic teachings of our religion . . . we would be in compliance with the law."[1]

— **Bishop William Weigand**
Catholic Diocese of Sacramento

"I am absolutely convinced that culture wars are just so Nineties."[2]

— **Senator Barack Obama**
Planned Parenthood Conference, July 17, 2007

"We're not giving unfettered access to the psyche of our son when he enters the school."

— **Tonia Parker**
The Boston Globe, April 29, 2005

I n the late 1990s, nine out of ten people enrolled in commercial health insurance plans in California had plans that covered contraceptives.[3] Among the 10 percent whose plans did not cover contraceptives were employees of the Catholic Church, which believes artificial contraception is a sin.

These employees were free to buy contraceptives anytime they wanted, but they had to use their own money.

Some liberals in the California legislature found this situation intolerable. They passed a law forcing employers—including some Catholic organizations—to provide their workers with insurance plans that covered prescription contraceptives if the plans they offered included coverage for any prescription drugs at all.[4] Consequently, they set up a moral struggle between the Catholic Church and the state of California that raised a question at the heart of liberty: Can government rightfully force a person to act against his conscience?

If the "free exercise" of religion our Constitution guarantees means anything, it means this: the state cannot compel people to commit acts they believe are immoral. Coercion of this sort is what Roman emperors tried to do to early Christian martyrs and what Henry VIII tried to do to Saint Thomas More. It is the soul of tyranny.

The Catholic Church has always taught that the use of artificial contraception is wrong. It is a teaching rooted in the Catholic understanding of the nature of human beings, the nature of their relationship with God, the nature of marriage, and the natural law itself. In *Humanae Vitae*, an encyclical letter published by Pope Paul VI in 1968, the church explained its duty to preach this doctrine no matter what popular opinion held or what the prevailing political powers demanded. The church made an argument that Western political philosophers from Cicero to the Founding Fathers would have readily understood.

"It is to be anticipated that perhaps not everyone will easily accept this particular teaching. There is too much clamorous outcry against the voice of the Church, and this is intensified by modern means of communication," said the encyclical.

But it comes as no surprise to the Church that she, no less than her divine Founder, is destined to be a "sign of contradiction." She does not, because of this, evade the duty imposed on her of proclaiming humbly but firmly the entire moral law, both natural and evangelical. Since the Church did not make either of these laws, she cannot be their arbiter—only their guardian and interpreter. It could never be right for her to declare lawful what is in fact unlawful, since that, by its very nature, is always opposed to the true good of man.[5]

When the contraception mandate came up in the California senate in 1999, Senator Ray Haynes, a Republican, tried but failed to amend it to bar coverage of contraceptives that worked as abortifacients (which prevent an embryo from implanting in the uterus) and also to exempt employers who did not want to pay for contraceptives for religious reasons. "There are a number of people whose religious beliefs would prohibit them from paying for this coverage," Haynes said, according to the Associated Press.[6]

Democratic State Senator Jackie Speier, the bill's sponsor, seemed confused about who would be imposing a mandate on whom under the regulation she proposed. As she presented it, the government would not be dictating something to employers, it would be preventing employers from dictating something to their workers. "Is it in the best interest of California if an employer, by his religious beliefs, can dictate how the employees conduct their affairs?"[7] she asked.

State Senator Ross Johnson deftly rebutted Speier's argument. "It is not a question of dictating one's religious beliefs on employees," Johnson said, according to the Los Angeles Times. "It's a question of the state compelling people to spend their money on programs that they do not, in good conscience, agree with."[8]

The law finally signed by Democratic Governor Gray Davis included a very narrow exemption for "religious organizations." But to qualify as "religious," an organization needed to be in the business of inculcating "religious values," employ primarily people of the same religion, serve primarily people of the same religion, and be organized under the specific section of the Internal Revenue Code used by churches.[9] A Catholic parish or convent would qualify, a Catholic hospital, university, or charitable organization would not.[10]

Catholic Charities—which employed many non-Catholics and served many non-Catholics by providing food, clothing, and shelter among other services—did not qualify as a "religious organization" under this rule. The law thus presented it with a stark choice: stop providing prescription drug coverage to its workers or start providing contraception coverage.[11]

The group sued to protect its religious freedom from an unjust law. Roman Catholic Bishop William Weigand of the Sacramento diocese explained why the church took this step. "This lawsuit has very little to do with health insurance and everything to do with our fundamental rights as Americans," he said. "It boils down to a very simple question. Under the Constitution, does the state of California have the right to tell its citizens how to practice their religion?"

"Healing the sick, offering charity to the poor and providing education to the young are fundamental to how Catholics practice their faith," said the bishop. "We don't ask anyone if they're Catholic first."

In other words," said the bishop, "if we turned our back on the basic teachings of our religion and employed only Catholics, provided charity and social services only to Catholics, educated only Catholics in our universities and treated only Catholics in our hospitals, we would be in compliance with the law."[12]

The question raised by the suit filed by Catholic Charities mattered not only to Catholics, but to anyone serious about protecting freedom of conscience. The Lutheran-Church Missouri Synod, the International Church of the Foursquare Gospel, and the Worldwide Church of God joined with the U.S. Conference of Catholic Bishops in presenting an amicus brief to the California Supreme Court in defense of Catholic Charities.

"Most of these amici do not share the Catholic Church's conviction about contraceptives. However, they recognize that this case seeks to establish a precedent dangerous to our national tradition of respecting the integrity of religious institutions against the intrusive power of the state," said the brief. "The state proposes a rule of law that forces a church institution, in violation of its own self-identity and constitution, to pay for something in its own workplace that the institution holds and teaches to be sinful."[13]

These church organizations foresaw that once this precedent was set, it could be used to justify additional governmental actions aimed at forcing religious groups to act in contradiction to their moral principles. "Today's case is about contraceptives," they said. "Tomorrow's will present some other issue that elicits public division, such as abortion, assisted suicide, cloning, or some issue of self-governance, such as the use of resources for evangelization or who a religious agency may hire to do ministry work. Indeed, the state's preposterous claim that Catholic Charities is not a religious organization at all shows how radical the state's agenda is."[14]

These church groups also rejected California's argument that the contraception mandate was acceptable because a religious organization could evade it by choosing not to cover any prescription drugs for its workers. "It is no answer to say that Catholic Charities can simply avoid the mandate by declining to provide its employees with prescription drug coverage," said the brief.

> As a matter of social justice, Catholic Charities considers it a religious duty to provide such coverage. And as a matter of the common good, how is the health and welfare of employees better off if there is no prescription drug coverage? One would hope that the state would find some mechanism to promote public health and resolve insurance problems without creating one that actually could reduce health and exacerbate the very problems the state seeks to solve. For us, this one factor speaks eloquently to the fact that the overriding concern is not contraceptive coverage but establishing a principle that the state can force a religion to submit to the state's will.[15]

The California Supreme Court swept aside these objections. It voted 6 to 1 to uphold the state's claimed authority to force Catholic Charities either to buy contraceptive coverage for its workers or strip their workers of all prescription coverage. The court did so even as it conceded that Catholic Charities, in keeping with its religious principles, could not provide contraception coverage to its workers. "We do not doubt Catholic Charities' assertion that to offer insurance coverage for prescription contraceptives to its employees would be religiously unacceptable," said the court. But Catholic Charities' desire to heed Catholic teaching was trumped, in the court's view, by the state's interest in eliminating "gender discrimination," and by the court's finding that the law did not specifically target Catholic employers but was a "neutral law of general applicability" aimed at all state employers.[16]

Catholic Charities appealed to the U.S. Supreme Court, which declined to take up the case. The contraception mandate stands.[17]

This mandate imposed an unacceptable choice not only on religious organizations, but also on private-sector employers and individuals. A business owner who believed artificial contraception was wrong was forced by this law to choose between providing no prescription drug coverage to his or her workers, or providing them with contraception coverage the owner morally opposed. By the same measure, insofar as workers paid for a part of their insurance premiums, they would also be forced to buy coverage for contraceptives even if they believed artificial contraception was wrong.

California's law was an act of moral extortion. It held the well-being of an employer's workers hostage, until the employer agreed to pay for contraception coverage. It was a direct attack on the employer's freedom of conscience and on the freedom of conscience of workers who objected to artificial contraception and did not want to pay for it. It was also a warning of things to come in the movement toward a federal law that would put the national government effectively in control of the nation's health care system.

Hyde and Go Seek

Seven years after the 1973 *Roe* v. *Wade* decision in which the Supreme Court preposterously declared that killing an unborn child was a mother's right, pro-abortion liberals went back to the court with another absurd proposition. Since abortion is a right, they said, the Constitution must require taxpayers to buy them for poor women.

This is almost the logical equivalent of saying that since gun ownership is a right, the Constitution must require taxpayers to buy guns for poor people—except owning guns truly is a right, and killing unborn children is not.[18] In fact, the Constitution, which expressly protects the right to keep and bear arms, does not require taxpayers to buy guns for poor people. And, even if it did protect a right to kill an unborn child, which it does not, such a right would give someone who wants an abortion no more claim to the property of pro-lifers than the Second Amendment gives members of the National Rifle Association a claim to the property of members of the Brady Campaign.

Nonetheless, the issue went all the way to the Supreme Court.

Three years after *Roe*, Republican Representative Henry Hyde of Illinois secured language in the annual funding bill for the Department of Health and Human Services (HHS) that prohibited any money appropriated in that bill from being used to pay for any part of any health care plan that covered abortion. This language prevented Medicaid from paying for most abortions. Initially, this funding ban exempted only abortions necessary to save the life of the mother. Later, it also exempted abortions in cases of rape and incest. But apart from these exceptions, for more than thirty years it remained illegal to use federal tax dollars to fund the killing of an unborn child.

The key language in recent versions of the Hyde Amendment has said: "None of the funds appropriated in this Act, and none of the funds in any trust fund to which funds are appropriated in this Act, shall be expended for health benefits coverage that includes coverage of abortion."[19]

Pro-abortion liberals tried to overturn Hyde in the federal courts. In 1980, the Supreme Court examined the issue in the case of *Harris* v. *McRae*. The so-called right to an abortion it had created in *Roe*, the court ruled, did not include a right to force taxpayers to pay for abortions. Three of the justices who had voted for *Roe*—Chief Justice Warren Burger, Justice Lewis Powell, and Justice Potter Stewart—joined the majority in *Harris* and voted against ordering government funding of abortion. Stewart wrote the opinion of the court.

"Although the liberty protected by the Due Process Clause affords protection against unwarranted government interference with freedom of choice in the context of certain personal decisions," Stewart wrote, "it does not confer an entitlement to such funds as may be necessary to realize all the advantages of that freedom. To hold otherwise would mark a drastic change in our understanding of the Constitution."[20]

To put it in terms reminiscent of Justice Samuel Chase's 1798 opinion in *Calder* v. *Bull*,[21] to hold otherwise would have meant that the Constitution was now interpreted to require the government take the property of A and give it to B—so long as B claimed A's money was needed to carry out a "right," such as purchasing an abortion. Establishing such a principle would trample on basic tenets of liberty, including not only the right to private property but freedom of conscience. Yet, in 1980, *Harris* v. *McRae* was decided by a one-vote majority.[22]

In the years following *Harris*, Congress routinely included the Hyde Amendment in the annual Health and Human Service appropriations as well as in other annual appropriations dealing with health care programs.[23] The amendment thus stopped the government from forcing pro-life Americans to pay for abortions except in the cases exempted under the amendment. But the control freaks did not give up.

When the Democratic leaders in Congress began pushing their national health care plan in 2009, they had a clever plan for evading the Hyde Amendment: they simply would not include it in the bill. Because the amendment's prohibition on abortion funding applied only to the appropriations bills that carried it, and only for the year that that bill covered, if Congress approved a health care bill that did not include the amendment, and that created new programs funded by other means than annual appropriations, those programs would not be prohibited from funding abortion.[24]

As originally drafted, both the House and Senate health care bills did just that. They created a system for using federal tax dollars to help middle-class Americans buy health insurance. Each bill would give Americans earning up to 400 percent of the poverty level ($88,200 for a family of four in 2009) a subsidy for buying insurance as long as they purchased a government-approved plan in a government-regulated insurance exchange. But neither bill included a Hyde-type provision prohibiting people from using these subsidies to buy insurance that covered abortion.[25]

Then Representative Bart Stupak, a Michigan Democrat, joined with Representative Joe Pitts, a Pennsylvania Republican, to disrupt this plan. They offered an amendment to the House bill that would permanently impose the Hyde Amendment's abortion-funding ban on all programs the bill created and funded. It said, "No funds authorized or appropriated by this act (or an amendment made by this act) may be used to pay for any abortion or to cover any part of the costs of any health plan that includes coverage of abortion" except in cases of rape, incest, or to save the life of the mother.[26]

House Speaker Nancy Pelosi, the California Democrat, tried to prevent the House from considering the Stupak-Pitts amendment when the House version of the bill came up for a final vote. But Stupak had enough Democratic votes to kill the overall bill if it did not include his amendment. So Pelosi relented. In the subsequent debate over Stupak-Pitts, opponents of the amendment made clear that they opposed it because they wanted the government to aid women in funding abortions.

"The Stupak-Pitts amendment would make abortion coverage virtually inaccessible to most women in the exchange," said Representative Carolyn Maloney, the New York Democrat. "It does so by: Banning abortion coverage in the exchange for women who receive subsidies, except by separate rider that they could only purchase with their own private funds."[27]

Representative Jerrold Nadler, another New York Democrat, put it this way: "Under this proposal, if a woman is of low or moderate income and receives tax credits to help her afford the premiums for a health insurance plan she purchases on the exchange, she cannot choose a plan that covers abortion services."[28]

If she wanted an abortion, she would have to buy it with her own money—not her neighbor's money.

Sixty-four Democratic representatives voted for Stupak-Pitts as the House approved it 240 to 194. But the Senate did not approve similar language. Instead, it played an elaborate shell game with abortion funding that was intended to give senators who supported the bill some political cover for voting to provide tax dollars for abortions.

First, the Senate tied any future regulation of abortion funding in the health insurance plans subsidized by the new health care law to the language Congress enacts each year in the HHS appropriation. If in some future year, Congress did not include the Hyde Amendment in an HHS appropriation, there would be no restriction at all on abortion funding in federally subsidized health insurance plans.[29]

But even if Congress continued to pass the Hyde Amendment as part of each year's annual HHS appropriation, there would still be no restriction on abortion funding in federally subsidized health care plans. Instead, there would be a meaningless "segregation" of funds.[30]

Because Representative Stupak and a number of other Democrats who supported the Stupak-Pitts amendment in the House bill caved and voted to pass the Senate bill through the House, the Senate bill is now law, and federal funding of abortion on demand will commence when the federal insurance subsidies authorized by the law start in 2014.[31]

Under this law, a person receiving a federal subsidy to buy health insurance will be allowed to use that subsidy to buy a plan that covers abortions. These abortion-providing plans, meanwhile, will be required to extract a special monthly fee of at least one dollar per month from every one of their enrollees regardless of "the enrollee's age, sex, or family status."[32] The plans will be required to deposit this special one-dollar-per-month fee into a special account theoretically dedicated to paying for the abortions they cover. The federal tax money these plans receive will go into another account and will theoretically be used to cover everything else the insurance plan does—except the abortions.[33] Apologists for this ploy argued that it would protect taxpayers from paying for the abortions. But that is plainly a fiction.

Suppose, for example, there is a Health Maintenance Organization named the Harry Blackmun HMO in honor of the Supreme Court justice who wrote the court's opinion in *Roe* v. *Wade*. The Blackmun HMO covers abortions and sells its plan on the government-regulated exchange to government-subsidized customers. One of its enrollees is a 62-year-old pro-life woman. She will be required to pay the HMO the one-dollar special fee that goes into the special account dedicated solely to paying for abortions. This is despite the fact that she will never seek an abortion.

The Blackmun HMO, meanwhile, builds a surgical center. In this center, it employs nurses, doctors, administrators and clerical personnel. It uses the center to perform procedures ranging from repairing a high school football player's injured finger to aborting a baby at seventeen weeks gestation. Using the taxpayer subsidies it receives from the U.S. Treasury, the Blackmun HMO pays for the room in which an abortion is performed, the lighting of the room, the heating and cooling of the room, the cleaning of the room, and the reusable surgical equipment used in the room. It also uses its tax subsidies to pay for the base salary of the doctor who performs the abortion, the nurse who assists in the abortion, the secretary who schedules the abortion, and the administrator who orders all the materials used in the abortion and manages the operations so the abortion can be efficiently done.

But the Blackmun HMO is a law-abiding contractor. It pays the specific fees for the actual killings of unborn children out of the special account the law says it must maintain for that purpose. This, we are supposed to believe, means the government did not make the taxpayers pay for abortion.

Under President Obama's health care law, the hypothetical 62-year-old woman described above would be forced to pay for the lethal abuse of an unborn child three times over. She would pay when her tax dollars are provided as subsidies to the Blackmun HMO. She would pay through her share of the premiums she pays to the Blackmun HMO. And she would pay through the one dollar special fee she provides to the Blackmun HMO's segregated account that is dedicated expressly for the purpose of funding the HMO's killing of unborn children.

It is true that the law provides that there will be at least one health care plan in every exchange that does not cover abortions. So, people who oppose abortion can still choose to join that plan or look for a plan outside the exchange that does not fund abortion. If they take this route, however, they still will not escape a federal mandate that they fund abortion. Rather than fund it through three channels, they will fund it through one: the taxes they pay to subsidize other people's premiums at the Blackmun HMO and other abortion-providing health care plans. Under President Obama's health care law, taxpayers cannot escape paying for abortions.

This law is an attack on the freedom of conscience, one that forces Americans to pay for the taking of innocent life.

Culture Wars

The Planned Parenthood activists gathered at Washington's posh Ritz-Carlton Hotel laughed and cheered as then-presidential candidate Barack Obama boasted of his efforts to promote legal abortion, sex education, and what he depicted as the "new day" that would soon be dawning in America. It was July 17, 2007, and Obama was predicting swift victory in the Culture War.

"At a time when the real war is being fought abroad, they would have us fight culture wars here at home," he said. "But I am absolutely convinced that culture wars are just so Nineties. Their days are growing dark. It is time to turn the page. We want a new day here in America."[34]

In that "new day," Obama would reveal a moment later in his speech, public schools would teach "age appropriate" sex education to kindergartners—a position that sparked predictable controversy.[35] A spokesman for

Obama's campaign attempted to frame that controversy as one that focused on the relative explicitness and extensiveness of the sex education he advocated for kindergartners, pointing out that the sex education Obama envisioned at that age level would be very limited and non-explicit.[36]

The more fundamental controversy, however, was not about the explicitness or extensiveness of the sex education Obama envisioned being taught in kindergarten or at any other grade level; it was about whose values the sex education would be used to promote.

During a question-and-answer session at the end of Obama's speech to the Planned Parenthood conference, the moderator called on a teenage girl in the audience who worked as a Planned Parenthood "peer educator" in Washington, D.C. "With the AIDS case rate in D.C. being ten times the national average," the teenager asked, "what would you do to make sure that schools and programs like mine are encouraged to treat, to teach, excuse me, medically accurate, age-appropriate, and responsible sex education?"[37]

Obama noted that he had been involved in the fight for sex education since serving as chairman of the Health and Human Services Committee in the Illinois Senate. Ambassador Alan Keyes, his opponent in the 2004 U.S. Senate race, Obama said, had attacked him during that campaign for supporting a bill in that committee that would have expanded sex education in the Illinois schools.

"I remember Alan Keyes—I ran against Alan Keyes," said Obama, "but I remember him using this in his campaign against me, saying, 'Barack Obama supports teaching sex education to kindergartners.'

"And you know," said Obama, "I didn't know what to tell him. But it is the right thing to do, to provide age-appropriate sex education, science-based sex education in the schools."

"You, as a peer, can have enormous power over your age cohort," Obama told the teen who asked the question. "But you've got to have some support from the schools, and you certainly shouldn't have to be fighting each and every instance by providing accurate information outside the classroom because inside the classroom the only thing that can be talked about is abstinence."[38]

ABCNews.com posted a video of Obama's answer to the girl's question along with a story that was headlined: "Sex Ed for Kindergartners 'Right Thing to Do,' Says Obama." The story said that when Obama's campaign was asked to clarify what Obama meant by "age appropriate" for kindergartners, the campaign referred to a news story published in the *Daily Herald*, a suburban Chicago newspaper, during the 2004 Senate campaign.[39]

"Democratic U.S. Senate nominee Barack Obama, addressing college students Tuesday in Lisle, moved to clarify that he does not support teaching explicit sex education to children in kindergarten," said the *Daily Herald* report.

"Nobody's suggesting that kindergartners are going to be getting information about sex in the way that we think about it," Obama said. "If they ask a teacher 'where do babies come from,' that providing information that the fact is that it's not a stork is probably not an unhealthy thing. Although again, that's going to be determined on a case by case basis by local communities and local school boards."[40]

Two days after Obama's speech to Planned Parenthood, campaign spokesman Bill Burton suggested to MSNBC that the sex education Obama envisioned for kindergartners was primarily about protecting them from predators. "You can teach a kid about what's appropriate and not appropriate to protect them from predators out there," an MSNBC blog quoted Burton as saying. But then, according to MSNBC, Burton "issued a document showing that the Oregon Department of Education has guidelines for sex education for children in grades K–3 (which includes understanding the difference between good touch and bad touch), and that the Sexuality Information and Education Council of the United States has curriculum for those in kindergarten."[41]

The Sexuality Information and Education Council of the United States (SIECUS) does, in fact, publish sex education guidelines for grades as low as kindergarten. These guidelines are available in a document—

"Guidelines for Comprehensive Sexuality Education: Kindergarten–12th Grade"—posted on the group's Web site. "Sexuality education is a lifelong process of acquiring information and forming attitudes, beliefs, and values," says an explanation of "sexuality education" on the SIECUS Web site. "It encompasses sexual development, sexual and reproductive health, interpersonal relationships, affection, intimacy, body image, and gender roles."[42]

The guidelines are broken down by four age levels: 5 through 8 years old, 9 through 12, 12 through 15, and 15 through 18. Sexual orientation is one topic covered at all four age levels, and relationships is another. The sexual orientation guidelines recommend discussing homosexuality, in general terms, with children ages 5 through 8. The relationships guidelines recommend telling 9 to 12 year olds that people may have two parents of the same sex or some other combination.[43]

The sex-ed bill Obama supported in the Illinois Senate did not get into this level of detail, but according to SIECUS itself, the bill did delete "all references to marriage in the Illinois sex education code."[44]

When Senator John McCain's presidential campaign later ran a television ad in the 2008 general election season criticizing Obama for backing this bill to extend sex education to kindergarten, SIECUS posted a statement that responded to McCain's ad and explained the bill Obama supported.

"The ad is referring to Senate Bill 99 (SB 99), which was assigned to the Health and Human Services Committee in the Illinois Senate in 2003," said SIECUS. "At the time, State Senator Barack Obama was the Chairperson of the committee. He did not sponsor the bill, but he did vote in favor of it."[45]

SIECUS explained how the bill dealt with marriage and the grade levels that would include sex education. "SB 99 proposed to make changes to Illinois' existing sex education law which requires instruction in grades six through 12 that includes teaching about prevention, transmission, and spread of AIDS," said SIECUS.

Illinois law also states that schools much [*sic*] teach "honor and respect for monogamous heterosexual marriage." SB 99 would

have eliminated all references to marriage in the Illinois sex education code, and required that all material used in classrooms be
age- and developmentally appropriate and medically accurate. It
would also have expanded sexuality education to students in
kindergarten through fifth grade and mandated that students be
taught age of consent, positive communications skills, and that
they [the pupil] have the power to control behavior.[46]

Byron York wrote an excellent analysis for *National Review* about the
dispute over Obama's support for this bill. York noted that the bill Obama
backed would have removed "value-laden language" from the existing Illinois sex-ed law. For example, it would have eliminated a sentence in the
law that said: "Course material and instruction shall teach honor and
respect for heterosexual marriage."[47]

While the Obama-backed bill did include language to allow parents to
remove their children from sex-ed classes and a provision that children
should be taught on avoiding abuse, the fact that the bill would strip existing law of its provision instilling respect for the institution of marriage
demonstrated that it was about far more than that. Clearly, in 2003 when
he supported SB99 in the Illinois Senate and in 2007 when he defended it
as a presdential canddate, Obama did not think the "culture wars" were
quite so Nineties.

King and King

Parents in Massachusetts—a state where the Supreme Judicial Court in
2003 ordered legal recognition for same-sex marriages[48]—were targeted in
the past decade by liberals seeking to seize control of their most sacred
parental duty: teaching right and wrong to their children.

One day in 2005, as it was later recorded in an opinion filed by the U.S.
Court of Appeals for the First Circuit, David and Tonia Parker's kinder-
garten-age son returned from the Estabrook Elementary School in Lexington, Massachusetts, toting something called a "Diversity Book Bag."

Inside was a little volume entitled *Who's In a Family?* In this case, the answer to that question was not simply mom, dad,and children, or perhaps grandparents and the other extended family members you might expect to find in a traditional family unit. The educators at Estabrook Elementary wanted to expose the kindgartners in their care to a broader understanding of family that included families in which both parents are the same sex. "The book," said the appeals court opinion, "says nothing about marriage."[49]

A year later, the second-grade son of Joseph and Robin Wirthlin came home from the same Massachusetts elementary school and told his parents that his teacher had read them a story that day in class. It was not about some sports hero or some great figure from American history. It was a book designed to expose children to a new sort of role model. Its title was *King and King*, and it told "the story of a prince, ordered by his mother to get married, who first rejects several princesses only to fall in love with another prince," the U.S. Court of Appeals for the First Circuit reported in the opinion it issued in the suit filed by the Wirthlin and Parker families against Lexington school officials. "A wedding scene between the two princes is depicted. The last page of the book shows the two princes kissing, but with a red heart superimposed over their mouths."[50]

In each instance, the parents wanted the school to inform them in advance if this sort of material was going to be presented to their children so they could opt them out of that particular element of the instruction, something Massachusetts law allowed in sex education classes. The school did not oblige, however, because it did not consider the instruction in question part of its sex education curriculum. "Massachusetts does have a statute that requires parents to be given notice and the opportunity to exempt their children from curriculum which primarily involves human sexuality education or human sexuality issues," the appeals court said. "The school system has declined to apply this statutory exemption to these plaintiffs on the basis that the materials do not primarily involve human sexual education or human sexuality issues."[51]

The Parkers, the court said, were worried that *Who's In a Family* was "part of an effort by the public schools 'to indoctrinate young children into the concept that homosexuality and homosexual relations or marriage are moral and acceptable behavior.' Such an effort, they feared, would require their sons to affirm a belief inconsistent with their religion."

The Wirthlins, said the court, objected to "what they considered to be indoctrination of their son about gay marriage in contravention of their religious beliefs."

"Both families," said the court, "assert that they are devout Judeo-Christians and that a core belief of their religion is that homosexual behavior and gay marriage are immoral and violate God's law."[52]

"I'm just trying to be a good dad," David Parker told the *Boston Globe* when the controversy first erupted.[53]

"We're not intolerant," Tonia Parker told the paper. "We love all people. That is part of our faith." But she was committed to defending her child. "We're not giving unfettered access to the psyche of our son when he enters the school," she said.[54]

These parents were not trying to stop the public schools from using these books to instruct other people's children. They just wanted a chance to remove their own children from that instruction to preserve their rights as parents to teach their children their own values and to protect their right to the free exercise of their religion. "The parents assert it is ironic, and unconstitutional under the Free Exercise Clause," said the court, "for a public school system to show such intolerance towards their own religious beliefs in the name of tolerance."[55]

But the court ruled against the two families, though it did not contest their claim that the school's action violated their religious convictions. "While we accept as true the plaintiffs' assertion that their sincerely held religious beliefs were deeply offended," said the court, "we find that they have not described a constitutional burden on their rights, or on those of their children."[56]

The U.S. Supreme Court declined to take up the case. The appeals court ruling stood.[57] Public schools in Massachusetts retained the power to use their classrooms, including their kindergarten classrooms, to propagandize children on the government's view of the morality of homosexual unions—and they could do so without necessarily notifying parents.

As this case was moving through the courts, the issue of what happened at Estabrook Elementary School came up in an MSNBC-sponsored Democratic presidential debate at Dartmouth College in New Hampshire. "For example, last year some parents of second-graders were outraged to learn their children's teacher had read a story about same-sex marriage, about a prince who marries another prince," Allison King of New England Cable News told the candidates. "Same-sex marriage is legal in Massachusetts but most of you oppose it. Would you be comfortable having this story read to your children as part of their school curriculum?"

She put the question first to Senator John Edwards of North Carolina. "Yes, absolutely," said Edwards.

Edwards said he was personally not in favor of same-sex marriage, and thought second grade "might be a little tough" as a venue for the issue, but seemed to approve of what happened at Estabrook as an example of the competition he thought ought to take place between parents and public schools over the fundamental moral values of children. "So, I don't want to make that decision [about same-sex marriage] on behalf of my children," said Edwards.

> I want my children to be able to make that decision on behalf of themselves, and I want them to be exposed to all the information, even in—did you say second grade? Second grade might be a little tough, but even in second grade to be exposed to all those possibilities, because I don't want to impose my view. Nobody made me God. I don't get to decide on behalf of my family or my children, as my wife Elizabeth has spoken her own mind on this issue. I don't get to impose on them what it is that I believe is right.[58]

A moment later, King turned to Obama for his view. "You know," said Obama, "I feel very similar to John."[59]

Section 2953 of President Obama's health-care law authorizes the secretary of Health and Human Services to provide grants to the states for "personal responsibility education"[60] programs for adolescents. These programs will include what the law calls "adulthood preparations subjects."[61] Six of these subjects are listed in the law itself, and states receiving grants will be required to provide instruction in at least three of them. There are multiple ironies to this list. A federal government, running record deficits and heading towards bankruptcy, suggests that grant recipients instruct adolescents in "financial literacy." A law passed by control freaks, who are ready to use the public schools to teach kindergartners values at odds with the ones they learn at home, calls for the government to instruct teens in "parent-child communications."

Then there is this suggested subject for "responsibility" instruction: "Healthy relationships, such as positive self-esteem and relationship dynamics, friendship, dating, romantic involvement, marriage, and family interactions."[62]

Now that the federal welfare state has reached this deeply into our lives, whose vision of life and marriage will prevail in federally subsidized instruction on marriage and family?

The ultimate strategic goal of the control freaks is to seize the hearts and minds of future generations. They cannot win the Culture War by teaching their values to their children alone; they must teach their values to everybody else's children as well. They want to separate America once and for all from our traditional understanding of the inalienable, God-given right to life and the sanctity of marriage. The problem with this is that our traditional understandings are true. They are rooted in natural law. They are at the very heart of the unchanging moral order our Founding Fathers honored and respected, and that they understood all men, all governments and all societies must obey.

If we turn our backs on the truths that the right to life begins at conception, and the state has a duty to protect it, and that marriage is the union of one man and woman, and the state has no authority to deny it, we will find no solid alternative foundation for our society. The role of the state will change from being the protector of our lives and families to being the definer of our lives and families.

We will have lost the thing of greatest value our pioneering forebears carried into the wilderness and carefully preserved for their children and for us—not a love of freedom, but a love of the truth that makes freedom possible.

Conclusion

What We Owe

As this book has shown, there are liberals in this country today who want government to control our lives. They want Americans to forget our constitutional and moral tradition and submit to dependence on the state and to a new order that devalues life and liberty. They cannot succeed if Americans choose again to control their own destiny, and to use the tools of government forged by the Founding Fathers to preserve the freedom that has been handed down from generation to generation ever since the Founding era.

But Americans can learn from the vices of the Founding Fathers as well as their virtues.

One of the saddest, yet most instructive, ironies in our history is that some of the Founders who most ardently defended representative government and the principle that all men have God-given rights, held some men as if they were property. Hypocrisy is nothing new among politicians.

Thomas Jefferson, who authored the Declaration of Independence, and James Madison, who authored the Bill of Rights, both owned slaves. Even as they produced the greatest charters of American freedom, they personally denied freedom to some Americans. They knew contemporaries who freed their slaves—such as George Washington, who freed his in his will—but they never did it themselves.

This does not mean the Declaration and the Constitution are flawed. It means that Jefferson and Madison were flawed, a reflection of the fact that all human beings are flawed and always will be. The Founders well understood this, which is why they structured our government the way they did, with power divided not only among the three branches of the federal government, but between the federal government and the states. They did not intend to leave liberty to the good will of those who governed, because they did not have faith in the good will of those who governed.

The flawed nature of man, as the Founders knew, also underscored the need to put faith in God, not in men, and to use as the ultimate guides for the laws of the nation not the whims of any passing era but the eternal rules of natural law.

In 1774, after the British Parliament closed the port of Boston in retaliation for the Boston Tea Party, John Dickinson, a Philadelphia lawyer famed for his eloquence, penned these timely words:

> *Honor, justice* and *humanity,* call upon us to hold and to transmit to our posterity that liberty which we received from our ancestors. It is not our duty to leave wealth to our children, but it is our duty to leave liberty to them. No infamy, iniquity, or cruelty, can exceed our own, if we, born and educated in a country of freedom, entitled to its blessings, and knowing their value, pusillanimously deserting the post assigned us by Divine Providence, surrender succeeding generations to a condition of wretchedness from which no human efforts, in all probability, will be sufficient to extricate them .... So alarming are the measures already taken for laying the foundations of a despotic authority of Great Britain over us, and with such artful and incessant vigilance is the plan prosecuted, that unless the present generation can interrupt the work, *while it is going forward,* can it be imagined that our children, debilitated by our imprudence and supineness, will be able to overthrow it, *when completed?*[1]

In one sense, Dickinson's words remind us that it is always 1774 in the quest for individual liberty. A supine people can never preserve freedom. But in another sense it is nothing like 1774 in America today precisely because of what we inherited from the Americans of that era. They gave us the finest Constitution ever written. On our behalf, they signed a Declaration that gives constant witness to the moral law on which our Constitution is based. No foreign parliament seeks today to impose its rule on us. We are not denied representation. The politicians who make our laws are elected by us, must answer to us, and can be removed by us.

The generations that went before us left us a nation both prosperous and free. We owe it to them and our children to do the same. Let's get to it.

Acknowledgments

O ver the years, I have had the honor and privilege of working for some wonderful mentors both in the conservative cause and in journalism. Pat Buchanan gave me the opportunity to work in two presidential campaigns, where ideas and first principles were the motivating factors in everything we did. Allan Ryskind and Tom Winter, whose *Human Events* was instrumental in inspiring and informing the Reagan Revolution, welcomed me in a later era as their colleague and friend at the first and greatest of all conservative periodicals. Because of these men I was able to pursue the vocation and cause I love. I am grateful to them.

I am also deeply grateful to Media Research Center Founder and President Brent Bozell and the other leaders of the MRC, including David Martin, for building and growing an institution that, as a bulwark of the Conservative Movement, embodies and advances on a daily basis the values and principles of the Founding Fathers, and that in CNSNews.com has created a news organization where those values and principles are respected. At CNSNews.com, I have learned and been inspired by the dedication and camaraderie of fellow workers, including Michael Chapman, Pete Winn, Susan Jones, Craig Bannister, Melanie Hunter-Omar, Fred Lucas, Penny Starr, Matt Cover, Nicholas Ballasy, Edwin Mora, Jonathan Schulter, and Chris Neefus.

I want to thank David Limbaugh for helping to make this book project a reality and Harry Crocker for seeing the potential in it and giving me the opportunity to publish it with Regnery.

Most importantly, I am thankful to my wife Julie and my five children, Maria, Anna, Theresa, Daniel, and Ben for their support and encouragement in this project.

Notes

Chapter 1

1. Frederick Jackson Turner, *The Frontier in American History* (New York: Henry Holt and Company, 1962), 37.

2. The White House, "February 10, 2009, Remarks by the President at Fort Myers Town Hall," http://www.whitehouse.gov/the-press-office/remarks-president-fort-myers-town-hall [accessed April 26, 2010].

3. CQ Transcriptions, "Secretary of Transportation Ray LaHood Delivers Remarks at The National Press Club on Stimulus Spending on Roads and Infrastructure," May 21, 2009. See also, Federal News Service, National Press Club Newsmaker Luncheon With Secretary of Transportation Ray LaHood; Subject: Update on the American Recovery and Reinvestment Act; Moderator: Donna Leinwand, President of the National Press Club; Location: The National Press Club, Washington, D.C., May 21, 2009. See also, "Sec. LaHood on U.S. Transportation Dept. Involvement in Stimulus Package," C-SPAN.org, Thursday, May 21, 2009; available at: http://cspan.org/Watch/Media/2009/05/21/HP/A/18891/Sec 1 LaHood 1 on 1 US 1 Transportation 1 Dept 1 Involvement 1 in 1 Stimulus 1 Package.aspx [accessed April 26, 2010].

4. Associated Press, "LaHood's talk of mileage tax nixed," MSNBC, February 20, 2009; available at: http://www.msnbc.msn.com/id/29298315/ [accessed April 26, 2010].

5. Ibid.

6. The White House, "February 20, 2009, Briefing by Press Secretary Robert Gibbs," http://www.whitehouse.gov/the-press-office/briefing-white-house-press-secretary-robert-gibbs-2202009 [accessed April 26, 2010].

7. Carle Hulse, "Obama's Inner Circle: Members and Maybes: Ray LaHood," *New York Times*, December 18, 2008, Section A, Column 0, National Desk; available at: http://query.nytimes.com/gst/full page.html?res=9C0DEEDC153AF93BA25751C1A96E9C8B63, 30.

8. Ibid.

9. Dennis Conrad, "Earmark rankings, Illinois 7th," The Associated Press, June 7, 2008; available at: http://www.pantagraph.com/news/article_645c8bdb-aad2-5645-b239-851555c7ac38.html [accessed April 28, 2010].

10. Citizens Against Government Waste "Porker of the Month: CAGW Names Transportation Secretary Ray LaHood Porker of the Month; available   at: http://www.cagw.org/newsroom/porker-of-the-month/2009/cagw-names-secretary-lahood.html [accessed April 26, 2010].

11. Carle Hulse, "Obama's Inner Circle: Members and Maybes," *op. cit.*

12. Ray LaHood, Statement of the Honorable Ray LaHood, Secretary of Transportation, Before the Committee on Appropriations Subcommittee on Transportation, Housing and Urban Development, and Related Agencies, United States House of Representatives, March 18, 2009; available at: http://appropriations.house.gov/Witness_testimony/TH/Honorable_Ray_%20Lahood_03_18_09.pdf [accessed April 26, 2010]. See also, Federal News Service, Hearing of the Transportation, Housing and Urban Development, and Related Agencies Subcommittee of the House Appropriations Committee; Subject: Livable Communities, Transit Oriented Development, and Incorporating Green Building Practices into Federal Housing and Transportation Policy; Chaired by: Representative John W. Oliver (D.-Ma.); Witness:

Ray LaHood, Secretary, Department of Transportation; Shaun Donovan, Secretary, Department of Housing and Urban Development, March 18, 2009.

13. United States Department of Transportation, "DOT Secretary Ray LaHood, HUD Secretary Shaun Donovan and EPA Administrator Lisa Jackson Announce Interagency Partnership for Sustainable Communities," June 16, 2009; available at: http://www.dot.gov/affairs/2009/dot8009.htm [accessed April 26, 2010].

14. Ronald D. Utt, Ph.D, "President Obama's New Plan to Decide Where Americans Live and How They Travel," Heritage Foundation, Backgrounder No. 2260, April 14, 2009; available at: http://www.heritage.org/Research/Reports/2009/04/President-Obamas-New-Plan-To-Decide-Where-Americans-Live-and-How-They-Travel [accessed April 28, 2010].

15. United States Department of Transportation, "DOT Secretary Ray LaHood, HUD Secretary Shaun Donovan and EPA Administrator Lisa Jackson Announce Interagency Partnership for Sustainable Communities," *op. cit.*

16. Ray LaHood, "Statement of the Honorable Ray LaHood Secretary of Transportation Before the Committee on Appropriations Subcommittee on Transportation, Housing and Urban Development, and Related Agencies United States House of Representatives," *op. cit.*

17. Ibid.

18. George F. Will, "Ray LaHood Transformed : Secretary of Behavior Modification," *Newsweek*, May 25, 2009; available at: http://www.newsweek.com/id/197925 [accessed April 26, 2010].

19. CQ Transcriptions, "Secretary of Transportation Ray LaHood Delivers Remarks at The National Press Club on Stimulus Spending on Roads and Infrastructure," May 21, 2009. See also, Federal News Service, National Press Club Newsmaker Luncheon With Secretary of Transportation Ray LaHood; Subject: Update on the American Recovery and Reinvestment Act; Moderator: Donna Leinwand,

President of the National Press Club; Location: The National Press Club, Washington, D.C., May 21, 2009. See also, "Sec. LaHood on U.S. Transportation Dept. Involvement in Stimulus Package," *op. cit.*

20. Samuel Eliot Morison, *The Oxford History of the American People* (New York: Oxford University Press, 1965), 169.

21. Ibid., 182.

22. John C. Miller, *Origins of the American Revolution* (Boston: Little Brown and Company, 1943), 74.

23. John Adams, *The Works of John Adams, Second President of the United States*, Vol. III, (Boston: Charles C. Little and James Brown, 1851), 462.

24. John C. Miller, *Origins of the American Revolution*, 53–78, 103, 201–31, 374–75; Samuel Eliot Morison, *The Oxford History of the American People*, 171–88.

25. The Avalon Project: Documents in Law, History and Diplomacy, "The Royal Proclamation—October 7, 1763: By the King. A Proclamation George R."; available at: http://avalon.law.yale.edu/18th_century/proc1763.asp [accessed April 26, 2010].

26. C. W. Butterfield, *The Washington-Crawford Letters: Being the Correspondence Between George Washington and William Crawford, From 1767 to 1781, Concerning Western Lands* (Cincinnati: Robert Clark & Co., 1877).

27. Ibid., 4.

28. Archibald Freeman and Arthur W. Leonard, *Conciliation with the Colonies: The Speech by Edmund Burke* (Boston, New York, Chicago: Houghton Mifflin and Company, 1915), 70. See also Frederick Jackson Turner, *The Frontier in American History*, 33. Turner called this Burke's "splendid protest."

29. John C. Miller, *Origins of the American Revolution*, 210.

30. Frederick Jackson Turner, *The Frontier in American History*, 206.

31. Ibid., 30.

32. Ibid., 153–54.

33. Ibid., 306–7.

34. Ibid., 37.

35. Ibid., 307, 309.

36. United States Department of Transportation, "Portland Streetcar suits this 'livable community," July 1, 2009; see the videotape of Secretary LaHood's remarks in Portland that are embedded here in the secretary's blog entry; available at: http://fastlane.dot.gov/2009/07/portland-streetcar-suits-this-livable-community.html [accessed April 27, 2010].

37. "Stimulus and Federal Transportation Projects," *Washington Journal*, C-SPAN, Broadcast April 14, 2009; available at: http://www.c-span-video.org/program/285255-2&start=1498.57&stop=1550.74 [accessed April 27, 2010].

38. "Road to the Future: Interview: Secretary Ray LaHood" Blueprint America (PBS), July 17, 2009; available at: http://www.pbs.org/wnet/blueprintamerica/reports/road-to-the-future/interview-secretary-of-transportation-ray-lahood/637/.

39. "Portland Streetcar Unveiling Event - Secretary LaHood's Remarks," July 1, 2009; video available at: http://www.youtube.com/watch?v=P4Tjj7ga5jE.

40. Jeff Mapes, "LaHood: It is Congress that needs the extension," *The Oregonian*, July 1, 2009; available at: http://blog.oregonlive.com/mapesonpolitics/2009/07/lahood_it_is_congress_that_nee.html [accessed April 28, 2010].

41. Tom McCall, Governor of Oregon, "The Oregon Land Use Story," Executive Department, Local Government Relations Division, Robert K. Logan, Administrator, Salem, Oregon, 97310; January 7, 1974. See also, Metro, "Abbott: A history of Metro," May 1991; available at: http://www.oregonmetro.gov/index.cfm/go/by.web/id=2937/level=4 [accessed April 28, 2010]; Randal O'Toole, "Debunking Portland: The City That Doesn't Work," Cato Institute, Policy Analysis No. 596, July 9, 2007; available at: http://www.cato.org/pubs/pas/pa-596.pdf [accessed April 28, 2010].

42. Metro, "Urban growth boundary," available at: http://www.oregon metro.gov/index.cfm/go/by.web/id=277/level=3 [accessed April 28, 2010].

43. Oregon Department of Land Conservation and Development, "Oregon's Statewide Planning Goals & Guidelines, Goal 14: Urbanization," OAR 660-015-0000(14); available at: http://www.oregon.gov/ LCD/docs/goals/goal14.pdf [accessed April 28, 2010].

44. Ibid.

45. Ibid.

46. "Transportation Planning," Department of Land Conservation and Development Department; available at: http://arcweb.sos.state.or.us/ rules/OARS_600/OAR_660/660_012.html.

47. Ibid.

48. Ibid.

49. Ibid.

50. "Sierra Club California: Urban Growth Management Policy Guidelines," Sierra Club; available at: http://www.sierraclub.org/ca/scc/ growth.asp

51. Ibid.

52. Ibid.

53. Ibid.

54. Joel Garreau, *Edge City: Life on the New Frontier* (New York: First Edition Anchor Books, 1992), 222.

55. Ibid., 239.

56. The White House, "February 10, 2009, Remarks by the President at Fort Myers Town Hall"; available at: http://www.whitehouse.gov/the-press-office/remarks-president-fort-myers-town-hall [accessed April 26, 2010].

57. "Election 2004: 2000 vote, county by county," *USA Today*, November 1, 2004; available at: http://www.usatoday.com/news/politicselections/ vote2004/countymap2000.htm [accessed April 28, 2010]. See also, "Election 2004: Latest vote, county by county," *USA Today*, November

16, 2004; available at: http://www.usatoday.com/news/politicselections/ vote2004/countymap.htm [accessed April 28, 2010]; "2008 election coverage; Behind the results," *USA Today*; available at: http://www.usatoday.com/news/politics/election2008/results.htm [accessed April 28, 2010] and David Leip's Atlas of U.S. Presidential Elections, available at: http://uselectionatlas.org [accessed April 28, 2010].

58. Jeff Maples, "It is Congress that needs the extension," *op. cit.* See also, "Road to the Future: Interview: Secretary Ray LaHood" *op. cit.*

Chapter 2

1. Henry R. Seager, *Social Insurance: A Program of Social Reform* (New York: Macmillan, 1910), 168.

2. "A Social Security Program Must Include All Those Who Need Its Protection," Radio Address on the Third Anniversary of the Social Security Act. August 15, 1938," FDR's Statements on Social Security, Social Security Administration, Social Security History; available at: http://www.ssa.gov/history/fdrstmts.html#radio [accessed May 15, 2010].

3. Merle Haggard and Dean Holloway, "Big City" (Nashville: Copyright © 1981 Sony/ATV Songs LLC).

4. Mark Levin, *Liberty and Tyranny: A Conservative Manifesto* (New York: Simon & Schuster, 2009).

5. "Henry Seager's 1910 Book on Social Security," Social Security Administration; available at: http://www.socialsecurity.gov/history/ seager.html [accessed May 11, 2010].

6. Ibid.

7. Thomas C. Leonard, "Retrospectives: Eugenics and Economics in the Progressive Era," *Journal of Economic Perspectives*, Vol. 19, No. 4, Fall 2005, pp. 207–24.

8. Thomas C. Leonard, "'More Merciful and Not Less Effective': Eugenics and American Economics in the Progressive Era," *History of Political Economy*, Vol. 35, No. 4, Winter 2003: 702.

9. Henry R. Seager, *Social Insurance: A Program of Social Reform* (New York: Macmillan, 1910), 104–5.

10. Ibid., 3.

11. Ibid., 4–5.

12. Ibid., 20.

13. Ibid., 118.

14. Ibid., 143.

15. "Message to Congress Reviewing the Broad Objectives and Accomplishments of the Administration. June 8, 1934," FDR's Statements on Social Security, Social Security Administration, Social Security History; available at: http://www.ssa.gov/history/fdrstmts.html#message1 [accessed May 16, 2010].

16. "Why Social Security," 1937, Social Security Administration, Social Security History; available at: http://www.ssa.gov/history/whybook.html [accessed May 16, 2010].

17. "'A Social Security Program Must Include All Those Who Need Its Protection,' Radio Address on the Third Anniversary of the Social Security Act. August 15, 1938," FDR's Statements on Social Security, Social Security Administration, Social Security History.

18. Edwin E. Witte, "Reflections on the Beginnings of Social Security," Remarks delivered at observance of 20th Anniversary of Social Security Act by Department of Health, Education and Welfare, Washington, D.C., on August 15, 1955, Social Security Administration, Social Security History; available at: http://www.ssa.gov/history/witte4.html [accessed May 16, 2010].

19. Thomas H. Eliot, "The Legal Background of the Social Security Act," delivered at a general staff meeting at Social Security Administration Headquarters, Baltimore, Maryland, Social Security Administration, on February 3, 1961; available at: http://www.ssa.gov/history/eliot2.html [accessed May 16, 2010].

20. H. R. Rep. No. 1711, 74th Cong., 1st Sess. 10 [1935]

21. *Railroad Retirement Board* v. *Alton Railroad Co.*, 295 U.S. 330 (1935); available at: http://supreme.justia.com/us/295/330/case.html [accessed May 16, 2010].

22. Ibid.

23. Ibid.

24. Robert G. Natelson, "The General Welfare Clause and the Public Trust: An Essay in Original Understanding," *The University of Kansas Law Review*, Vol. 52, 2003-2004, p. 55.

25. In contrast to the Roosevelt administration's position in 1935 that the General Welfare Clause empowered the federal government to pay farmers not to farm, James Madison and Thomas Jefferson had firmly asserted in the Founding era that the clause gave the federal government no power to take action outside the scope of the other enumerated powers. As Natelson pointed out in his essay in the *University of Kansas Law Review*, many who opposed ratification of the Constitution during the time when the states were holding their ratifying conventions, argued that the General Welfare Clause could be interpreted to give the federal Congress the power to legislate on virtually anything. But Madison rebutted this argument in Federalist 41, which was published in the midst of the ratification process on January 19, 1788. To reassure people that the General Welfare Clause would not give the federal Congress the unlimited power opponents of the Constitution claimed, Madison wrote:

"It has been urged and echoed, that the power 'to lay and collect taxes, duties, imposts and excises, to pay the debts and provide for the common defense and general welfare of the United States,' amounts to an unlimited commission to exercise every power which may be alleged to be necessary for the common defense or general welfare. No stronger proof could be given of the distress under which these writers labor for objections, than their stooping to such a misconstruction.

"Had no other enumeration or definition of the powers of the Congress been found in the Constitution, than the general expression just cited, the authors of the objection might have had some color for it, though it would have been difficult to find a reason for so awkward a form of describing an authority to legislate in all possible cases. ...

"But what color can the objection have when a specification of the objects alluded to by these general terms immediately follows, and is not even separated by a longer pause than a semicolon? For what purpose could the enumeration of particular powers be inserted, if these and all others were meant to be included in the preceding general power?"

26. Federalist #45, James Madison.
27. *The Debates in the Several State Conventions, On The Adoption of the Federal Constitution, As Recommended by the General Convention at Philadelphia in 1787*, Vol. IV, ed. Jonathan Elliot (Washington: Printed for the Editor, 1836), 137; available at: http://memory.loc.gov/cgi-bin/ampage?collId=lled&fileName=004/lled004.db&recNum=148&itemLink=r%3Fammem%2Fhlaw%3A@field%28DOCID%2B@lit%28ed0041%29%29%230040002&linkText=1 [accessed May 16, 2010].
28. Ibid.
29. Ibid., 138.
30. *The Debates in the Several State Conventions, On The Adoption of the Federal Constitution, As Recommended by the General Convention at Philadelphia in 1787*, Vol. III, 441; available at: http://memory.loc.gov/cgi-bin/ampage [accessed May 16, 2010].
31. Ibid., 441–42.
32. Ibid.
33. Kurt T. Lash, "The Original Meaning of an Omission: The Tenth Amendment, Popular Sovereignty, and 'Expressly' Delegated Powers," *Notre Dame Law Review*, Vol. 83:5, 2008, p. 1895; available at: http://www.nd.edu/~ndlrev/archive_public/83ndlr5/Lash.pdf [accessed May 16, 2010].
34. Ibid., 1912.

35. "Jefferson's Opinion on the Constitutionality of a National Bank: 1791," The Avalon Project: Documents in Law, History and Diplomacy; Yale Law School, Lillian Goldman Law Library; available at: http://avalon.law.yale.edu/18th_century/bank-tj.asp [accessed May 16, 2010].

36. Ibid.

37. Ibid.

38. Ibid.

39. "Hamilton's Opinion as to the Constitutionality of the Bank of the United States: 1791," The Avalon Project: Documents in Law, History and Diplomacy; Yale Law School, Lillian Goldman Law Library; available at: http://avalon.law.yale.edu/18th_century/bank-ah.asp [accessed May 16, 2010].

40. Ibid.

41. Ibid.

42. Alexander Hamilton, "Report on the Subject of Manufactures," December 5, 1791, Online Library of Liberty; available at: http://oll.libertyfund.org/?option=com_staticxt&staticfile=show.php%3Ftitle=875&chapter=63882&layout=html&Itemid=27 [accessed May 11, 2010].

43. Ibid.

44. 29 U.S. 1 (1936).

45. Joseph Story, *Commentaries on the Constitution of the United States*, Vol. II (Boston: Hilliard, Gray, and Company.

46. Ibid.

47. Franklin D. Roosevelt, XXXII President of the United States L 1933-1945, Fireside Chat, March 9, 1937; available at: http://www.presidency.ucsb.edu/ws/index.php?pid=15381 [accessed May 16, 2010].

48. Ibid.

49. William E. Leuchtenburg, *The Supreme Court Reborn: The Constitutional Revolution in the Age of Roosevelt*, (New York, Oxford: Oxford University Press, 1995), pp.142.

50. 301 U.S. 548 (1937).

51. 301 U.S. 619 (1937).

52. 301 U.S. 610 (1937).

53. William E. Leuchtenburg, *The Supreme Court Reborn: The Constitutional Revolution in the Age of Roosevelt* (New York: Oxford University Press, 1995), 143–144.

54. Thomas H. Eliot, "The Legal Background of the Social Security Act," *op. cit.*

55. Data available at: http://www.ssa.gov/history/idapayroll.html

56. Ibid.

57. Congressional Record, March 2, 1994, p. S2194; available at: http://thomas.loc.gov/cgi-bin/query/F?r103:31:./temp/~r103cBP68f: e6482: [accessed May 17, 2010].

58. "The Social Security Program Today," Social Security USA—The Program & Its Administration, SSA History; available at: http://www.socialsecurity.gov/history/ssa/usa1964-1.html [accessed May 17, 2010].

59. Historical Tables: Budget of the U.S. Government, Fiscal Year 2011 (Office of Management and Budget), 21.

60. Historical Debt Outstanding, 1900-1949, Treasury Direct; available at: http://www.treasurydirect.gov/govt/reports/pd/histdebt/histdebt_histo3.htm [accessed May 17, 2010].

61. Ibid.

62. Historical Tables: Budget of the U.S. Government, Fiscal Year 2011 (Office of Management and Budget), 21–23.

63. "The 2009 Annual Report of the Board of Trustees of the Federal Old-Age and Survivors Insurance and Federal Disability Insurance Trust Funds" (Washington, D.C.: U.S. Government Printing Office, 2009), 137.

64. Congressional Record, June 17, 1935, p. 9423.

65. "The First Social Security Beneficiary," Social Security Online; available at: http://www.ssa.gov/history/imf.html [accessed May 11, 2010].

66. "The Social Security Program Today," Social Security USA—The Program & Its Administration, SSA History, *op. cit.*

67. The First Social Security Beneficiary," Social Security Online, *op. cit.*

68. "Income of the Population 55. or Older, 2006," Social Security Administration; SSA Publication No. 13-11871, February 2009.

69. "Our Real Federal Financial Condition," Peter G. Peterson Foundation; available at: http://www.pgpf.org/about/nationaldebt/ [accessed May 17, 2010].

70. Merle Haggard, Dean Holloway, "Big City" (Nashville, TN: Copyright © 1981 Sony/ATV Songs LLC).

Chapter 3

1. Matt Cover, "Senate Judiciary Chairman Unable to Say Where Constitution Authorizes Congress to Order Americans to Buy Healthcare," CNSNews.com, October 22, 2009; available at: http://www.cnsnews.com/news/article/55910 [accessed May 11, 2010].

2. Terence P. Jeffrey, "Sen. Hatch Questions Constitutionality of Obamacare: If Feds Can Force Us to Buy Health Insurance 'Then There's Literally Nothing the Federal Government Can't Force Us to Do,'" CNSNews.com, November 26, 2009; available at: http://www.cnsnews.com/news/article/56447 [accessed May 11, 2010].

3. "President's Weekly Address: Americans Tired of Politicians Who Talk the Talk but don't Walk the Walk," Political Buzz; transcript and audio available at: http://political-buzz.com/2010/02/13/presidents-weekly-address-americans-tired-of-politicians-who-talk-the-talk-but-dont-walk-the-walk/ [accessed June 3, 2010].

4. Matt Cover, "Senate Judiciary Chairman Unable to Say Where Constitution Authorizes Congress to Order Americans to Buy Healthcare," *op. cit.*

5. Matt Cover, "When Asked Where the Constitution Authorizes Congress to Order Americans to Buy Health Insurance, Pelosi Says: 'Are You Serious?'" CNSNews.com, Oct. 23, 2009; available at: http://www.cnsnews.com/news/article/55971http://www.cnsnews.com/news/article/55971 [accessed May 20, 2010].

6. CBO Memorandum, "The Budgetary Treatment of an Individual Mandate to Buy Health Insurance," Congressional Budget Office, August 1994; available at: http://www.cbo.gov/ftpdocs/48xx/doc4816/doc38.pdf [accessed May 11, 2010].

7. Edwin Mora, "Sen. Reed: Forcing People to Buy Health Insurance is Constitutionally Justified Because It's Like Making People 'Sign Up for the Draft,'" CNSNews.com, November 26, 2009; available at: http://www.cnsnews.com/news/article/56971 [accessed May 11, 2010].

8. Nicholas Ballasy, "Sen. Akaka Says 'I'm Not Aware' of Constitution Giving Congress Authority to Make Individuals Buy Health Insurance," CNSNews.com, November 26, 2009; available at: http://www.cnsnews.com/news/article/57024 [accessed May 11, 2010].

9. Matt Cover, "Sen. Bob Casey: Health Care Mandate Constitutional But Not Sure If There's 'Specific Constitutional Provision,'" CNSNews.com, December 24, 2009; available at: http://www.cnsnews.com/news/article/59011 [accessed May 20, 2010].

10. Edwin Mora, "Sen. Ben Nelson: 'I'm Not Going to Be Able to Answer That Question' of Where Constitution Authorizes Congress to Force Americans to Buy Health Insurance," CNSNews.com, November 11, 2009; available at: http://www.cnsnews.com/news/article/57007 [accessed May 11, 2010].

11. Nicholas Ballasy, "Sen. Landrieu Declines to Say Where Constitution Authorizes Congress to Force Americans to Buy Health Insurance, Saying She'll Let 'Constitutional Lawyers on Our Staff' Handle That," CNSNews.com, December 11, 2009; available at: http://www.cnsnews.com/news/article/58401 [accessed May 20, 2010].

12. Edwin Mora, "Sen. Conrad 'Assumes' Constitution's Commerce Clause Gives Congress Power To Mandate Buying Health Insurance,'" CNSNews.com, December 23, 2009; available at: http://www.cnsnews.com/news/article/58988 [accessed May 11, 2010].

13. Matt Cover, "Sen. Brown: Constitution Gives Congress Power to Mandate Health Insurance In 'Same Place' As Medicare," CNSNews.com, December 29, 2009; available at: http://www.cnsnews.com/news/article/ 59068 [accessed May 11, 2010].

14. Matt Cover, "Sen. Sanders: Constitutional Authority for Congress' Health Insurance Mandate 'Probably' Same As Medicare," CNSNews.com, December 24, 2009; available at: http://www.cns news.com/news/article/59002 [accessed May 11, 2010].

15. Nicholas Ballasy, "Congress Mandating That People Buy Health Insurance Like States Requiring Driver's Licenses, Warner Says," CNSNews.com, November 13, 2009; available at: http://www.cns news.com/news/article/57085 [accessed May 11, 2010].

16. Edwin Mora, "Sen. McCaskill Doesn't Say Where Congress Gets Power To Mandate Health Insurance, But Cites Auto Insurance At State Level," CNSNews.com, December 28, 2009; available at: http://www.cnsnews.com/news/article/59036 [accessed May 11, 2010].

17. Edwin Mora, "Sen. Merkley: Authority to Force People to Buy Health Insurance is Part of Congress's 'Very First Enumerated Power,'" CNSNews.com, November 26, 2009; available at: http://www.cns news.com/news/article/56968 [accessed May 11, 2010].

18. Fred Lucas, "Sen. Feinstein 'Assumes' Commerce Clause Gives Congress Unlimited Authority to Mandate Health Insurance," CNSNews.com, December 23, 2009; available at: http://www.cns news.com/news/article/58937 [accessed May 11, 2010].

19. Nicholas Ballasy, "House Judiciary Chairman Says Constitution's Non-Existent 'Good and Welfare Clause' Authorizes Congress to Force Americans to Buy Health Insurance," CNSNews.com, March 23, 2010; available at: http://www.cnsnews.com/news/article/63182 [accessed May 11, 2010].

20. Nicholas Ballasy, "Sen. Burris Cites Unwritten Constitutional 'Health' Provision to Justify Forcing Americans to Buy Health Insurance," CNSNews.com, November 26, 2009; available at: http://www.cns news.com/news/article/56629 [accessed May 11, 2010].

21. The White House, "Briefing by White House Press Secretary Robert Gibbs," March 22, 2010; transcript available at: http://www.white house.gov/the-press-office/briefing-white-house-press-secretary-robert-gibbs-32210 [accessed May 20, 2010]. See also: Terence P. Jeffrey, "A Tyrannical Act," *Human Events*, March 24, 2010; available at: http://www.humanevents.com/article.php?id=36178 [accessed May 11, 2010].

22. Ibid.

23. Fred Lucas, "White House Not Worried About States' Constitutional Challenge to Health Care," CNSNews.com, March 23, 2010; available at: http://www.cnsnews.com/news/article/63208 [accessed May 11, 2010]. See also: "Virginia Attorney General to file suit against federal government over passage of health care bill," press release, Commonwealth of Virginia, Office of the Attorney General; available at: http://www.vaag.com/PRESS_RELEASES/Cuccinelli/32210_Health_Care_Bill.html [accessed May 20, 2010].

24. Terence P. Jeffrey, "Sen. Hatch Questions Constitutionality of Obamacare: If Feds Can Force Us to Buy Health Insurance 'Then There's Literally Nothing the Federal Government Can't Force Us to Do,'" *op. cit.*

25. "An Analysis of Health Insurance Premiums Under the Patient Protection and Affordable Care Act," Congressional Budget Office, Letter to Sen. Evan Bayh, November 30, 2009; available at: http://www.cbo.gov/ftpdocs/107xx/doc10781/11-30-Premiums.pdf [accessed May 20, 2010]. For the annual incomes that correlate to the federal poverty level see: "The 2009 HHS Poverty Guidelines," available at: http://aspe.hhs.gov/poverty/09poverty.shtml [accessed May 20, 2010]. These guidelines were in effect until May 31, 2010. They listed an income of $22,050 as the poverty level for a family of four. So a family earning 400 percent of this would earn $88,200.

26. "Estimated Premiums for 'Bronze' Coverage Under the Patient Protection and Affordable Care Act," Congressional Budget Office, Letter to Sen. Olympia Snowe, January 11, 2010; available at: http://www. cbo.gov/ftpdocs/108xx/doc10884/01-11-Premiums_for_Bronze_Plan. pdf [accessed May 20, 2010].

27. "An Analysis of Health Insurance Premiums Under the Patient Protection and Affordable Care Act," *op. cit.*

28. Ibid.

29. The White House, "Remarks by the President and Vice President at Signing of the Health Insurance Reform Bill," March 23, 2010, available at: http://www.whitehouse.gov/the-press-office/remarks-president-and-vice-president-signing-health-insurance-reform-bill [accessed May 20, 2010]. See also: Terence P. Jeffrey, "Obama's Defining Lie," *Human Events*, April 1, 2010; available at: http://www.human events.com/article.php?id=36283 [accessed May 11, 2010].

30. Data available at: http://www.cbo.gov/ftpdocs/103xx/doc10310/06-15-HealthChoicesAct.pdf [accessed May 11, 2010].

31. "Responses to Questions About CBO's Preliminary Estimate of the Direct Spending and Revenue Effects of H.R. 4872, the Reconciliation Act of 2010," Congressional Budget Office, Letter to Rep. Paul Ryan, March 19, 2010; available at: http://www.cbo.gov/ftp docs/113xx/doc11376/RyanLtrhr4872.pdf [accessed May 20, 2010].

32. Ibid.

33. Ibid.

34. "President's Weekly Address: Americans Tired of Politicians Who Talk the Talk but don't Walk the Walk," *op. cit.*

35. Terence P. Jeffrey, "Obama Defeats FDR (In Spending Other People's Money)," *Human Events*, February 17, 2010; available at: http://www.humanevents.com/article.php?id=35673 [accessed May 11, 2010]. Data are from: Historical Tables: Budget of the U.S. Government, Fiscal Year 2011 (Office of Management and Budget), 24–27.

36. Ibid.

37. "An Analysis of the President's Budgetary Proposals for Fiscal Year 2011," Congress of the United States, Congressional Budget Office, March 2010; available at: http://www.cbo.gov/ftpdocs/112xx /doc11280/03-24-apb.pdf [accessed May 21, 2010].

38. Posted by John T. Woolley and Gerhard Peters, "The President's News Conference," April 8, 1965, The American Presidency Project; available at: http://www.presidency.ucsb.edu/ws/index.php?pid=26881 [accessed May 11, 2010].

39. Posted by John T. Woolley and Gerhard Peters, "Remarks With President Truman at the Signing in Independence of the Medicare Bill," July 30, 1965, The American Presidency Project; available at: http://www.presidency.ucsb.edu/ws/index.php?pid=27123 [accessed May 11, 2010].

40. "Our Real Federal Financial Condition," Peter G. Peterson Foundation; available at: http://www.pgpf.org/about/nationaldebt/ [accessed May 21, 2010].

41. Ibid.

42. U.S. Treasury Department, "2009 Financial Report of the United States Government," available at: http://fmsq.treas.gov/fr/09frusg/ 09frusg.pdf, p. ii [accessed May 21, 2010].

43. Statement of the Comptroller General of the United States, Government Accountability Office, February 26, 2010; available at: http://www.gao.gov/financial/fy2009/09gao1.pdf [accessed May 11, 2010].

44. Ibid.

45. "Our Real Federal Financial Condition," Peter G. Peterson Foundation; available at: http://www.pgpf.org/about/nationaldebt/ [accessed May 21, 2010].

46. "Estimated Financial Effects of the 'Social Security Personal Savings Guarantee and Prosperity Act of 2005'—INFORMATION," Memorandum to Representative Paul Ryan, Senator John Sununu, from Steve Gross, chief actuary of the Social Security Administration, April

20, 2005; available at: http://www.ssa.gov/OACT/solvency/index.html [accessed May 21, 2010]. This memo from the actuary of the Social Security Administration describes how the Ryan-Sununu Social Security reform proposal would have worked and concluded, "Under the plan specifications described below the Social Security program would be expected to be solvent and meet its benefit obligations throughout the long-range period 2004 through 2078 and beyond."

47. Ibid.

48. Matt Cover, "Pelosi Confirms New Medicare Tax on 'Unearned Income, Whatever Category That Is,'" CNSNews.com, March 19, 2010; available at: http://www.cnsnews.com/news/article/63036 [accessed May 11, 2010].

Chapter 4

1. Exodus 20:17

2. Lance Banning, ed., *Liberty and Order: The First American Party Struggle* (Indianapolis: Liberty Fund, 2004); available at: http://app.library-ofliberty.org/?option=com_staticxt&staticfile=show.php%3Ftitle=875 &chapter=63884&layout=html&Itemid=27 (accessed May 24, 2010).

3. Paul R. Ehrlich, Anne H. Ehrlich, and John P. Holdren, *Human Ecology: Problems and Solutions* (San Francisco: W.H. Freeman and Company, 1973), 279.

4. Lance Banning, ed., *Liberty and Order, op. cit.*

5. 3 U.S. 386 (1798).

6. For the basic facts of the *Kelo* v. *New London* case see the petitioners' and respondents' briefs presented to the United States Supreme Court: William H. Mellor, Scott G. Bullock, and Dana Berliner of the Institute for Justice, and Scott W. Sawyer of the Sawyer Law Firm LLC, "Brief of the Petitioners," Supreme Court of the United States, No. 04-108; available at: http://www.oyez.org/sites/default/files/cases/2000-2009/2004/2004_04_108/briefs/Petitioners'%20brief.pdf [accessed May 24, 2010]; Wesley Horton, Daniel J. Krisch of Horton, Shields and

Knox, P.C.; Thomas J. Londregan, Jeffrey T. Londregan of Conway & Londregan, P.C.; Edward O'Connell and David P. Condon of Waller, Smith and Palmer, P.C., "Brief of the Respondents," Supreme Court of the United States, No. 04-108; available at: http://www.oyez.org /sites/default/files/cases/2000-2009/2004/2004_04_108/briefs/Respondent's%20brief.pdf [accessed May 24, 2010].

7. Matthew Dery, "Win or Lose, We Take Pride In Our Fight For Our Homes," New London Day, February 20, 2005; available at: http://www.theday.com/article/20050220/DAYARC/302209990 [accessed May 25, 2010].

8. Day Staff Writer, "Defendants in Eminent Domain Case Are Linked By Belief in Right to Property," *New London Day*, July 25, 2001; available at: http://www.theday.com/article/20010725/DAYARC/307259955 [accessed May 25, 2010].

9. William H. Mellor, Scott G. Bullock, and Dana Berliner of the Institute for Justice, and Scott W. Sawyer of the Sawyer Law Firm LLC, "Brief of the Petitioners," Supreme Court of the United States, No. 04-108 [accessed May 24, 2010]; Wesley Horton, Daniel J. Krisch of Horton, Shields and Knox, P.C.; Thomas J. Londregan, Jeffrey T. Londregan of Conway & Londregan, P.C.; Edward O'Connell and David P. Condon of Waller, Smith and Palmer, P.C., "Brief of the Respondents," Supreme Court of the United States, No. 04-108.

10. For a breakdown of how the Supreme Court voted in *Kelo* v. *City of New London* as well as links to the opinion and major briefs and the oral argument in the case, see the Web page on the case at Oyez.org; available at: http://www.oyez.org/cases/2000-2009/2004/2004_04_108 [accessed May 25, 2010].

11. 545 U. S. 649 (2005).

12. Ibid.

13. Ibid.

14. Press Release, Quinnipiac University Polling Institute, "Connecticut Voters Say 11–1 Stop Eminent Domain Quinnipiac University Poll

Finds; Saving Groton Sub Base Is High Priority," July 28, 2005; available at: http://www.quinnipiac.edu/x1296.xml?ReleaseID=821 [accessed April 19, 2009]. [Hereinafter Quinnipiac University Press Release.]

15. Press Release, "President-elect Obama speaks on an American Recovery and Reinvestment Plan in Ohio," Change.gov; available at: http://change.gov/newsroom/entry/president-elect_obama_speaks_on_an_american_recovery_and_reinvestment_plan_/ [accessed May 12, 2010].

16. The White House, "Press Briefing by Press Secretary Robert Gibbs," January 26, 2009; available at: http://www.whitehouse.gov/the-press-office/press-briefing-12609 [accessed May 25, 2010].

17. "The Inefficiency of Targeted Tax Policies," Joint Economic Committee Report, Jim Saxton, Chairman, April 1997; available at: http://www.house.gov/jec/fiscal/tx-grwth/targets.htm [accessed May 12, 2010].

18. Lance Banning, ed., *Liberty and Order, op. cit.*

19. Federalist #62.

20. Rick Klein, "Kennedy Faces Fight on Cape Wind," *Boston Globe*, April 27, 2006; available at: http://www.boston.com/news/nation/articles/2006/04/27/kennedy_faces_fight_on_cape_wind/ [accessed May 25, 2010].

21. Robert F. Kennedy Jr., "An Ill Wind Off Cape Cod," *New York Times*, December 16, 2005; available at: http://www.nytimes.com/2005/12/16/opinion/16kennedy.html [accessed May 13, 2010].

22. Juliet Eilpperin, "Offshore wind farm near Cape Cod, first in U.S., gets federal approval," *Washington Post*, April 28, 2010; available at: http://www.washingtonpost.com/wp-dyn/content/article/2010/04/28/AR2010042804398.html?sid=ST20100 42806249 [accessed May 25, 2010].

23. "Annual Estimates of the Loss of Households' Purchasing Power Under H.R. 2454," Letter to the Honorable Christopher Smith,

Congressional Budget Office, April 20, 2010. At the request of Representative Chris Smith (R, NJ), the CBO estimated the lost purchasing power of American households as a result of the American Clean Energy and Security Act of 2009, which would cap carbon emissions in the United States. "Measured in terms of the 2010 economy, the average loss per household would be $90 for 2012, $550 for 2030, and $930 for 2050; it would average about $460 per year over the 2012-2050 period," said CBO.

24. "Proceedings of the First International Scientific Meeting on the Polar Bear at Fairbanks, Alaska, 6–10, September, 1965," U.S. Department of Interior, Bureau of Sport Fisheries and Wildlife, and The University of Alaska, 56; available at: http://pbsg.npolar.no/export/sites/pbsg/en/docs/PBSG00proc.pdf [accessed May 25, 2010].

25. Ibid., 7.

26. Ibid., 11.

27. Ibid., 45.

28. Ibid., 66.

29. Compiled and edited by Jon Aars, Nicholas J. Lunn, and Andrew E. Derocher, "Proceedings of the 14th Working Meeting of the IUCN/SSC Polar Bear Specialist Group, 20-24 June, 2005, Seattle, Washington, USA, Occassional Paper of the IUCN Species Survival Commission No. 32; available at: http://pbsg.npolar.no/export/sites/pbsg/en/docs/PBSG14proc.pdf [accessed May 25, 2010].

30. Ibid., 20.

31. Ibid., 33.

32. Center for Biological Diversity, "Action Timeline"; available at: http://www.biologicaldiversity.org/species/mammals/polar_bear/action_timeline.html [accessed May 25, 2010].

33. "Before the Secretary of the Interior: Petition to List the Polar Bear (Ursus maritimus) As a Threatened Species Under the Endangered Species Act," Center for Biological Diversty, February 16, 2003; available at: http://www.biologicaldiversity.org/species/mammals/polar_bear/pdfs/15976_7338.pdf [accessed May 25, 2010].

34. 515 U.S. 687 (1995).

35. "Before the Secretary of the Interior: Petition to List the Polar Bear (Ursus maritimus) As a Threatened Species Under the Endangered Species Act," Center for Biological Diversty, *op. cit.*

36. Ibid.

37. Ibid.

38. Eugene H. Buck, CRS Report for Congress, "Polar Bears: Proposed Listing Under the Endangered Species Act," Updated March 30, 2007; available at: http://www.fas.org/sgp/crs/misc/RL33941.pdf [accessed May 13, 2010].

39. U.S. Department of the Interior, "Remarks by Secretary Kempthorne, Press Conference On Polar Bear Listing, May 14, 2008," available at: http://www.doi.gov/archive/secretary/speeches/081405_speech.html [accessed May 25, 2010].

40. "Q & A: Professor Phil Jones," BBC, February 13, 2010; available at: http://news.bbc.co.uk/2/hi/8511670.stm [accessed May 13, 2010]. The BBC asked Jones: "Do you agree that from 1995 to the present there has been no statistically significant global warming?" Jones answered: "Yes, but only just. I also calculated the trend for the period 1995 to 2009. This trend (0.12C per decade) is positive, but not significant at the 95% significance level. The positive trend is quite close to the significance level. Achieving statistical significance in scientific terms is much more likely for longer periods, and much less likely for shorter periods."

41. Press Release, "Harvard Kennedy School's John P. Holdren Named Obama's Science Advisor," Belfer Center for Science and International Affairs, December 20, 2008; available at: http://belfercenter.ksg.harvard.edu/publication/18738/harvard_kenned y_schools_john_p_holdren_named_obamas_science_advisor.html?bre adcrumb=%2Fexperts%2F946%2Fsasha_talcott%3Fback_url%3D%2 52Fpublication%252F20069%252Fon_eve_of_nuclear_security_sum mit_faster_broader_global_effort_needed_to_secure_all_nuclear_mat erials_in_four_years%26back_text%3DBack%2520to%2520publicatio n%26page%3D3 [accessed May 13, 2010].

42. The Office of the President Elect, Change.gov, "Remarks of the President-Elect Barack Obama, Science Team Rollout Radio Address, Friday, December 17, 2008, Chicago, Illiniois: available at: http://change.gov/newsroom/entry/the_search_for_knowledge_truth_a nd_a_greater_understanding_of_the_world_aro/ [accessed May 25, 2010]. See also, Terence P. Jeffrey, "The Global Redistributionist at Obama's Left Hand," CNSNews.com, August 5, 2009; available at: http://www.cnsnews.com/public/content/article.aspx?RsrcID=52051 [accessed May 13, 2010].

43. Paul Ehrlich, *Population Bomb* (Buccaneer Books, 1997).

44. Ibid.

45. John P. Holdren, "Population and the American Predicament: The Case Against Complacency," Caltech Population Program Occasional Papers, The California Institute of Technology, Pasadena, California, 1973; available at: http://www.eric.ed.gov/ERICDocs/ data/ericdocs2sql/content_storage_01/0000019b/80/39/60/78.pdf [accessed May 25, 2010].

46. Thomas Robert Malthus, *An Essay on the Principle of Population* (W.W. Norton and Company, 2003).

47. Paul R. Ehrlich, Anne H. Ehrlich, and John P. Holdren, *op.cit.*, see, for example, pp. 12–13.

48. Ibid., 12, 206–7.

49. Ibid., 12.

50. Ibid., 12–13.

51. Ibid., 221.

52. Ibid., 277.

53. Ibid., 278.

54. Kenneth Ewart Boulding, "The Economics of the Coming Spaceship Earth," in Environmental Quality in a Growing Economy, ed. H. Jarrett (Baltimore: Resources for the Future/Johns Hopkins University Press, 1966), 3–14. See also: Paul R. Ehrlich, Anne H. Ehrlich, and John P. Holdren, *op.cit.*, 260–62.

55. Paul R. Ehrlich, Anne H. Ehrlich, and John P. Holdren, op.cit., p. 274.

56. Ibid., 278.

57. Ibid., 279.

58. Ibid.

59. Ibid., 262.

60. Ibid., 263.

61. Ibid., 264.

62. Ibid., 266.

63. Ibid.

64. Ibid., 265.

65. Julian L. Simon, "Resources, Population, Environment: An Oversupply of False Bad News," *Science, New Series*, Vol. 208, No. 4451, (June 27, 1980), 1431–37; and also Julian L. Simon,*The Ultimate Resource* (Princeton, NJ: Princeton University Press, 1981).

66. Julian Simon, *The Ultimate Resource*, 3–29.

67. Ibid., 54–69.

68. Ibid., 42–53; 216; 257–288; 343–348.

69. Ibid., 42–53.

70. Ibid., 49.

71. Ibid., 44.

72. Ibid., 196–203; 222; 271; 332–48.

73. Ibid., 345–46.

74. Ibid., 348.

75. Ed Regis, "The Doomslayer," *Wired*, Issue 5.02, February 1997; available at: http://www.wired.com/wired/archive/5.02/ffsimon.html?topic 1 topic_set= [accessed May 25, 2010].

76. John Tierny, "Betting on the Planet," *New York Times*, December 2, 1990; available at: http://www.nytimes.com/1990/12/02/magazine/betting-on-the-planet.html?sec=&spon=&pagewanted=all [accessed May 13, 2010].

77. Ibid.

78. John P. Holdren., Gretchen C. Daily, and Paul R. Ehrlich, "The Meaning of Sustainability: Biogeophysical Aspects," in *Defining and Measuring Sustainability: The Biogeophysical Foundations*, ed. Mohan

Munasinghe and Walter Shearer (Washington, D.C.: Distributed for the United Nations University by The World Bank, 1995), 13.

79. Ibid., 12–13.

80. Ibid., 14–15.

81. U.S. Senate Committee on Commerce, Science and Transportation, Hearings, Executive Session, Feb. 12, 2009, 10:00 AM, Archived Webcast, Exchange Between Senator David Vitter and John P. Holdren was transcribed from the video by the author; exchange is found between 1:16:06 in the video and 1:26:16; available at: http://commerce.senate.gov/public/index.cfm?p=Hearings&ContentRecord_id=e24ac4c4-1119-4ad2-8c0d-4b210ed8340c&ContentType_id=14f995b9-dfa5-407a-9d35-56cc7152a7ed&Group_id=b06c39af-e033-4cba-9221-de668ca1978a&MonthDisplay=2&YearDisplay=2009 [accessed May 25, 2010]; see also, Christopher Neefus, "Obama's Top Science Adviser to Congress: Earth Could Be Reaching Global Warming 'Tipping Point' That Would Be Followed by a Dramatic Rise in Sea Level," CNSNews.com, December 10, 2009; available at: http://www.cnsnews.com/news/article/58316 [accessed May 13, 2010].

82. Terence P. Jeffrey, "Rockefeller Refers to Obama's Science Czar as 'Walking on Water,'" CNSNews.com, August 19, 2009; available at: http://www.cnsnews.com/news/article/52757 [accessed May 13, 2010].

Chapter 5

1. The video of President Obama's full January 27, 2010, State of the Union Address as broadcast by CBS is available on YouTube. Justice Alito's reaction can be seen on this recording at approximately the 46:33 mark; available at: http://www.youtube.com/watch?v=rTMrs9vpoqg [accessed May 26, 2010]. An Associated Press video of the particular segment of the speech where Justice Alito reacts to President Obama is also, posted on YouTube; available at: http://www.youtube.com/watch?v=k92SerxLWtc [accessed May 26, 2010]. The Associated Press reported that Alito "appeared to mouth

the words 'not true' or 'simply not true.'" See: "Alito disparages Obama's Supreme Court criticism," Associated Press, *Boston Herald*, January 28, 2010; available at: http://bostonherald.com/news/us_politics/view/20100128alito_disparages_obamas_supreme_court_criticism/. *The New York Daily News* reported that Alito "appeared to mouth 'Not true.'" See: Neil Nagraj, "Justice Alito mouths 'not true' when Obama blasts Supreme Court ruling in State of the Union address," NYDailyNews.com, January 28, 2010; available at: http://www.nydaily news.com/news/politics/2010/01/28/2010-01-28_jutice_alito_mouths_ not_true_when_obama_blasts_supreme_court_ruling_in_state_of.html.

2. 558 U.S. _ (2010). Concurring opinion of Chief Justice John Roberts.

3. "Editorializing by Broadcast Licensees," 13 F.C.C. 1246; 1949, p. 1264; available at: http://fcc.gov/ftp/Bureaus/Mass_Media/Databases/documents_collection/490608.pdf [accessed May 26, 2010].

4. The White House, "Remarks by the President in the State of the Union Address," January 27, 2010; available at: http://www.whitehouse.gov/the-press-office/remarks-president-state-union-address [accessed May 26, 2010].

5. See note 1, chapter 5.

6. Federalist #45.

7. *The Debates in Several State Conventions On the Adoption of the Federal Constitution As Recommended by the General Convention in Philadelphia in 1787*, ed. Jonathan Elliot (Washington: Printed for the Editor, 1836), 462; available at: http://memory.loc.gov/cgi-bin/query/D?hlaw:1:./temp/~ammem_zSOT:: [accessed May 26, 2010].

8. Ibid., 469.

9. Brief for Appellant at [_]-[_], *Citizens United* v. *Fed. Election Comm'n*, 130 S.Ct. 876 (2010) (No. 08-205); available at: http://www.abanet.org/publiced/preview/briefs/pdfs/07-08/08-205_Appellant.pdf [accessed May 13, 2010].

10. "Just Veto Them, Mr. President," *Human Events*, July 25, 2006; available at: http://www.humanevents.com/article.php?id=16193 [accessed May 11, 2010].

11. "Citizens United v. Federal Election Commission—Oral Argument," Oyez; transcript available at: http://www.oyez.org/cases/2000-2009/2008/2008_08_205/argument [accessed May 11, 2010].

12. Ibid.

13. 558 U.S. _ (2010).

14. Ibid.

15. Representative Wallace White explained the purpose and results of the 1925 radio conference in a speech on the floor of the U.S. House of Representatives. The speech appears in the Congressional Record for March 12, 1926, pp. 5478–80; See also: Steven J. Simmons, *The Fairness Doctrine and the Media* (Berkeley, Los Angeles, London: University of California Press, 1978), 16–22.

16. U.S. Congress. 67 Congressional Record, House, p. 5479.

17. Ibid., 5480. See also, Terence P. Jeffrey, "Silencing the Opposition," Townhall.com, March 18, 2009; available at: http://townhall.com/columnists/TerryJeffrey/2009/03/18/silencing_the_opposition [accessed May 11, 2010].

18. Ibid.

19. U.S. Congress. 67 Congressional Record, Senate, p. 12335.

20. House Rept. No. 464, 69th Cong., first sess. (1926); Minority views of Representative Davis, p. 16, as quoted in "Legislative History of the Fairness Doctrine: Staff Study for the Committee on Interstate and Foreign Commerce, House of Representatives, Ninetieth Congress, Second Session, February 1968" (Washington: U.S. Government Printing Office, 1968).

21. U.S. Congress. 67 Congressional Record, Senate, 12501.

22. Ibid.

23. Ibid. See also, Terence P. Jeffrey, "Silencing the Opposition," Townhall.com, March 18, 2009; available at: http://townhall.com/columnists/TerryJeffrey/2009/03/18/silencing_the_opposition [accessed May 11, 2010].

24. "Legislative History of the Fairness Doctrine: Staff Study for the Committee on Interstate and Foreign Commerce, House of Representa-

tives, Ninetieth Congress, Second Session, February 1968," (Washington: U.S. Government Printing Office, 1968). See also: Steven J. Simmons, *The Fairness Doctrine and the Media*, 25–26.

25. Ibid.

26. "Regulation of Radio Communication, Conference Report," 69th Congress, 2nd Session, House of Representatives, Report No. 1886, January 27, 1927.

27. Terence P. Jeffrey, "Silencing the Opposition," *Townhall* Magazine, February 2009, available at: http://townhall.com/columnists/TerryJeffrey/2009/03/18/silencing_the_opposition [accessed May 11, 2010].

28. Federal Communications Commission, "Message from the President of the United States Recommending that Congress Create a New Agency to Be Known as The Federal Communications Commission," February 26, 1934, 73rd Congress, 2nd Session, Senate, Document No. 144; available at: http://www.fcc.gov/Bureaus/OSEC/library/legislative_histories/40.pdf [accessed May 27, 2010].

29. "Legislative History of the Fairness Doctrine: Staff Study for the Committee on Interstate and Foreign Commerce," House of Representatives, Ninetieth Congress, Second Session, February 1968, (Washington: U.S. Government Printing Office, 1968).

30. Ibid.

31. Public Law No. 416, June 19, 1934, 73d Congress.

32. "In the matter of the application of Great Lakes Broadcasting Co.," 3 FRC *Annual Report* 32 (1929).

33. Ibid. See also, Terence P. Jeffrey, "Silencing the Opposition," *op. cit.*

34. "Radio: Sinking of the Mayflower," *Time*, June 13, 1949; available at: http://www.time.com/time/magazine/article/0,9171,800314,00.html. See also, Steven J. Simmons, *The Fairness Doctrine and the Media*, 37–38. See also, "Legislative History of the Fairness Doctrine: Staff Study for the Committee on Interstate and Foreign Commerce, House of Representatives, Ninetieth Congress, Second Session, February 1968," (Washington: U.S. Government Printing Office, 1968). See also, Fred W. Friendly, *The Good Guys, the Bad Guys, and the First*

Amendment (New York: Vintage Books, A Division of Random House, 1976), 21–22. See also, The "Separate Views of Commissioner Jones" in "Appendix Before the Federal Communications Commission In the Matter of Editorializing Broadcast License," Federal Communications Commission, March/April 1948; available at: http://www.fcc.gov/Bureaus/Mass_Media/Databases/documents_collection/490608.pdf [accessed May 11, 2010].

35. "Legislative History of the Fairness Doctrine: Staff Study for the Committee on Interstate and Foreign Commerce," Steven J. Simmons, *The Fairness Doctrine and the Media*, 37–38.

36. "Radio: Sinking of the Mayflower," *Time*, June 13, 1949; available at: http://www.time.com/time/magazine/article/0,9171,800314,00.html [accessed June 4, 2010].

37. Brief for the Federal Respondents in Opposition at [_]-[_], *Syracuse Peace Council v. Fed. Communications Comm'n*, 493 U.S. 1019 (1990) (No. 89-312). Available at: http://justice.gov/odg/briefs/1989/sg89039-0.txt [accessed May 27, 2010]. See also: "Legislative History of the Fairness Doctrine: Staff Study for the Committee on Interstate and Foreign Commerce."

38. "Appendix Before the Federal Communications Commission In the Matter of Editorializing Broadcast License," Federal Communications Commission, March/April 1948; available at: http://www.fcc.gov/Bureaus/Mass_Media/Databases/documents_collection/490608.pdf [accessed May 11, 2010].

39. *Commissioners of the FCC: 1927-1994*, ed. Gerald V. Flannery (Lanham, Maryland: University Press of America, 1995), 96–98.

40. "Appendix Before the Federal Communications Commission In the Matter of Editorializing Broadcast License," Federal Communications Commission, March/April 1948; "Dissenting Views of Commissioner Hennock," available at: http://www.fcc.gov/Bureaus/Mass_Media/Databases/documents_collection/490608.pdf [accessed May 11, 2010].

41. "Appendix Before the Federal Communications Commission In the Matter of Editorializing Broadcast License," *op. cit.*

42. *Commissioners of the FCC: 1927-1994*, ed. Gerald V. Flannery, 84–86.

43. "Appendix Before the Federal Communications Commission In the Matter of Editorializing Broadcast License." "Additional Views of Commissioner E.M. Webster," available at: http://www.fcc.gov/ Bureaus/Mass_Media/Databases/documents_collection/490608.pdf [accessed May 11, 2010].

44. Biographical Directory of the United States Congress, "Jones, Robert Franklin, (1907-1968)," available at: http://bioguide.congress. gov/scripts/biodisplay/pl?index=J000249 [accessed May 27, 2010].

45. "Appendix Before the Federal Communications Commission In the Matter of Editorializing Broadcast License," and "Separate Views of Commissioner Jones"; available at: http://www.fcc.gov/Bureaus/ Mass_Media/Databases/documents_collection/490608.pdf [accessed May 11, 2010].

46. Fred W. Friendly, *The Good Guys, The Bad Guys And The First Amendment: Free Speech Vs. Fairness in Broadcasting* (New York: Vintage Books, A Division of Random House, 1976), 39.

47. Ibid., 41–42.

48. Brief for the Federal Respondents in Opposition at [_]-[_], *Syracuse Peace Council v. Fed. Communications Comm'n*, 493 U.S. 1019 (1990) (No. 89-312). Available at: http://justice.gov/odg/briefs/1989/sg89039-0.txt [accessed May 27, 2010].

49. Kenneth R. Noble, "Reagan Vetoes Measure to Affirm Fairness Policy for Broadcasters," *New York Times*, June 21, 1987.

50. H.R. 501, 109th Congress, 1st Session (2005).

51. John Gizzi, "Pelosi Supports 'Fairness Doctrine,'" *Human Events*, June 25, 2008; available at: http://www.humanevents.com/article. php?id=27185 [accessed May 11, 2010].

52. Interview with Jeff Bingaman by Jim Villanucci, KKOB (Albequerque), posted October 22, 2008; recording available at: http://www. youtube.com/watch?v=cKCWiFA0Eq0 [accessed May 11, 2010].

53. Congressional Record, Senate, July 13, 2007, S9194.

54. Ibid.

55. House Roll Call 599, June 28, 2007.

56. John Halpin, James Heidbreder, Mark Lloyd, Paul Woodhull, Ben Scott, Josh Silver, and S. Derek Turner, "The Structural Imbalance of Political Talk Radio," Center for American Progress, June 20, 2007; available at: http://www.americanprogress.org/issues/2007/06/talk_radio.html [accessed May 11, 2010].

57. Ibid.

58. Julian L. Simon, *The Ultimate Resource* (New Jersey: Princeton University Press, 1981).

Chapter 6

1. The Declaration of Independence,

2. Alexander Hamilton, "The Farmer Refuted," February 5, 1775, in *The Works of Alexander Hamilton*, Vol. 1, ed. Henry Cabot Lodge (New York and London: G.P. Putnam's Sons, 1904), 53–177; available at: http://oll.libertyfund.org/index.php?option=com_staticxt&staticfile=show.php%3Ftitle=1378&layout=html#chapter_64144 [accessed May 28, 2010].

3. The American Presidency Project, "Remarks at the Saddleback Civil Forum on the Presidency in Lake Forest California," August 16, 2008; available at: http://www.presidency.ucsb.edu/ws/index.php?pid=77822 [accessed May 28, 2010].

4. Jill L. Stanek of Mokena, Illinois, who worked as a nurse at Christ Hospital in Oak Lawn, Illinois, described this scene in a written statement presented to the Subcommittee on the Constitution of the Committee on the Judiciary on July 20, 2000. Stanek said in her statement to the subcommittee: "I am a Registered Nurse who has worked in the Labor & Delivery Department at Christ Hospital in Oak Lawn, Illinois, for the past five years. Christ Hospital performs abortions on women in their second or even third trimesters of pregnancy. Sometimes the babies being aborted are healthy, and sometimes they are not. The method of abortion that Christ Hospital uses is called

'induced labor abortion,' also now known as 'live birth abortion.' This type of abortion can be performed different ways, but the goal always is to cause a pregnant woman's cervix to open so that she will deliver a premature baby who dies during the birth process or soon afterward. The way that induced abortion is most often executed at my hospital is by the physician inserting a medication called Cytotec into the birth canal close to the cervix. Cytotec irritates the cervix and stimulates it to open. When this occurs, the small, preterm baby drops out of the uterus, oftentimes alive. It is not uncommon for one of these live aborted babies to linger for an hour or two or even longer. One of them once lived for almost eight hours. In the event that a baby is aborted alive, he or she receives no medical assessments or care but is only given what my hospital calls 'comfort care.' 'Comfort care' is defined as keeping the baby warm in a blanket until he or she dies, although even this minimal compassion is not always provided. It is not required that these babies be held during their short lives. One night, a nursing co-worker was taking an aborted Down's Syndrome baby who was born alive to our Soiled Utility Room because his parents did not want to hold him, and she did not have time to hold him. I could not bear the thought of this suffering child dying alone in a Soiled Utility Room, so I cradled and rocked him for the 45 minutes that he lived. He was 21 to 22 weeks old, weighed about 1/2 pound, and was about 10 inches long. He was too weak to move very much, expending any energy he had trying to breathe. Toward the end he was so quiet that I couldn't tell if he was still alive unless I held him up to the light to see if his heart was still beating through his chest wall. After he was pronounced dead, we folded his little arms across his chest, wrapped him in a tiny shroud, and carried him to the hospital morgue where all of our dead patients are taken." Prepared Statement of Jill L. Stanek, Mokena, IL., 67-226, Born Alive Infant Protection Act of 2000, Hearing Before the Subcommittee on the Constitution of the Committee on the Judiciary, House of Representatives, One Hundred Sixth Congress, Second

Session, On H.R. 4292, July 20, 2000, Serial No. 120; available at: http://commdocs.house.gov/committees/judiciary/hju67226.000/hju67 226_0f.htm [accessed May 28, 2010]. Stanek also described the event in an interview with author, see: Terence P. Jeffrey, "Delivery Nurse Describes Obama's Efforts to Stop a Law to Protect Babies Who Survived Abortion," CNSNews.com, January 29, 2009; available at: http://www.cnsnews.com/news/article/42688 [accessed May 28, 2010]. Stanek repeated her testimony before the House Subcommittee in 2001; see Born Alive Infant Protection Act of 2001, Hearing Before the Subcommittee on the Constitution of the Committee on the Judiciary, House of Representatives, One Hundred Seventh Congress, First Session, On H.R. 2175, July 12, 2001, Serial No. 32; available at: http://commdocs.house.gov/committees/judiciary/hju73696.000/hju73 696_0.HTM [accessed May 28, 2010].

5.   On April 23, 1999, Jill Stanek wrote a letter to chairman of the OB-GYN department, the vice president for Religion & Health, the director of Women's & Infants Health Services, and the chair of the ethics committee for Christ Hospital & Medical Center complaining about the induced-labor abortions conducted at the hospital. In the letter she said: ". . . [B]ut I believe it is incongruent with our Mission Statement to intervene directly to take their lives. Rather, we should teach parents alternative approaches and frames of mind to bringing defective children into the world which would be consistent with our medical ethics, our Mission Statement, and our hospital's strong Judeo-Christian base. This approach would be to encourage treatment of these children as imperfect but still as special as you or I, as we are all created in the image of God. I am aware of a couple to whom abortion was recommended because of a congenital defect in their child. They chose, however, to carry their baby to term and were able to hold and love her for the 20 minutes that she lived. This is an example of the guidance a Christian hospital should give." The letter is included in: Born Alive Infant Protection Act of 2001, Hearing Before the Sub-

committee on the Constitution of the Committee on the Judiciary, House of Representatives, One Hundred Seventh Congress, First Session, On H.R. 2175, July 12, 2001, Serial No. 32; available at: http://commdocs.house.gov/committees/judiciary/hju73696.000/hju73 696_0.HTM [accessed May 28, 2010].

6. Prepared Statement of Jill L. Stanek, Mokena, IL., 67-226, Born Alive Infant Protection Act of 2000, Hearing Before the Subcommittee on the Constitution of the Committee on the Judiciary, House of Representatives, One Hundred Sixth Congress, Second Session, On H.R. 4292, July 20, 2000, Serial No. 120; available at: http://commdocs.house.gov/committees/judiciary/hju67226.000/hju67 226_0f.htm [accessed May 28, 2010]. See also, Born Alive Infant Protection Act of 2001, Hearing Before the Subcommittee on the Constitution of the Committee on the Judiciary, House of Representatives, One Hundred Seventh Congress, First Session, On H.R. 2175, July 12, 2001, Serial No. 32, *op. cit.*

7. Prepared Statement of Allison Baker, Charlottesville, VA, 67-226, Born Alive Infant Protection Act of 2000, Hearing Before the Subcommittee on the Constitution of the Committee on the Judiciary, House of Representatives, One Hundred Sixth Congress, Second Session, On H.R. 4292, July 20, 2000, Serial No. 120; available at: http://commdocs.house.gov/committees/judiciary/hju67226.000/hju67 226_0f.htm [accessed May 28, 2010].

8. Ibid.

9. The National Institutes of Health's "Facts About Down Syndrome" describes three prenatal tests for Down Syndrome: amniocentesis, chorionic villus sampling, and percutaneous umbilical blood sampling (PUBS). The sheet says "amniocentesis cannot be done until the 14th to 18th week of pregnancy, and it usually takes additional time to determine whether the cells contain extra material from chromosome 21." Chorionic villus sampling is "conducted at 9 to 11 weeks of pregnancy," the NIH says, but "carries a 1-2% risk of miscarriage." "PUBS," says the NIH,

"cannot be performed until later in the pregnancy, during the 18th to 22nd weeks, and carries the greatest risk of miscarriage." See: National Institutes of Health, Eunice Kennedy Shriver National Institute of Child Health and Human Development, "Facts About Down Syndrome"; available at: http://www.nichd.nih.gov/publications/ pubs/downsyndrome. cfm#Prenatal [accessed May 28, 2010]. The NIH says that ultrasound and "maternal serum alpha fetoprotein" (MSAFP) are the most common tests for spina bifida and that amniocentesis can also be used to diagnose the defect. Both MSAFP and amniocentesis are done in the second trimester. "The most common screening methods used to look for spina bifida during pregnancy are second trimester maternal serum alpha fetoprotein (MSAFP) screening and fetal ultrasound," says the NIH Spina Bifida Fact Sheet. See: National Institutes of Health, National Institute of Neurological Disorder and Stroke, "Spina Bifida Fact Sheet"; available: http://www.ninds.nih.gov/disorders/spina_bifida/detail_spina_bifida. htm#106493258 [accessed May 28, 2010].

10. National Institutes of Health, Eunice Kennedy Shriver National Institute of Child Health and Human Development, "Facts About Down Syndrome"; available at: http://www.nichd.nih.gov/publications/ pubs/downsyndrome.cfm#Prenatal [accessed May 28, 2010].

11. National Institutes of Health, National Institute of Neurological Disorder and Stroke, "Spina Bifida Fact Sheet"; available at: http://www.ninds.nih.gov/disorders/spina_bifida/detail_spina_bifida.ht m#106493258 [accessed May 28, 2010].

12. Ibid.

13. Prepared Statement of Jill L. Stanek, Mokena, IL., 67-226, Born Alive Infant Protection Act of 2000, Hearing Before the Subcommittee on the Constitution of the Committee on the Judiciary, House of Representatives, One Hundred Sixth Congress, Second Session, On H.R. 4292, July 20, 2000, Serial No. 120; *op. cit.* See also: Born Alive Infant Protection Act of 2001, Hearing Before the Subcommittee on the Constitution of the Committee on the Judiciary, House of Representatives,

One Hundred Seventh Congress, First Session, On H.R. 2175, July 12, 2001, Serial No. 32. *op. cit.*

14. Ibid.

15. Terence P. Jeffrey, "Delivery Nurse Describes Obama's Efforts to Stop a Law to Protect Babies Who Survived Abortion," CNSNews.com, January 29, 2009; available at: http://www.cnsnews.com/news/article/42688 [accessed May 28, 2010]. See also Stanek's April 23, 1999, letter to leaders of Christ Hospital cited in note 5, chapter 6.

16. Office of the Attorney General, State of Illinois, Letter from Chief Deputy Attorney General Carole R. Doris to Ms. Karen Hayes, Director, Concerned Women for America, July 17, 2000. The letter is reproduced in: Born Alive Infant Protection Act of 2001, Hearing Before the Subcommittee on the Constitution of the Committee on the Judiciary, House of Representatives, One Hundred Seventh Congress, First Session, On H.R. 2175, July 12, 2001, Serial No. 32; available at: http://commdocs.house.gov/committees/judiciary/hju73696.000/hju73696_0.HTM [accessed May 28, 2010].

17. State of Illinois, 92nd General Assembly, Regular Session, Senate Transcript, 20th Legislative Day, March 30, 2001; State Senator Barack Obama discusses the committee testimony on the issue on pages 85–87.

18. On March 30, 2001, State Senator Barack Obama voted "present" on Senate Bill 1095, the Born Alive Infant bill, sponsored by Senator Patrick O'Malley. The bill would have defined all born babies as "persons," stating: "In determining the meaning of any statute or of any rule, regulation, or interpretation of the various administrative agencies of this State, the words 'person', 'human being', 'child', and 'individual' include every infant member of the species homo sapiens who is born alive at any stage of development." A "present" vote has the same effect as a "no" vote in the Illinois senate, because a bill needs to secure a majority of the full membership of that legislative body to be passed. The transcript of the Senate debate cited above demonstrates

that Obama was the only member of the Illinois senate to speak against Senate Bill 1095. The vote is recorded at: Illinois Senate, 92nd General Assembly, Roll Call, SB1095, Third Reading, O'Malley, Born Alive Infant Defined, Sequence No. 30, March 30, 2001, 11:40 a.m., PG17. The text of SB1095 is available on the Illinois General Assembly Web site at: http://www.ilga.gov/legislation/legisnet92/sbgroups/sb/920SB1095LV.html [accessed May 30, 2010]. In 2002, Obama voted "No" on the Born Alive Infant Bill. The vote is recorded at: Illinois Senate, 92nd General Assembly, Senate Vote, Senate Bill No. 1662, Third Reading, April 4, 2002. The text of SB1662 is available on the Illinois General Assembly Web site at: http://ilga.gov/legislation/legisnet92/sbgroups/sb/920SB1662LV.html [accessed May 30, 2010]. On March 31, 2003, State Senator Barack Obama brought up the Born Alive Infant bill, Senate Bill 1082, now sponsored by Senator Rich Winkel, in the Illinois Senate Health and Human Services Committee, which Obama chaired. The bill was defeated, 4–6, with Obama voting "No." The text of SB1082 is available at the Illinois General Assembly Web site at: http://www.ilga.gov/legislation/fulltext.asp?DocName=09300S-B1082&GA=93&SessionId=3&DocTypeId=SB&LegID=3910&DocNum=1082&GAID=3&Session [accessed May 30, 2010]. The vote was recorded in an official "Senate Committee Action Report" that has been posted by National Right to life. National Right to Life has published an index with links to major documents related to Barack Obama's handling of this legislation. The index is available at: http://www.nrlc.org/ObamaBAIPA/Index.html [accessed May 30, 2010]. The 2003 vote on the bill in the Health and Human Services Committee that Obama chaired was reported at the time by the Associated Press. See: Kristy Hessman, "Lawmakers Approve Abortion-Friendly Legislation," Associated Press, March 13, 2003. See also, Terence P. Jeffrey, "More on Obama and Babies Born Alive," CNSNews.com, Wednesday, January 16, 2008; available at: http://www.cnsnews.com/news/article/44500 [accessed May 29, 2010].

FactCheck.org did an analysis of Obama's votes on these, "Obama and 'Infanticide': The facts about Obama's votes against 'Born Alive' bills in Illinois," August 25, 2008; available at: http://www.factcheck.org/elec tions-2008/obama_and_infanticide.html [accessed May 30, 2010].

19. State of Illinois, 92nd General Assembly, Regular Session, Senate Transcript, 20th Legislative Day, March 30, 2001, p. 85.

20. Ibid., 85–86.

21. Ibid., 86.

22. On April 18, 2007, the day the Supreme Court issued its opinion in *Gonzales* v. *Carhart*, upholding the constitutionality of the Partial-Birth Abortion Ban Act of 2003, Senator Barack Obama issued a statement saying he "strongly disagreed" with the ruling. His statement is posted on the Web site Organizing for America; available at: http://my.barackobama.com/page/community/post_group/ObamaHQ/ CZsK [accessed May 29, 2010].

23. Speaking to the Planned Parenthood Action Fund on July 17, 2007, Senator Barack Obama said: "Well, the first thing I'd do as president is sign the Freedom of Choice Act. That's the first thing that I'd do." Video of Senator Obama making this statement is posted on YouTube; available at: http://www.youtube.com/watch?v=pf0XIRZSTt8 [accessed May 29, 2010].

24. The American Presidency Project, Remarks at the Saddleback Civil Forum on the Presidency in Lake Forest California, August 16, 2008; available at: http://www.presidency.ucsb.edu/ws/index.php?pid=77822 [accessed May 28, 2010].

25. The White House, "Executive Order—Removing Barriers to Responsible Scientific Research Involving Human Stem Cells," March 9, 2009; available at: http://www.whitehouse.gov/the-press-office/remov-ing-barriers-responsible-scientific-research-involving-human-stem-cells [accessed May 30, 2010].

26. The White House press office put out a list of attendees and participants in the Executive Order signing ceremony that included six Nobel Laureates. A White House blog posting included an official

White House photograph with a caption that said ten Nobel Laureates were in attendance. See: The White House, Office of the Press Secretary, "Participants and Attendees at President Barack Obama's signing of Stem Cell Executive Order and Scientific Integrity Presidential Memorandum," March 9, 2009; available at: http://www.white-house.gov/the-press-office/participants-and-attendees-president-barack-obamas-signing-stem-cell-executive-orde [accessed May 30, 2010]. The caption of a photo of the event posted on the White House Web site blog stated the following: "Surrounded by a group comprised of 30 members of Congress and 10 Nobel Laureates, President Barack Obama offers remarks and then signs the Stem Cell Executive Order and Presidential Memorandum on Scientific Integrity in the East Room of the White House on Monday, March 9, 2009"; available at: http://www.whitehouse.gov/blog/2009/03/09/ldquoa-debt-gratitude-so-many-tireless-advocatesrdquo [accessed May 30, 2010].

27. The event was televised by C-SPAN, and the video is available in the C-CPAN video library. See: C-SPAN Video Library, "U.S. Science Policy, Mar 9, 2009"; available at: http://www.c-spanvideo.org/program/284502-1 [accessed May 30, 2010].

28. The White House, Remarks of President Barack Obama—As Prepared for Delivery, Signing of Stem Cell Executive Order and Scientific Integrity Presidential Memorandum, Washington, D.C., March 9, 2009; available at: http://www.whitehouse.gov/the-press-office/remarks-president-prepared-delivery-signing-stem-cell-executive-order-and-scientifi [accessed May 30, 2010].

29. The Declaration of Independence.

30. Thomas Jefferson, letter to Henry Lee, Monticello, May 8, 1825, in *The Works of Thomas Jefferson*, Vol. XII, ed. Paul Leicester Ford (New York and London: G.P. Putnam's Sons, The Knickerbocker Press, 1905), 250; available at: http://oll.libertyfund.org/?option=com_staticxt&staticfile=show.php%3Ftitle=808&chapter=88496&layout=html&Itemid=27. See also, Clinton Rossiter, *Seedtime of the*

Republic: The Origin of the American Tradition of Political Liberty (New York: Harcourt, Brace & World, Inc., 1953), 355–56.

31. According to Henry Cabot Lodge, who edited the works of Alexander Hamilton, Hamilton was born on January 11, 1757, and published "The Farmer Refuted" on February 5, 1775, less than a month after his 18th birthday. See: Henry Cabot Lodge, ed., *The Works of Alexander Hamilton*, Vol. 1 *op. cit.*, xxi, 55; available at: http://oll.liberty-fund.org/index.php?option=com_staticxt&staticfile=show.php%3Ftitle=1378&layout=html#chapter_64144 [accessed May 28, 2010]. Hamilton biographer Forrest McDonald writes: "In the winter of 1774-75 he [Hamilton] published two major political tracts, *A Full Vindication of the Measures of the Congress* and *The Farmer Refuted*, in a polemical battle with the Anglican minister and Tory Samuel Seabury. Hamilton's pair of articles, totaling around 60,000 words, were dashed off in about two weeks apiece and published anonymously: when their authorship became known, there was general astonishment that one so young could have written them." See: Forrest McDonald, *Alexander Hamilton: A Biography* (New York, London: W.W. Norton & Company, 1982), 13.

32. Richard B. Vernier, ed., *The Revolutionary Writings of Alexander Hamilton*, with a Foreword by Joyce O. Appleby (Indianapolis, IN: Liberty Fund, 2008), 16, 40; available at: http://oll.libertyfund.org/index.php?option=com_staticxt&staticfile=show.php%3Ftitle=2121&Itemid=28 [accessed May 30, 2010]. See also: Forrest McDonald, *Alexander Hamilton, op. cit.*, 13.

33. Henry Cabot Lodge, ed., *The Works of Alexander Hamilton*, Vol. 1, p. 62.

34. Ibid., 63.

35. Ibid.

36. Ibid., 113.

37. Hamilton biographer Forrest McDonald writes: "Similarly, writing in 1794 in denunciation of the Whiskey Rebellion, Hamilton would use

the name 'Tully' to invoke 'memory of Cicero's invective against the horrid conspiracy of Cataline.'" McDonald, in a footnote, credits this point to Douglas Adair, "A Note on Certain of Alexander Hamilton's Pseudonyms," *William and Mary Quarterly*, 12:284, 285 (April 1955). Forrest McDonald, *Alexander Hamilton, op. cit.*, 86, 383. Hamilton's four essays on the Whiskey Rebellion, signed by "Tully," appear in: Henry Cabot Lodge, ed., *The Works of Alexander Hamilton*, Vol. 6, *op. cit.*, 410–26; available at: http://oll.libertyfund.org/index.php?option=com_staticxt&staticfile=show.php%3Ftitle=1383&layout=html. In 1795, in an essay defending the treaty John Jay had negotiated with Great Britain, Hamilton referred to another writer "who disgraces the name of Cicero by adopting it." See: Henry Cabot Lodge, ed., *The Works of Alexander Hamilton*, Vol. 5, *op. cit.*, 473; available at: http://oll.libertyfund.org/index.php?option=com_staticxt&staticfile=show.php%3Ftitle=1382&layout=html [accessed May 31, 2010]. In the outline for his speech to the convention of 1787, in which he introduced his own proposal for a constitution, Hamilton included a line of references ("Aristotle — Cicero — Montesquieu — Neckar") immediately after the note "British constitution best form." See Henry Cabot Lodge, ed., *The Works of Alexander Hamilton*, Vol. 1, *op. cit.*, 374; available at: http://oll.libertyfund.org/index.php?option=com_staticxt&staticfile=show.php%3Ftitle=1378&layout=html [accessed May 31, 2010].

38. Russell Kirk, *The Roots of American Order*, Third Edition (Washington, D.C.: Regnery Gateway, 1991), 105. In *The Roots of American Order*, Kirk discusses "Cicero and the Law of Nature" on pp. 106–13.

39. Clinton Rossiter, *Seedtime of the Republic, op. cit.*, 438. Rossiter writes: "First, the colonists were, as we have insisted repeatedly conscious conservatives. In proclaiming the doctrines of natural law and contract, they held fast to their colonial and English heritage. Not indifference or poverty of intellect, but pride and a sense of history persuaded the colonists to take their stand at the end of the heroic line of Protagoras, Cicero, Aquinas, Hooker, Locke, and Burlamaqui."

40. Marcus Tullius Cicero, *Treatise on the Laws*, in *The Political Works of Marcus Tullius Cicero: Comprising His Treatise on the Commonwealth; and His Treatise on The Laws*, Vol. 2, trans. Francis Barham, Esq. (London: Edmund Spettigue, 1841-42); available at: http://oll.libertyfund.org/index.php?option=com_staticxt&staticfile=show.php%3Ftitle=545&layout=html [accessed May 31, 2010].

41. Marcus Tullius Cicero, Treatise on the Republic, in *The Political Works of Marcus Tullius Cicero: Comprising His Treatise on the Commonwealth; and His Treatise on The Laws*, Vol. 1, trans. Francis Barham, Esq., 270. All but fragments of Cicero's Republic had been lost by the time of the American Revolution. In 1822, however, a fuller copy of it that had been found in the Vatican library was published. Barham writes: "The celebrated treatise of Cicero, 'De Republica;' or the Commonwealth, so highly extolled by ancient writers, and so diligently sought by the scholars of modern Europe, was at length rescued from the slumber of ages, by Angelus Maio, librarian of the Vatican, formerly of the Ambrosian library of Milan, and now raised to the dignity of a Roman cardinal.... Before this, nothing was known of 'The Commonwealth,' save a few fragments which had been preserved in the writings of Macrobius, Lactantius, Augustin, Nonius, and others. Maio published his recovered MSS. (containing the main part of "The Commonwealth,") at Rome, in 1822.... The work has also been translated at New York, in the United States, 1829; if we may trust the *Cyclopædia Americana*, by Mr. Featherstonhaugh.... It is no wonder, therefore, that the recovery of Cicero's 'Commonwealth' by Maio in 1822, made a most immense stir in the literary world. It was criticised and quoted by all the leading periodicals of Europe and America. Senators and lawyers instantly availed themselves of the long-lost, latefound treasure; and it diffused new light and energy through every department of political science." Russell Kirk, who quotes this passage from *The Republic*, writes in a footnote on page 107 of *The Roots of American Order*: "Of The Republic, however, the Americans of Convention times

knew only the portion called, 'The Dream of Scipio,' and some fragments; for a fuller surviving manuscript of that book—much of which
is missing even today—was not discovered until 1820, in the Vatican."
Kirk also says (on page 108 of *The Roots of American Order*): "In
Cicero's writings, they found powerfully expressed the idea of the law
of nature, essential to an understanding of the American social order;
here they studied his book *The Laws*." Russell Kirk, *The Roots of American Order*, 3rd edition (Washington, D.C.: Regnery Gateway, 1991).

42. Ibid.

43. "For as we cannot call the recipes of ignorant empirics, who give poi-
sons instead of medicines, the prescriptions of a physician, we cannot
call that the true law of the people, whatever be its name, if it enjoins
what is injurious, let the people receive it as they will," wrote Cicero.
"For law is the just distinction between right and wrong, conformable
to nature, the original and principal regulator of all things, by which
the laws of men should be measured, whether they punish the guilty
or protect the innocent." Marcus Tullius Cicero, *Treatise on the Laws*,
in *The Political Works of Marcus Tullius Cicero: Comprising His Treatise on the Commonwealth; and His Treatise on The Laws* Vol. 2, trans.
Francis Barham, Esq., *op. cit.*

44. The White House, Remarks of President Barack Obama—As Prepared
for Delivery, Signing of Stem Cell Executive Order and Scientific
Integrity Presidential Memorandum, Washington, D.C., March 9,
2009; available at: http://www.whitehouse.gov/the-press-office/remarks-
president-prepared-delivery-signing-stem-cell-executive-order-and-sci-
entifi [accessed May 30, 2010].

45. Ibid.

46. Ibid.

47. Ibid.

48. Article available at: http://www.breitbart.com/article.php?id=D96QJ
LPO0 [accessed June 1, 2010].

49. The White House, Remarks of President Barack Obama—As Prepared
for Delivery, Signing of Stem Cell Executive Order and Scientific

Integrity Presidential Memorandum, Washington, D.C., March 9, 2009, *op. cit.*

50. The terms "reproductive cloning" and "therapeutic cloning" were used in U.S. House floor debate on the merits of a cloning ban on July 31, 2001. See for example the speech of Democratic Representative Louise Slaughter of New York at Congressional Record, House, July 31, 2001, p. H4907. In the same debate, Democratic Representative Diana DeGette used the terms "reproductive cloning" and "therapeutic cloning" in the same sense. DeGette said: "Reproductive cloning practices which must be banned are an attempt to create a new human being and, as we heard in hearings throughout the spring, there are fringe groups who would like to clone humans. This is wrong, and it must be stopped. Conversely, somatic cell nuclear transfer, or so-called 'therapeutic cloning,' is the way to take stem cell research and all of its promise from the lab to the patient who has diabetes, Parkinson's Disease, Alzheimer's, spinal cord injury, and other health problems." See Congressional Record, House, July 31, 2001, p. H4909.

51. Republican Senator Bob Smith of New Hampshire used the phrase "clone and kill" in Senate debate on August 2, 2001. See Congressional Record, Senate, August 2, 2001, p. S7864; previously available at: 1 0 1 2 1 0&WAISaction=retrieve. A February 10, 2003, statement by the National Right to Life Committee that was entered into the Congressional Record also uses the phrase "clone and kill." See the Congressional Record, February 27, 2003, p. H1400. Republican Representative Chris Smith used the phrase "clone and kill" on the House floor that same day. See Congressional Record, February 27, 2003, p. H1428; previously available at: http://frwebgate5.access.gpo.gov/cgi-bin/PDFgate.cgi?WAISdocID=32419249259 1 0 1 2 1 0&WAIS-action=retrieve [accessed May 31, 2010].

52. CRS Report for Congress, Judith A. Johnson, Specialist in Life Sciences, Domestic Social Policy Division, Erin Williams, Specialist in Bioethical Policy, Domestic Social Policy Division, "Stem Cell Research," updated August 13, 2004, (Congressional Research Service,

The Library of Congress); available at: http://www.fas.org/spp/civil/crs/RL31015.pdf [accessed May 31, 2010].

53. Ibid.

54. H.R. 2560, "The Human Cloning Prohibition Act of 2007"; available at: http://thomas.loc.gov/cgi-bin/query/z?c110:H.R.2560 [accessed May 31, 2010].

55. Congressional Record, House, July 31, 2001, p.H4909; previously available at: http://frwebgate1.access.gpo.gov/cgi-bin/PDFgate.cgi?WAISdocID=325678495847 1 0 1 2 1 0&WAISaction=retrieve [accessed May 31, 2010].

56. Ibid.

57. Ibid.

58. Congressional Record, House, June 6, 2007, p. H6038; available at: http://frwebgate5.access.gpo.gov/cgi-bin/PDFgate.cgi?WAISdocID=32592660071 1 0 1 2 1 0&WAIS-action=retrieve [accessed May 31, 2010].

59. H.R. 4808, "Stem Cell Research Advancement Act of 2009"; available at: http://www.opencongress.org/bill/111-h4808/show [accessed June 1, 2010].

60. Ibid.

Chapter 7

1. "Diocese of Sacramento Will Appeal Catholic Charities Lawsuit to U.S. Supreme Court," *Business Wire*, June 1, 2004; available at: http://www.allbusiness.com/legal/trial-procedure-appeals/5612645-1.html [accessed May 31, 2010].

2. Barack Obama, speech before the Planned Parenthood Action, July 17, 2007; video available at: http://www.imoneinamillion.com/video.php?candidate=obama_speech [accessed May 31, 2010]. The words were transcribed by the author. They appear on the tape at the cited link at 11:13 into the recording.

3. *Catholic Charities of California, Inc.,* v. *The Superior Court of Sacramento County,* In The Supreme Court of California, Filed 3/1/04; available at: http://caselaw.lp.findlaw.com/data2/californiastatecases/s099822.pdf [accessed May 31, 2010].

4. Ibid. See also: Steve Lawrence, "Frequently vetoed birth control legislation passes Senate," Associated Press, April 13, 1999. See also, Mary Ann Ostrom, "State May Require Pill Coverage Test of Wills on Religious-Exemption Issue Leaves Outcome in Doubt," *San Jose Mercury News,* April 20, 1999, p.1A. See also, Mark Gladstone and Carl Ingram, "California and The West; Senate, Assembly OK Bills Requiring Insurers to Cover Birth Control," *Los Angeles Times,* September 8, 1999, Part A, p. 3.

5. Pope Paul VI, *Humanae Vitae,* July 25, 1968; available at: http://www.vatican.va/holy_father/paul_vi/encyclicals/documents/hf_p -vi_enc_25071968_humanae-vitae_en.html

6. Steve Lawrence, "Much-vetoed birth control legislation passes Senate," Associated Press, April 12, 1999.

7. Ibid.

8. Carl Ingram, "California and The West; Senate Votes to Force Insurers to Cover Birth Control Pills; Health: Bill, Which Goes to the Assembly, is The Latest in a Five-Year Campaign to Require Contraception Coverage. Ex-Gov. Wilson Vetoed Earlier Versions," *Los Angeles Times,* April 13, 1999, Part A, p. 3.

9. *Catholic Charities of California, Inc.,* v. *The Superior Court of Sacramento County, op.cit.*

10. Ibid. See also: "Diocese of Sacramento Will Appeal Catholic Charities Lawsuit to U.S. Supreme Court," *op.cit.*

11. Patricia Zapor, "Court says Catholic agency must provide birth control coverage," Catholic News Service, March 2, 2004; available at: http://www.catholicnews.com/data/stories/cns/20040302.htm

12. "Diocese of Sacramento Will Appeal Catholic Charities Lawsuit to U.S. Supreme Court," *op.cit.*

13. *Catholic Charities of Sacramento, Inc. v. Superior Court of the State of California,* #S099822, Supreme Court of the State of California; available at United States Conference of Catholic Bishops website: http://www.usccb.org/ogc/amicuscuriae5.shtml

14. Ibid.

15. Ibid.

16. *Catholic Charities of California, Inc., v. The Superior Court of Sacramento County, op.cit.*

17. Gina Holland, "U.S. Supreme Court declines religious dispute over contraceptives," *Associated Press Worldstream,* October 4, 2004.

18. The author made the same comparison between the alleged duty of the taxpayers to fund someone in exercising their claimed "right" to an abortion and funding someone in their Second Amendment right to keep and bear armes in his *Creators Syndicate* column. See: Terence P. Jeffrey, "Would Kerry buy poor people guns?" October 13, 2004; available at: http://townhall.com/columnists/TerryJeffrey/2004/10/13/would_kerry_buy_poor_people_guns?page=full&comments 1 tr ue [accessed June 2, 2010].

19. The National Committee for a Human Life Amendment has published a fact sheet, explaining the basic history and language of the Hyde Amendment over the years. See National Committee for a Human Life Amendment, "The Hyde Amendment," April 2008; available at: http://www.nchla.org/datasource/ifactsheets/4FSHydeAm22a.08.pdf [accessed June 3, 2010].

20. *Harris* v. *McRae,* 448 U.S. 297(1980); available at: http://supreme.justia,com/us/448/297/case.html [accessed June 2, 2010].

21. In the 1798 case of *Calder* v. *Bull,* which arose from a dispute over a person's will in the state of Connecticutt, Justice Samuel Chase wrote that it was "political heresy" to believe that either the federal or state governments in the United States had been empowered to enact any legislation that violates basic principles of justice. He included in this context legislation that would redistribute property. "An act of the leg-

islature (for I cannot call it a law) contrary to the first principles of the social compact cannot be considered a rightful exercise of legislative authority. The obligation of a law in governments established on express compact and on republican principles msut be determined by the nature of the power on which it is founded. A few instances will suffice to explain what I mean. A law that punished a citizen for an innocent action, or in other words for an act which when done was in violation of no existing law, a law that destroys or impairs the lawful private contracts of citizens; a law that makes a man a judge in his own cause, or a law that takes property from A. and gives it to B. It is against all reason and justice for a people to entrust a legislature with such powers, and therefore it cannot be presumed it has done it. The genius, the nature, and the spirit of our state governments amount to a prohibition of such acts of legislation, and the general principles of law and reason forbid them. The legislature may enjoin, permit, forbid, and punish; It may declare new crimes and establish rules of conduct for all its citizens in future cases; it may command what is right and prohibit what is wrong, but it cannot change innocence into guilt or punish innocence as a crime or violate the right of an antecedent lawful private contract or the right of private property." *Calder* v. *Bull*, 3 U.S. 386 (1798); available at: http://supreme.justia.com/us/3/386/case.html [accessed June 2, 2010].

22. *Harris* v. *McRae*, 448 U.S. 297(1980); available at: http://supreme.justia.com/us/448/297/case.html [accessed June 2, 2010)]. See also Oyez.org, *Harris* v. *McRae*, available at: http://oyez.org/cases/1970-1979/1979/1979_79_1268 [accessed June 2, 2010].

23. The National Committee for a Human Life Amendment, see note 20, chapter 7. For a liberal view on the background of the Hyde Amendment see: The Guttmacher Report on Public Policy, Heather Boonstra and Adam Sonfield, "Rights Without Access: Revisiting Public Funding of Abortion for Poor Women;" available at: http://www.guttmacher.org/pubs/tgr/03/2/gr030208.pdf [accessed June 2, 2010].

24. United States Conference of Catholic Bishops, Secretariat of Pro-Life Activities, "Issues of Life and Conscience in Health Care Reform: A Comparison of the House and Senate Bills," January 20, 2010; available at: http://www.usccb.org/healthcare/life_conscience.pdf [accessed June 2, 2010]. United States Conference of Catholic Bishops, Letter to Members of the United States Senate, December 22, 2009, Signed by Bishop William F. Murphy of the Diocese of Rockville Centre, Chairman of the Committee on Domestic Justice and Human Development; Cardinal Daniel DiNardo, Archdiocese of Gavleston-Houston, Chairman Committee on Pro-Life Activities; Bishop John Wester, Diocese of Salt Lake City, Chairman Committee on Migration; available at: http://www.usccb.org/healthcare/letter-to-senate-20091222.pdf [accessed June 2, 2010]. United States Conference of Catholic Bishops, Office of Media Relations, "Bishop Urge Passage of Stupak-Ellsworth Anti-Abortion Amendment for Health Reform Bill," November 7, 2009; available at: http://www.usccb.org/comm/archives/2009/09-229.shtml [accessed June 2, 2010]. United States Conference of Catholic Bishops, "Bishops to House: Keep Abortion Funding Out of Health Reform, Make Health Care Available to Vulnerable," November 6, 2009; available at: http://www.usccb.org/comm/archives/2009/09-228.shtml [accessed June 2, 2010]. See also, Terence P. Jeffrey, "Congressman Says He Now Has 'About 40 Likeminded Democrats' Who Will Vote to Kill Health Bill If He Doesn't Get Floor Vote on Pro-Life Amendment," CNSNews.com, October 23, 2009; available at: http://www.cnsnews.com/news/article/56023 [accessed June 2, 2010]; and Terence P. Jeffrey, "Obama Told House Democrat He Wasn't Talking About House Health Bill When He Told Congress 'Our Plan' Doesn't Fund Abortion," CNSNews.com, October 26, 2009; available at: http://www.cnsnews.com/news/article/56109 [accessed June 2, 2010].

25. Ibid.

26. House Rules Committee, "Part C-Text of the Amendment by Rep.Stupak to be Made in Order;" available at: http://www.rules. house.gov/111/SpecialRules/hr3962/111_part3_hr3962.pdf [accessed June 2, 2010].

27. Congressional Record, House, November 7, 2009, p.H12924; available at: http://frwebgate.access.gpo.gov/cgi-bin/getpage.cgi [accessed June 2, 2010].

28. Ibid., p.H12923.

29. One Hundred Eleventh Congress of the United States of America, "Patient Protection and Affordable Care Act," pp.778–781; available at: http://frwebgate.access.gpo.gov/cgi-bin/getdoc.cgi?dbname=111_ cong_bills&docid=f:h3590enr.txt.pdf [accessed June 2, 2010].

30. Ibid.

31. United States Conference of Catholic Bishops, Secretariat of Pro-Life Activities, "Abortion Funding in Senate Health Care Reform Bill," March 4, 2010. This fact sheet on the final Senate health bill that was passed by the House and enacted into law provided a no-nonsense analysis of the abortion funding elements in the bill. It said:

"Congress and the public agree that the federal government should not fund elective abortions. For over three decades this policy has been reflected in the Hyde amendment to the Labor/HHS appropriations bill and many similar laws. While the House-approved health care reform bill (H.R. 3962) follows this longstanding policy, in key respects the Senate bill (H.R. 3590) does not:

"Federal funds in the Senate bill can be used for elective abortions. For example, the bill authorizes and appropriates $7 billion over five years for services at Community Health Centers. (This would rise to $11 billion under President Obama's new proposal.) These funds are not covered by the Hyde amendment (as they are not appropriated through the Labor/HHS appropriations bill governed by the Hyde amendment), and not covered by the bill's own abortion limitation in

Sec. 1303 (as that provision relates only to tax credits or cost-sharing reductions for qualified health plans, and does not govern all funds in the bill). So the funds can be used directly for elective abortions.

"The Senate bill uses federal funds to subsidize health plans that cover abortions. Sec. 1303 limits only the direct use of a federal tax credit specifically to fund abortion coverage; it tries to segregate funds within health plans, to keep federal funds distinct from funds directly used for abortions. But the credits are still used to pay overall premiums for health plans covering elective abortions. This violates the policy of current federal laws on abortion funding, including the Hyde amendment, which forbid use of federal funds for any part of a health benefits package that covers elective abortions. By subsidizing plans that cover abortion, the federal government will expand abortion coverage and make abortions more accessible.

"The Senate bill uses federal power to force Americans to pay for other people's abortions even if they are morally opposed. The bill mandates that insurance companies deciding to cover elective abortions in a health plan 'shall . . . collect from each enrollee in the plan (without regard to the enrollee's age, sex, or family status) a separate payment' for such abortions. While the bill states that one plan in each exchange will not cover elective abortions, every other plan may cover them—and everyone purchasing such a plan, because it best meets his or her family's needs, will be required by federal law to fund abortions. No accommodation is permitted for people morally opposed to abortion. This creates a more overt threat to conscience than insurers engage in now, because in many plans receiving federal subsidies everyone will be forced to make separate payments solely and specifically for other people's abortions. Saying that this payment is not a 'tax dollar' is no help if it is required by the government.

"The House bill simply follows current law. The Stupak/Pitts provision in the House-passed health bill (also offered but rejected in the Senate as the Nelson/Hatch/Casey amendment) solves these problems by following longstanding current laws such as the Hyde amendment: No funds authorized or appropriated in the entire bill may be used for elective abortions or health plans that cover them. People are not forced to pay for other people's abortions, and those who want abortion coverage may buy it separately without using federal funds. This policy would maintain longstanding federal precedent, ensuring that this is a health bill and not an abortion bill." Available at: http://www.usccb. org/healthcare/030410facts.pdf [accessed June 2, 2010].

32. One Hundred Eleventh Congress of the United States of America, "Patient Protection and Affordable Care Act," "SEC. 1303. Special Rules," p.780; available at: http://frwebgate.access.gpo.gov/cgi-bin/getdoc.cgi?dbname=111_cong_bills&docid=f:h3590enr.txt.pdf [accessed June 2, 2010].

33. Ibid., 778–81; available at: http://frwebgate.access.gpo.gov/cgi-bin/getdoc.cgi?dbname=111_cong _bills&docid=f:h3590enr.txt.pdf [accessed June 2, 2010]. United States Conference of Catholic Bishops, Secretariat of Pro-Life Activities, "Issues of Life and Conscience in Health Care Reform: A Comparison of the House and Senate Bills," January 20, 2010; available at: http://www.usccb.org/healthcare/life_conscience.pdf (accessed June 2, 2010).

34. Barack Obama, speech before the Planned Parenthood Action, *op. cit.*

35. "Sex Ed for Kindergarteners 'Right Thing to Do,' Says Obama," ABC News, July 18, 2007; available at: http://blogs.abcnews.com/political radar/2007/07/sex-ed-for-kind.html [accessed Jun 3, 2010]. See also: Lisa Wangsness, "Romney, Obama spar over sex-education in public schools," *Boston Globe*, July 25, 2007, available at: http://www. boston.com/news/nation/articles/2007/07/25/romney_obama_spar_over_sex_education_in_public_schools/ [accessed June 3, 2010].

36. Mark Murray, "Obama and sex ed for kids," First Read on msnbc.com, July 19, 2007; available at: http://firstread.msnbc.msn.com/_news /2007/07/19/4430240-obama-and-sex-ed-for-kids [accessed June 8, 2010].

37. Senator Barack Obama's speech before the Planned Parenthood Action Fund, ABC News video as posted on YouTube, "Barack Obama

on sex education kindergarten;" available at: http://www.youtube.com/ watch?v=EwNV069wLGU [accessed June 3, 2010]. The teenager's words were transcribed by the author.

38. Ibid. Obama's words transcribed by the author.

39. "Sex Ed for Kindergarteners 'Right Thing to Do,' Says Obama," ABC News, *op. cit.*

40. Eric Krol, "Obama clarifies sex-ed views at Benedictine," *Daily Herald*, October 6, 2004, p. 17.

41. Mark Murray, "Obama and Sex Ed for Kids," MSNBC.com, July 19, 2007; available at: http://firstread.msnbc.msn.com/archive/2007/07/ 19/277886.aspx

42. Sexuality Education Q & A, SIECUS, http://www.siecus.org/ index.cfm?fuseaction=page.viewpage&pageid=521&grandparentID=4 77&parentID=514 [accessed June 3, 2010].

43. "Guidelines for Comprehensive Sexuality Education: Kindergarten Through 12th Grade," 3rd Edition, National Guidelines Task Force (Sexuality Information and Education Council of the United States, 2004); available at: http://www.siecus.org/_data/global/images/guidelines.pdf [accessed June 3, 2010].

44. "Political Ad Distorts Illinois Sex Education Bill," SIECUS, http://www.siecus.org/index.cfm?fuseaction=Feature.showFeature&featureid=1483&pageid=483&parentid=478 [accessed June 3, 2010].

45. Ibid.

46. Ibid.

47. Byron York, "On Sex-Ed Ad, McCain Is Right," *National Review*, September 16, 2008; available at: http://article.nationalreview.com/ 371243/on-sex-ed-ad-mccain-is-right/byron-york [accessed June 3, 2010].

48. *Goodrich* v. *Department of Public Health*, 798 N.E. 2d 941 (Mass. 2003): available at: http://fl1.findlaw.com/news.findlaw.com/cnn/docs/conlaw/goodridge111803opn.pdf [accessed June 3, 2010[.

49. United States Court of Appeals for the First Circuit, *Parker* v. *Hurley*, January 31, 2008; available at: http://www.ca1.uscourts.gov/pdf.opin-

ions/07-1528-01A.pdf [accessed June 3, 2010]. See also: "Culture Wars A Father's Protest," *ABC News World News Tonight*, Elizabeth Vargas, Jake Tapper, October 19, 2005; Laura Crimaldi, "Lexington school calls cops on dad irate over gay book," *Boston Herald*, April 28, 2005; "Man arrested after dispute over gay lifestyle teachings pleads innocent," Associated Press, April 28, 2005; Maria Cramer and Ralph Ranalli, "Arrested Father Had Point to Make, Disputed Schools Lesson in Diversity," *Boston Globe*, April 29, 2005, p. B1; Fox News Network, *The O'Reilly Factor*, "Personal Story: Interview With David Parker, Brian Camenker," May 10, 2005; Bill O'Reilly, "Back Off and Give Young Kids a Break," *Fort Lauderdale Sun Sentinel*, May 14, 2005.

50. United States Court of Appeals for the First Circuit, *Parker* v. *Hurley*, January 31, 2008; available at: http://www.ca1.uscourts.gov/ pdf.opinions/07-1528-01A.pdf [accessed June 3, 2010]. See also: Tracy Jan, "Parents Rip School Over Gay Storybook," *Boston Globe*, April 20, 2006, p.B1; James Vaznis and Tracy Jan, "In Storm Over Gay Books, A Principal Holds Ground," *Boston Globe*, April 27, 2006; p. B1; Fox News Network, *The O'Reilly Factor*, "Parents Suing Massachusetts School Over Book Portraying Homosexuality," May 3, 2006; James Vaznis, "Lawsuit Invokes Religious Freedom; Parents Say Beliefs Ignored by School," *Boston Globe*, May 4, 2006, p.1; Jay Lindsay, "Gay Marriage opponents say ruling stifles their rights in schools," Associated Press, May 5, 2006.

51. United States Court of Appeals for the First Circuit, *Parker* v. *Hurley*, *op. cit.*

52. Ibid.

53. Maria Cramer and Ralph Ranalli, "Arrested Father Had Point to Make, Disputed Schools Lesson in Diversity," *op. cit.*

54. Ibid.

55. United States Court of Appeals for the First Circuit, *Parker* v. *Hurley*, *op. cit.*

56. Ibid.

57. Lisa Keen, "U.S. Supreme Court refuses Lexington case Parents challenge gay-related books," *Boston Globe*, October 9, 2008, p.B2; available at: http://www.boston.com/news/education/k_12/articles/2008/ 10/09/us_supreme_court_refuses_lexington_case/ [accessed June 3, 2010].

58. September 26 Democratic debate transcript, MSNBC, available at: http://www.msnbc.msn.com/id/21327206/ns/politics-the_debates/page /11/ [accessed June 3, 2010].

59. Ibid.

60. One Hundred Eleventh Congress of the United States of America, "Patient Protection and Affordable Care Act," pp.229–234; available at: http://frwebgate.access.gpo.gov/cgi-bin/getdoc.cgi?dbname=111_ cong_bills&docid=f:h3590enr.txt.pdf [accessed June 2, 2010].

61. Ibid., 231.

62. Ibid., 232.

Conclusion

1. *Essay on the Constitutional Power of Great Britain Over the Colonies in America; With the Resolves of the Committee for the Province of Pennsylvania, and the Instructions of Their Representatives in Assembly* (Printed at Philadelphia, In the Year 1774), 312; available at: http://books.google.com/books?id=Nfwnq6-1cAkC&printsec=frontco ver&dq=%22Essay 1 on 1 the 1 Constitutional 1 Power 1 of 1 Great 1 Britain 1 Over 1 the 1 Colonies 1 in 1 America%22&lr=&as_drrb_is=q &as_minm_is=0&as_miny_is=&as_maxm_is=0&as_maxy_is=&as_brr =0&cd=1#v=onepage&q&f=false [accessed June 8, 2010]. See also: H. Niles, *Principles and Acts of the Revolution in America: Or, An Attempt to Collect and Preserve Some of the Speeches, Orations, Proceedings, With Sketches and Remarks on Men and Things, And Other Fugitive and Neglected Pieces, Belonging to the Revolutionary Period in*

the United States, (Baltimore, 1822), 176; available at: http://
books.google.com/books?id=YpjJdFJRY9MC&printsec=frontcover&d
q=%22Principles 1 and 1 Acts 1 of 1 the 1 Revolution 1 in 1 America%
22&lr=&as_drrb_is=q&as_minm_is=0&as_miny_is=&as_maxm_is=0
&as_maxy_is=&as_brr=0&cd=3#v=onepage&q&f=false [accessed
June 8, 2010].

Index